IT'S NOT ALWAYS EASY
"DOING WHAT COMES NATURALLY . . ."

- "I'm too tired for sex."

- "My husband is the problem; fix *him*."

- "My wife is the problem; fix *her*."

- "We're always fighting; who wants to make love?"

- "He wants it five times a week. I'd be happy with five times a month."

- "We still enjoy sex, but our bodies aren't what they used to be."

- "I'm not feeling too sexy since the birth of our second child."

- "I don't know how to please my partner, and I'm afraid to ask."

Could any of these voices be yours? Whether you have a serious sexual concern or simply want to make your intimate relationship more rewarding, Dr. Domeena Renshaw, the founder and director of the Loyola Sex Therapy Clinic, has the solution in . . .

SEVEN WEEKS TO BETTER SEX

- A step-by-step method to liberate your sensual self
- The seven R's of a relationship—and how to build loving intimacy
- Loveplay exercises, real-case histories, revealing questionnaires, and more

Seven Weeks to Better Sex

Domeena Renshaw, MD

Director of the Loyola Sex Therapy Clinic

written with Pam Brick

Illustrations by Don R. Tate

A Dell Trade Paperback

A DELL TRADE PAPERBACK

Published by
Dell Publishing
a division of
Bantam Doubleday Dell Publishing Group, Inc.
1540 Broadway
New York, New York 10036

The information in this book reflects current medical knowledge. The recommendations and information are appropriate in most cases; however, they are not a substitute for professional diagnosis and treatment. For specific information, the AMA suggests that you consult a physician.

The names of organizations, products, or alternative therapies appearing in this book are given for informational purposes only. Their inclusion does not imply AMA endorsement, nor does the omission of any organization, product, or alternative therapy indicate AMA disapproval.

Edited excerpts and case histories have been reprinted from the following medical and health care journal articles with the permission of the publishers:

ARCHIVES OF GENERAL PSYCHIATRY: M. H. Hollender and A. J. Mercer, "Wish to Be Held and Wish to Hold in Men and Women" (vol. 33, January 1976, pp. 49–51), copyright © 1976 American Medical Association.

JOURNAL OF SCHOOL HEALTH: D. C. Renshaw, "Understanding Masturbation" (vol. 46, February 1976, pp. 98–101), copyright © 1976 American School Health Association, Kent, Ohio.

JOURNAL OF NEUROLOGY, NEUROSURGERY & PSYCHIATRY: M. Hamilton, "Rating Scale for Depression" (vol. 23, 1960, pp. 56–62), copyright © 1960 British Medical Association.

MEDICAL ASPECTS OF HUMAN SEXUALITY: D. C. Renshaw: "Sexuality in Children" (reprint, October 1971); "Types of Female Orgasm" (vol. 9, August 1975, pp. 29–30); "Sexual Problems in Stroke Patients" (vol. 9, December 1975); "Stimulation Most Pleasurable to Women" (vol. 10, January 1976, p. 26); "I'm Just Not Interested in Sex, Doctor" (vol. 12, May 1978, pp. 32–41); "Communication in Marriage" (vol. 17, June 1983, pp. 199–220); "Intimacy and Intercourse" (vol. 18, February 1984); "Inappropriate Guilt" (vol. 19, May 1985, pp. 187–201), copyright © Reed-Elsevier Medical Publishing.

RESIDENT & STAFF PHYSICIAN: D. C. Renshaw, "Sex and the Cardiac Patient" (February 1988), copyright © 1988 Romaine Pierson Publishers, Inc.

SEXUAL AND MARITAL THERAPY: D. C. Renshaw and L. Yarzagaray, "Neurological Diseases and Sexuality" (vol. 6, no. 2, 1991), copyright © 1991 Association of Sexual and Marital Therapists.

SOUTH AFRICAN MEDICAL JOURNAL: D. C. Renshaw, "Sex and Drugs" (August 19, 1978, pp. 322–26), copyright © 1978 Medical Association of South Africa.

The following books were used as sources for certain components of the sex therapy program:

Fritz Perls, *Gestalt Approach & Eyewitness to Therapy* (Palo Alto, Cal.; Science & Behavior Books, 1973) (see page 172, "The Gestalt Exercise").

David D. Burns, *Feeling Good: The New Mood Therapy* (New York: Morrow, 1980) (see page 217, "How to Correct Negative Thinking").

ISBN: 0-440-50752-9

Printed in the United States of America

Reprinted by arrangement with Random House, Inc.

Published simultaneously in Canada

February 1996

10 9 8 7 6 5 4 3

BVG

To my husband, Robert

American Medical Association
Physicians dedicated to the health of America

Executive Staff
James S. Todd, MD—Executive Vice President
Heidi Hough—Publisher, Consumer Publishing

Editorial Staff
Pam Brick—Senior Editor
Dorothea Guthrie—Managing Editor
Dennis Krauss, MD—Medical Consultant, Urology
Elliot Levine, MD—Medical Consultant, Gynecology
Robin Fitzpatrick Husayko—Editor
Debra Smith—Editorial Assistant

Acknowledgments

I would like to acknowledge and thank the following people whose work has inspired me and helped me shape the Loyola Sex Therapy Program: William Masters and Virginia Johnson; Frederick Perls, the father of Gestalt therapy; William Hartman; David D. Burns; Max Hamilton; and Marc Hollender, MD.

I also want to thank Elliot Levine, MD, and Dennis Krauss, MD, for reviewing the drafts of this book.

Finally, I wish to thank the many patients whose lives have touched mine and enriched my experience. Just as I have learned from my patients, the readers of this book will gain much from accounts of others who have experienced sexual problems and have found solutions through therapy and their own committed efforts.

I have made every effort to protect the privacy of our patients and to preserve the confidentiality of the physician/patient relationship. Some of the case histories in this book are based on real patients, to reflect genuine experience; these patients' identities have been thoroughly disguised to protect their privacy. Other case histories represent a composite of people and situations I have encountered in my work. I have constructed these composites to illustrate and clarify specific problems that are common to a great many people. None of the case histories in this book describes actual people or events; any resemblance to real people is purely coincidental. Likewise, none of the letters found throughout this book are the private correspondence of patients; they are based on feelings expressed by patients with whom we have worked.

—DOMEENA RENSHAW, MD

Contents

Introduction

You Can Be Your Own Sex Therapist

How This Book Can Help You Have a Better Sex Life

"We've been married three years and I've never had an orgasm."

"With two little kids, we're too tired to have sex."

"I don't really enjoy sex; I just want to get it over with."

"I'm too hurt and angry to make love."

People with sexual problems don't make news. We hear all about the people who are sexually active or who flaunt exotic sex, but nobody talks about the people who have problems with sex, or questions, or shame. Each time I'm interviewed on a TV talk show I get thousands of letters from people who are frustrated because they can't find help for their sexual problems. I wrote this book for those people. And I wrote this book for you.

You may not have a sexual problem that is as serious as some of those presented in this book. In fact, you may not have a sexual problem at all. You may just want to enrich your sexual relationship. You can find that kind of help here too. Completing the questionnaires and exercises I've included will reveal many things about yourself that you and your partner may never have thought about or known. And doing the loveplay at home will bring you closer together.

This book is designed to help couples who are in a committed relationship overcome sexual roadblocks and understand their sexual problems. If you and your partner are having sex problems, you will take a big step toward resolving them by reading this book. But you can't improve your sex life just by reading. You must also do the exercises I recommend. The good news is that sexual problems are treatable. You *can* overcome them. But the success of treatment depends not on this book or on me, but on you. The more faithful you are in doing the exercises in this program, the more likely that your sexual problems will be resolved, provided there are no underlying physical causes for them.

Who Am I to Tell You How to Improve Your Sex Life?

I have directed the Loyola Sex Therapy Clinic for the last twenty-three years. In that time, my colleagues and I have helped more than fifteen hundred couples overcome their sexual difficulties. You're probably wondering how I became an expert on sexual problems. It certainly was not by the direct route. Here's a brief biography. I was born and raised in South Africa. At age fifteen, I decided I wanted to become a doctor after my father and I witnessed a car accident. We found one of the passengers thrashing and groaning on the ground, complaining of a broken leg. But I could see that the man's leg was not broken because he was able to move it. So I began talking to him, assuring him that he was fine and trying to convince him that he could walk. After a while, the man sat up, stood, and then walked away from the scene of the accident.

I had never even heard the term "psychiatry," but that experience fascinated me. That man had gone from a state of panic and fear to one of calm, just by talking it out. I wanted to know more about the way the mind works. Boldly, I told my parents I wanted to go to medical school. But they would not hear of it—their daughter was supposed to stay at home. My parents threatened to disinherit me, said they'd never speak to me again, and declared I would be responsible for their early deaths from stroke. All this clamorous family opposition prepared me to become a calm and effective therapist.

Eleven years later, at age twenty-six, I had finally saved enough money to begin taking classes at the University of Cape Town Medical School. While I was there, I met Dr. Paul Dudley White, the renowned heart specialist, who asked me to do a residency in pediatrics at Boston Children's Hospital. That's how I first came to the United States. I completed my residency in Boston and then, a week before I was about to leave for home, I met my future husband, Robert. He wrote to me every day while I was working in a missionary hospital in South Africa. Three years later, he came to Africa to marry me. We returned to the United States and, after completing my specialty training in psychiatry, I got a position in the psychiatry department at Loyola Medical School, just outside of Chicago.

How did the sex clinic get started? By geographic chance. But it also fulfilled an unmet need. In the early seventies, the psychiatry department was sandwiched between the gynecology and urology departments. The gynecology department began sending me women who couldn't have an orgasm and the urology department started referring men who couldn't get an erection. But sex education, it seemed, was a problem for both patients and doctors. My psychiatrists-in-training would say, "She couldn't have an orgasm, so I sent her home" or "He had premature ejaculation, so I sent him home." I said to the doctors, "What do you mean, you sent them home? Why didn't you treat them?" They answered, "We don't know how." As a full-time faculty member, I realized if I didn't teach the doctors, no one would. So I studied Masters and Johnson's newly published sex therapy techniques and adapted them for use in our program here at Loyola. Over the years, I have enlarged and refined the program to make it as meaningful as possible for couples who need help.

When I opened the Loyola Sex Therapy Clinic in 1972, I predicted that I would treat all the people in town who had sexual problems and train so many other therapists that I'd put myself out of business in two years. No such luck! Twenty-three years later there is still an eight-month wait for couples to begin sex therapy at Loyola. And many more couples write to say they do not have access to sex therapy where they live. The need is strong. That's why I wrote this book. So I could help you help yourself at home.

What Is Sex Therapy?

In the Loyola sex therapy program, couples are paired with teams of two therapists. Each therapy team includes one man and one woman and at least one of the two is a medical doctor. Each couple and their therapist team meet once a week, in the evening, for seven weeks. I can't meet with every couple individually, but I supervise the therapists (I call them cotherapists) and talk directly to the couples in a lecture format every week. The therapists and I are not really the ones who perform magic in our clinic—the couples themselves are making miracles happen. That's why the therapy can work for you at home; this book will give you the right tools, but then it's up to you to work with them. If your partner is reluctant at first, don't wait for him or her to begin. Take the initiative yourself by reading this book and doing some of the solo exercises. Then get your partner involved.

Sex therapy combines sex education and relationship therapy with sexual activity at home (I call it home loveplay), which progresses weekly from caressing without touching the genitals all the way to intercourse. (All of the couples' sexual activity is done in the privacy of their own home. We *never* use sexual surrogates. I consider the practice unethical.) Many sexual problems arise from sexual misinformation—

or no information at all. Sex education and home loveplay can help couples "unlearn" unsatisfying sexual behavior patterns in a brief period of seven weeks. These techniques can help you too. This book will show you how.

The home loveplay exercises are the key to success in sex therapy. In this book, you'll learn how to do the same home loveplay exercises done by the couples who go through our sex therapy clinic so you can duplicate the program at home.

You'll also complete the same questionnaires our couples use at the clinic. These can give you better insight into your sexuality and your relationship. You will also do the same exercises during the middle weeks of sex therapy. These are designed to evoke your feelings about your relationship—feelings you may have forgotten from long ago. Using these techniques, sex therapy treats the whole person: body, mind, and feelings. Again I must stress that you both need to participate in the exercises and the home loveplay; just reading the book is a good start, but not enough to help you achieve the results you want.

That brings me to another point. Sex therapy is couple therapy. That means that both of you must "be your own sex therapists" together. In our clinic, we say that the relationship is the patient, not the individual partners. You may think "Jack is the one with the sex problem, not me" or "Cindy has a hang-up, so I don't have to go through sex therapy." Wrong! When a sexual problem exists, it affects both of you. Your *relationship* is what you are trying to improve. So both of you must do the exercises, the questionnaires, and the loveplay to benefit from the program. Sex therapy is a commitment, and both of you must be willing to set aside time for it.

Although the couples we treat in our sex therapy clinic are married, you don't have to be married to benefit from this book. Single or married, young or old, heterosexual or homosexual—the important thing is that you and your partner are committed to each other and to your relationship.

An affair—whether sexual or emotional—is a major barrier to closeness. A relationship outside of your primary relationship betrays your commitment and destroys trust, which is difficult to regain. If you are sexually involved with someone other than your primary partner, you must break off this relationship before you can honestly begin sex therapy. That's a basic rule for ethical conduct. Otherwise, you're playing a dishonest game.

Being your own sex therapist will be different from going to our clinic because you are on your own. You won't have two therapists to report to every week. No book can completely replicate the experience of attending our clinic. On the other hand, you will get much information in this book about sexual problems, their causes, and their treatments. And you won't have to travel to Chicago to see me!

You will learn that large doses of humor can help you get through some of the more embarrassing or difficult parts of sex therapy at home. For example, if you are fumbling with a new sexual position, laughter can make the attempt fun instead of turning it into an uncomfortable moment or a blaming session. Humor helps take the edge of seriousness off your sexual encounters with your partner so you both can relax, feel better, and get closer.

Success Stories

Overall, sex therapy has an 80 percent success rate in reversing sexual problems, such as the inability to reach orgasm in women and erection problems and premature ejaculation in men. But there is no magic formula—couples must faithfully do the exercises I describe in this book to resolve their problems. If you and your partner struggle with a sexual problem, this book will show you that you are not alone. No matter what your problem is, help is available. Our approach works. Here are some success stories:

• Dennis, age thirty-nine, had had sporadic erection problems throughout his fifteen years of marriage to Marie. He worried constantly about his performance in bed, and it affected not only his sex life but their entire relationship. During the seven-week sex therapy program, he learned how to overcome his performance anxiety. Now his erection problems have vanished and the couple enjoys a regular sex life for the first time in their marriage. "It's been like a second courtship," says Dennis. "We wish we'd known about sex therapy ten years ago."

• Laura was a forty-two-year-old travel agent who had never experienced an orgasm. She had come from a sheltered environment in which her family never discussed sexuality. Although intelligent and successful, Laura knew very little about her own body and its sexual responses. During sex therapy, she got a thorough education in sexual anatomy and learned how to explore her body to find out what she needed to become aroused. She also learned how to communicate her needs and desires to her husband. By the sixth week of therapy, she had reached orgasm for the first time in her life.

• Eric and Maggie entered sex therapy because they both had lost interest in sex. The couple had three-year-old twins and both worked full time. In addition, Eric was training for a half-marathon running race, something Maggie saw as an unnecessary intrusion on their already limited time together. Eric and Maggie were exhausted and irritable. Sex was always the last thing on their list of "must-dos." In sex therapy, they discovered how fatigue and anger were affecting their sex drives. They learned to compromise in sharing the time they needed for each other, and their interest in sex blossomed as the weeks passed.

Before I close, I want to acknowledge and extend my gratitude to William Masters and Virginia Johnson, who risked their careers to scientifically study human sexuality in the 1960s. They developed many of the techniques I use in my sex therapy clinic—techniques you'll find in this book—including sensate focus (which is the part of the program I've developed called home loveplay) and the squeeze technique. Without Masters and Johnson's landmark studies, we would have far less information about human sexuality to work with than we do today.

—DOMEENA RENSHAW, MD

Part 1

The Inside Facts About Sex Problems

1

What Causes Sex Problems?

In more than twenty years of treating patients with sexual problems, be assured that I have just about seen it all. That's why I can say with confidence that, no matter what difficulties you are experiencing, you are not alone. Many other people have the same problems you have. Do not feel ashamed or embarrassed about your circumstances. Lots of people have much to learn about their sexuality.

Regardless of what may have caused your or your partner's particular sexual problem, there is an excellent chance that your symptoms can be reversed through sex therapy, medical treatment, or the two combined. The outlook is good. But you must keep your end of the bargain by doing the exercises I outline in part 2 of this book, especially the home loveplay exercises (see page 116). I know that these exercises have helped thousands of people. They can help you too. The success of your self-help sex therapy program depends on your efforts and those of your partner in the privacy of your own home.

I hope this book will help you explore the root of your difficulties.

If you feel you need personalized, professional help at any time while you are reading this book, do not hesitate to seek it. The best way to find out the name of a competent and experienced therapist in your community is to call your local hospital and ask to speak to a social worker in the social services department. Social workers are trained professionals and sympathetic listeners who know what resources are available locally. They also know the personality and qualifications of each practitioner, so they can guide you to the therapist who can best handle your problem.

Having said all that, now I'll tell you the most common causes of sexual problems that I have seen in my many years of practice with more than three thousand patients.

Sexual Illiteracy:
A Lack of Knowledge and Experience

Many people believe that the legacy of the sexual revolution of the late 1960s is a complete understanding of our sexuality, but, in fact, the extent of sexual ignorance remains staggering. For example, although in 1966 Masters and Johnson revealed a very significant natural difference in timing between the cycle of sexual arousal in a man and that in a woman (see page 35), this difference is still not widely known to the general public. Couples who come to our sex therapy clinic hold a wide range of inaccurate beliefs. An impotent man once told me he thought his body had only a certain number of climaxes and that he had used them up. His wife would not allow him to masturbate because she wanted to salvage "all that was left" for herself.

Twenty percent of the female patients I see don't know where their clitoris is. I've had female patients who were physicians, nurses, and college professors who didn't know how to find their own clitoris. There are people who have MDs, PhDs, all kinds of Ds, who have no accurate knowledge of sexuality. Sexual problems and sexual ignorance are quite democratic. They cross all boundaries of race, religion, education, socioeconomic class, and age. Much of sex therapy, therefore, is education—the sex education most of us never got as children.

Children are alert, curious, and incredibly observant. For them, peer pressure is intense and important—whether it is in Little League or sexual conduct. When children tell each other about sex, they emphasize the mechanics of performance—how to do it and how to hide it from their parents. The information gleaned from peers is often so inaccurate and unreliable that even the most basic sex facts the child learns are wrong. For many people, these inaccuracies remain uncorrected for years. If their parents won't talk about sex, children will never learn about personal responsibility for sex; the right of refusal; privacy; or the meaning of affection, caring, and commitment.

The child's curious exploration of his or her own body is a normal part of development. Specialists call it "developmental sexplay," and it normally occurs from birth, through puberty, and into adult life. Children experiment with and learn from siblings and friends. Parents usually teach sexual restraint and respect for privacy, but some of these restraints may seem like punishment and can inhibit the child. The child may read them as negative messages about sexuality that generate shame and guilt in spite of the parents' good intentions.

Early sexplay is an essential and normal part of healthy human sexual development. For some children, never having been permitted sexual exploration of their own bodies may be as problematic as sexually abusive experiences are for others. About 50 percent of my patients who have sexual problems do not remember having any early sexplay or masturbation experience. Some report that they had no genital contact at all until marriage. Others engaged in a minimal amount of self-exploration; their problems are usually more readily reversible than those of men and women who never explored their sexuality.

"How I wish I had known what I know now when I was fifteen," said a college-educated twenty-nine-year-old woman who was four years into her second marriage before she sought help. "My mother kept saying to me over and over as I grew up that she'd throw me out if I ever got pregnant. That's all I remember about sex education at home. School? You're joking. We had this talk about menstruation, and the teacher said never to put anything inside because it would tear the vagina. I was terrified of touching down there."

Could accurate sex education have helped this woman and the many thousands like her? Yes. Sex education could also have prevented years of the kind of distress and sexual disability experienced by Diane and Len. She was twenty-nine; he was forty-five. They had been married for seven years, and it was the first marriage for both of them. Diane had valued virginity; the couple had courted for a year and a half without having sex. After they got married the couple's sexual relations were difficult. Diane felt ashamed about her lack of skill in the bedroom. She never reached orgasm during intercourse (which is not unusual or abnormal—only 20 to 30 percent of women can; see page 39). Len could not bring her to orgasm manually because she would not let him touch her genital area. They began to avoid sex with each other; Len masturbated in private. The slides I showed on sexual anatomy during the first week of the sex clinic were the first pieces of sexual information Diane had ever received in her life. At first she was embarrassed, but eventually, with support and encouragement, Diane overcame her sexual shame and was able to reach orgasm.

But it's not easy to leap from the second dimension of looking at sexual information on a slide or in a book to the third dimension of your own body. If you are a woman and you don't understand something you have read—in this book or any other—ask your gynecologist. You can say something like, "I'd like to know exactly where my clitoris is. Will you show me?" Your doctor can take your hand and place your own finger on your clitoris so you can feel its position in your genital area. Take along a small mirror to help you see what your doctor is showing you. It's the job of the "body doctor" to teach you about your body. Your personal doctor may be uncomfortable with this suggestion, but I encourage you to bring it up anyway and see how he or she responds. Take this book along and say, "Dr. Renshaw suggested I ask for your help." Likewise, if you are a man and you don't understand something you have read in this or any other book about sex, be sure to talk to your doctor.

If you don't feel comfortable asking your doctor to teach you about your sexual anatomy, please read chapter 2, "The Sex Education You Never Had," especially carefully so you can teach yourself. Take your time and look at the pictures to learn the location of each part of your body. Better still, go over the pictures with your partner so you can learn together.

A communication breakdown between partners can stem from sexual ignorance. Often, neither partner in a couple can admit to sexual ignorance or tell the other what he or she likes or dislikes in bed. Each of you may be afraid to suggest new and untried sexual positions or activities because your partner might ask where you gained such sexual knowledge. As a couple, you get stuck, unable to vary your means of stimulation or change a rigid routine of unfulfilling sexual exchange.

To become responsible for your own sexuality, you have to tell your partner exactly what you like and dislike, want and don't want in bed. But the way you say it makes all the difference between open dialogue and open hostility. I suggest that couples express themselves to each other in first-person statements (see page 140 for an explanation of what I call "I" language). For example, instead of accusingly saying, "You don't know how to please a woman. You're too rough," you could say, "I would really like it if you caressed me more gently." This newly learned communication skill often helps reduce resentment and resolve conflict in areas of the couple's life other than sex, such as housekeeping or child care.

Sexual Inhibition: Don't Look or Touch

Sexual inhibition is closely related to inadequate sexual knowledge. They both spring from mislabeling the genitals as bad or sinful or from a lack of forthright acceptance of sexuality during a person's formative years. The capacity to receive pleasure is not one we easily learn in our work-ethic culture. We've been heavily brainwashed with sexual negatives that can later cause severe inhibitions. Looking, touching, and talking about our sexual selves becomes unthinkable, so we suppress or avoid doing so.

A person's religious beliefs and a family custom of modesty deserve respect. But these influences can become exaggerated and impede sexual functioning. Early rearing has made some people so embarrassed about their body that they never allow their partner to see it. For some of my patients who have always slept in a nightgown or pajamas, my suggestion that they go to bed in the nude is a real novelty.

When I was a girl in South Africa, a nun in my convent school told me it was a mortal sin to look at my body. Nowhere does this exist in Catholic doctrine! When I told my mother about this, she said, "Sister is just an old maid who doesn't know better." Mother was the authority who corrected my misinformation. But the way parents react to sexual references from their children can fluctuate. When I came home another day and told my mother that a fourteen-year-old girl in my class was pregnant, she became upset and told me never again to use the word "pregnant." Well-meaning parents can sometimes overreact to their child's natural curiosity, causing confusion and sexual shame.

Christine and Jonathan, two of our former patients, serve as a good example of the way inhibition can hinder a person's sexual responses. Christine was a shy and sexually inexperienced college student when she met Jonathan, who was ten years her senior. In spite of being older, Jonathan was as unskilled in the ways of making love as Christine, and together they fumbled through their first attempts at loveplay after marriage. But soon Christine started to feel embarrassed and repelled by genital touch. And Jonathan was so self-conscious about his sexual ineptitude that he stopped initiating sex altogether. By the time they entered sex therapy, the couple had given up trying to have intercourse. They hadn't made love for over nine months.

Sex had been a taboo subject in Christine's home when she was growing up. Her parents never spoke about the subject and discouraged Christine from dating in high school, allowing her to socialize only in groups. When she began dating in college, she was uncomfortable about being alone with men. Her shyness made her seem formal and reserved.

Jonathan shared a similar background. He attended an all-male Catholic high school and entered a seminary immediately after graduating because he wanted to become a priest. Although he eventually changed his mind about the priesthood and finished college at a coed university, Jonathan had been sheltered from the opposite sex during his adolescence and young adulthood. He lacked experience with women and felt self-conscious about his inexperience. He also believed premarital sex was wrong.

This couple needed basic education about their bodies and the way they worked. But they also needed reassurance that the shame they had been taught to feel about their normal and natural sexual urges could be overcome. We asked Christine to practice masturbating every other day so she could learn about her body's sexual responsiveness. We also told both partners to talk to each other candidly about what each wanted the other to do in bed. With patience, persistence, and some personalized follow-up therapy, Christine and Jonathan slowly began to enjoy their natural sex drive and were able to see it as an important part of their life together.

Christine and Jonathan may seem like extreme examples of sexual inhibition, but many of our patients have experienced sexually unfulfilling adult relationships because of the taboos their parents, peers, and teachers taught them. Learned inhibition even prevents many people from exploring their own bodies. But a knowledge of the sex organs and how they work is as essential as an awareness of one's own thoughts and feelings. Many people avoid the journey into their own sexuality. That's why people who are sexually inhibited benefit from a thorough physical and sexological examination (see page 144) of their body, including their genitals, by their doctor. A thorough examination can defuse your anxiety and encourage you to explore and accept your own sexuality.

Masturbation allows you to have a private experience of arousal and orgasm that can be experienced later with a committed partner. The home loveplay exercises prescribed during sex therapy (see page 116) can be difficult for many sexually inhibited people. Because values are inextricably bound to sexual behavior, a visit with your priest, minister, rabbi, or other trusted confidant may be helpful. Once you explain that you are doing these exercises to correct your sexual problems within a committed relationship, you will probably receive assurance that your conduct is morally acceptable. If you instead meet with resistance, use your own best judgment about this very personal decision. And remember that I have given you permission to learn about your body.

Fatigue: "We're Just Too Tired to Make Love"

Fatigue is a message from your body to your mind saying "Please rest." Physical exhaustion from the demands of your job, young children, running a household, caring for an older relative, and other major commitments can act as an effective suppressor of your sex drive. Usually, when your body is tired, the last thing it wants to do is make love, although sexual release can be a wonderful relaxant. Today, many women must work outside the home to help make ends meet. So she is tired and he is tired. Two tired partners rarely find the thought of an emotionally or physically demanding sexual encounter appealing. Sleep becomes a priority.

John and Lorna were a young couple who had a two-and-a-half-year-old child and a three-month-old baby. Lorna worked part-time as a paralegal, and John put in long hours at a bank. "We didn't have sex for about three months after the second baby came because I was sore and tired," said Lorna. "Now, every time we try to make love, the baby starts crying. Then the two year old wakes up and wants to come into our bed. We're both awake half the night and then we have to work and I take care of the kids. I'm afraid we'll never have the energy or privacy to make love until the kids are in high school," she said with a sad laugh.

This is an all-too-common situation in today's world. Fortunately for John and Lorna and thousands of other similar couples, the sexual problems of people with young children are temporary—even though "temporary" can sometimes feel like an eternity. Eventually, your kids *will* sleep through the night and your sexual encounters *will* become easier to arrange. You'll find ways to carve out small segments of privacy, "which is almost as exciting as when we were teenagers," as one man told me. But you will still have to deal with the fatigue caused by your job and your other responsibilities.

Fatigue can make the extra effort needed to satisfy your partner's sexual demands a resented burden ("another job I have to do") that can result in a loss of interest in sex. It is completely normal to be uninterested in sex when you are physically exhausted. But there is a way to rest your body *and* satisfy your sexual drive. I advised Lorna to tell John, "Let me sleep for ninety minutes, then wake me up and we can both enjoy making love" (see page 72 for more ideas about what you can do "When You're Too Tired for Sex"). Remember that other causes of sexual problems have much more serious and long-lasting effects than does fatigue, which is a reversible state.

Interpersonal Conflict:
You Can't Make Love Until You Make Peace

Some couples display an ongoing pattern of destructive conflict that manifests itself either as open fighting or angry withdrawal. In either case, the fight becomes the center of their emotional relationship. It can even replace foreplay or lovemaking. I have seen many couples who don't even see the pattern until a therapist brings it to their attention. Although both partners may tell me they want help, neither may be ready to give up the fighting, which has become the focus of their relationship.

A couple may reinforce their antagonism by avoiding sex or making negative remarks or comparisons that deeply hurt the other person. Unresolved anger or lingering anxieties can cause a number of sexual problems, including erection problems, loss of desire, or deliberate withholding of sex.

Couples cannot make love until they make peace. Differences between people are usually neither good nor bad. They're simply differences. Your task as a couple is to negotiate and compromise so each person's most central needs can be met in the relationship. Anger, tenseness, or feelings of resentment almost always block normal sexual arousal. I often see such a response in women whose partners ignore them until bedtime. He may have been sitting in front of the TV all evening ignoring her, but then he expects instant and silent intercourse as soon as they get into bed. She pushes him away, saying "I'm not an inflatable doll." Both end up hurt and angry.

The bedroom is not the place to fight. I encourage couples to get up out of bed to discuss and resolve their differences in the living room or kitchen. Make your bedroom a special place of closeness and good feelings. Working out your problems in another room gives you the chance to say "Let's go to bed now and leave these issues behind."

Some people seek sex therapy with a hidden agenda for failure. I once counseled a couple whose names were Bob and Lydia. Bob had partial erections once a week, but he never approached Lydia for sex. He did not know that longer, stronger, direct-on-the-penis foreplay would help him improve his erections. Lydia did not know that Bob masturbated in secret. He claimed she had dragged him to therapy. "Fix him" was her message. "No way" was his. Each came to therapy determined to blame rather than to learn how to change. They could have mutually masturbated or had oral sex as pleasurable options, but she wanted intercourse or nothing. Sex therapy did not help Bob and Lydia because neither partner would even try to give the other pleasure through such natural, alternative methods as body massage. Both lost out on the pleasure of affectionate touch. Nobody "won."

At times, sex therapy can reverse sexual symptoms but may not save a relationship. Couples who successfully resolve the sexual symptom that brought them to therapy may later break up because other problems, such as money, alcohol or other drug abuse, or infidelity, remain unreconciled. But no therapist or family member can make the decision for a person to stay in a relationship or leave it. Only the partners in a relationship can save or sever it. They may have to struggle with the decision for a long time before they can cope with the consequences (see page 107 for advice on making a decision to end a relationship).

Boredom:
The Thrill Is Gone

Like brushing your teeth or setting the alarm clock, sex can become as predictable an event as nightfall. A routine of sex before sleep often becomes exaggerated to the point of monotony when preceded by such overused verbal cues as "Tonight?" or "Are you ready?" uttered without tenderness or humor. As one lady put it, "He pinches my left nipple, kisses my cheek, and then enters. That's it! Then it's over and I finish myself when he's asleep. What's in it for me? Three kids. Sex is an overrated bore. Who needs it?" Devoid of emotion, a mechanical sex routine becomes empty for both.

Underlying all boredom is conscious or unconscious anger because your expectations are being unmet. You go to a movie or a party to enjoy yourself and leave saying "It was boring" because you thought you would have a good time and then didn't. It's the same thing in the bedroom. Sex is supposed to be a thrill, a joy, but after years of doing it the same old way, the thrill has gone and the joy is elusive. This problem affects most couples who have been in a committed relationship for several years.

Some people in long-term relationships mourn losing the thrill of conquest that comes with bedding a new sex partner. Such people see seduction as an ego booster and miss the excitement and emotional high they get from sex with new partners. They may have an affair or yearn for an open marriage, in which both partners are free to date and have sex with other people. But let me assure you that, in my many years of practice, I have never seen a happy open marriage. Promiscuity within a committed relationship only fosters insecurity and a lack of trust.

Distorted Body Image:
Making Peace With Your Body

I am constantly amazed at how many people are dissatisfied with the way their body looks. "I'm not tall enough." "My thighs are fat." "I have cellulite." "Who could love my bad skin?" Men frequently worry about the size of their penis. Many women are concerned that their breasts are too small—or too large. When you get into bed with your partner, it can be distracting if you are thinking "I'm lumpy here and I'm dumpy there" or "My muscles are flabby." So you've got to make peace with your body. The mind and body are interrelated, so what happens in your mind affects what happens in your body. When you worry too much about the way you look, your body cannot relax and respond sexually. Later in this book, I'll guide you through an exercise that can help you overcome a distorted body image (see the section "The Fantastic Voyage" on page 167).

Many older people lament the loss of their youthful figures. "I can't get over the fact that I don't look eighteen anymore," said Marge, a suburban homemaker age fifty-four. She and her husband, Harry, came to our sex therapy clinic because of Marge's lack of interest in sex.

Marge felt that she had let herself go over the years, and she was ashamed of her body. "My body has gone to flab," she said. "How could Harry want me anymore?" Harry was a mail carrier for the post office and the walking and lifting he had to do on the job, coupled with golf on the weekends, gave his lean body a strength and vigor Marge's body lacked. "I love to cook," said Marge. "And I love to eat, but I never think about exercising."

We encouraged Marge to begin a physical activity she liked. She joined a local YMCA and made it part of her daily routine to take an exercise class or swim before she started her housework. Over the six weeks of sex therapy, she lost about eight pounds and her body became firmer. But most important, she learned to accept her less-than-perfect body for what it was. "I'll never be eighteen again and that's OK, but at least I know now that I can accept my fifty-four-year-old body and that Harry loves me the way I am," Marge said. It was a joy to hear Marge say she felt more relaxed during sex and that she wanted to try new sexual positions. Needless to say, Harry was happier too.

There are accurate body images, and there are unrealistic ones. We can entirely misperceive our bodies. A person who was overweight as an adolescent might retain that negative body image even after slimming down as an adult. People with anorexia nervosa, an eating disorder characterized by extreme weight loss, see themselves as much heavier than they are. In counseling for eating disorders, these people are sometimes asked to lie down on a large sheet of white paper and then trace the outline of their body. An anorectic's perception of the size of the outline is always larger than the reality.

An informal study I did with women who had anorexia showed that many of them had difficulty conceiving a child. Many had stopped ovulating because their weight had dropped so low. While they said they wanted a child, most of them resisted the idea of gaining twenty-five pounds or more during pregnancy. They balked at the notion of getting stretch marks that, to them, looked as large as railroad tracks. So they avoided a mature sexual exchange altogether so they could also avoid the unwanted "side effect" of having a child.

At the other end of the spectrum, real obesity (defined as being at least 20 percent over the average weight for a person's height and age) can cause physical problems that affect sexual performance. I once treated a man whose pendulous abdomen hung halfway down his thighs. He could feel his erection, but could not see it because his penis was buried in fat. He needed suggestions so he could find a special position for intercourse. The anxiety and fear of rejection that can accompany obesity can also affect sexual performance.

A person who is overweight often has difficulty finding a sexual partner, so the solitary obese person may overcompensate by seeking pleasure in excessive eating. "I don't have anybody, but I don't need anybody because eating is pleasure enough," he or she may say. Faced with a real sexual opportunity, obese people may find they have a high level of desire, but are inhibited, inexperienced, and uninformed about sex. Sexual problems such as erection difficulty, inability to have an orgasm (in a woman), or painful sex may appear.

Rita was a thirty-six-year-old married woman who had never had an orgasm. She was five feet two inches tall and weighed 196 pounds. Rita confessed such hatred of her body that she had never been naked with her husband in ten years of marriage. The couple's lovemaking took place exclusively in the dark, under the covers, in nightclothes.

I gave Rita a simple thirty-minute exercise to do every night for one week. She and her husband were to lie naked next to each other and take turns touching each other's bodies all over, except for the breasts and genitals. The purpose of this exercise was to learn relaxation and gain body awareness through affectionate massage. But Rita was so ashamed of her body that she couldn't do the exercise. She told me she felt she couldn't tackle her sexual problem until she lost weight.

Rita joined a supportive weight-loss program and eventually lost forty pounds. When she felt encouraged by the first twenty-pound loss, we began working together on her sexual problem. After a few months of mutual loveplay exercises (the same ones you will learn in part 2 of this book) with her husband, along with sexual self-exploration, Rita experienced an orgasm for the first time in her life. "It wasn't as big a deal as I thought it would be," she laughed with relief. "I expected a giant earthquake."

Our culture's unrealistic views of how a body should look or function affects us all every day. A Swedish bikini team frolics on TV while superslim models grace the pages of every magazine, but there are few famous plumpies. Women young and old strive to be thin. When they fail, they may lose interest in sex or insist on "lights out" before they will take off their clothes so they can hide an imperfect body in the darkness.

The struggle to look good can become extreme, and it's not just limited to women. Many men diet continually because they think they're overweight. Others take powerful steroids to increase their muscle mass so they can look tougher, stronger, bigger, and sexier. These steroids can cause impotence, cancer, and even death. Bought on the street, such drugs can be contaminated with harmful substances. Users seriously jeopardize their health for the sake of vanity.

Body image can even be affected by a minor flaw that the person perceives as glaring. I remember one couple in particular. Jerry, age thirty-three, was a successful business owner, but he had severe acne on his back that resisted all treatment he had received from his dermatologist. The acne created an extreme lack of confidence and fear of rejection in bed. Immediately after sex, Jerry would wrap a sheet around himself like a toga so his wife would not see the skin eruptions and scars. I helped him work through his anxiety about his condition in individual counseling, but his lack of confidence remained, although lessened. Such body image problems as these can directly affect sexual performance, causing avoidance of sex, difficulty having an erection, or lack of interest in sex.

When you and your partner make peace with your bodies the way they are, you can be sexual no matter what you look like. How? By accepting yourself as you are today, even after years of self-rejection. Realize that the inside person is much more important than the outside person. Sexual self-confidence grows from the inside.

Performance Anxiety:
Second-Guessing Your Sexual Self

Our culture has an overly driven concern about competition, achievement, and speed. We often carry these concerns into the bedroom. Many people tell me they tend to "watch" themselves perform during sex instead of relaxing and enjoying the sexual moment. Such "spectatoring" can build anxiety and impede the relaxed physical responses you need for erection or orgasm. Men in particular may experience erection problems because of such performance anxiety. "Will I get my erection?" "What if I ejaculate too quickly?"

The harder a man tries to have a full erection, the less erect his penis becomes. This paradox continues until the man relaxes. Relaxation exercises (see page 160) can help quell the turbulent negative thoughts and questions that men experience when they anxiously watch themselves perform in bed.

One of my patients, Abby, was an Orthodox Jew. In this faith, a woman cannot have sex with her husband when she is menstruating, so Abby and her husband, Phil, abstained at that time. But Abby had been spotting almost all month, every month, for about two years. There were only a few days every month in which Abby and Phil could have sex. Phil became so nervous about having to perform only on the permitted days that he began having erection problems. He was also angry because he suspected Abby might be using her spotting as an excuse to refrain from sex because she refused to see her gynecologist. There was high tension between them.

During the first two weeks of this couple's sex therapy, I suggested that they engage only in loveplay without intercourse, especially on the days when Abby was neither menstruating nor spotting. This strategy eliminated the pressure to perform, so it built Phil's confidence and increased his capacity for arousal. Loveplay emphasized Phil's sensual pleasure rather than penetration and taught him to relax and enjoy the pleasurable sensations experienced during loveplay. This process—

called "sensate focus"—is the same one you will go through when you begin to do what I call your "home loveplay." It will help you concentrate on the pleasurable sensations you feel instead of focusing on erection and penetration. (See page 116 for an explanation of how home loveplay exercises work.)

Abby finally agreed to see her doctor, who treated her disorder, and her spotting diminished. Phil's mistrust and anger subsided when he found out her physical problem was real. After about six months, Phil was able to sustain a good erection and have intercourse with Abby again.

Guilt:
Gain Perspective, Then Let It Go

Guilt differs from regret, which is the discomfort you feel when you have left something undone or have done something minor you wish you hadn't, such as forgetting a birthday or anniversary. Guilt is also different from irritability, anxiety, depression, agitation, and low self-esteem—although guilt sometimes causes some of these feelings. Guilt is an internal, private, negative feeling of wrongdoing in which you say, "I dislike myself for this behavior." Guilt can be immediate or delayed, appropriate or inappropriate.

When sexual urges evolve in total ignorance, they can produce unnecessary guilt. People develop endless misconceptions when they learn such global negatives as "Don't touch down there." "It's bad, dirty, sinful." "Masturbation breeds insanity; it damages your health, your eyes, your mind." "You shouldn't enjoy sex." "Don't get pregnant." For some people, even the normal, pleasurable sexual exchange in a loving relationship can stir up painful guilt feelings. Take the case of a woman who was raised with repeated warnings about getting pregnant out of wedlock. She may continue to feel guilty about having sex after she gets married because she still associates the sex act with her past fear of pregnancy.

Guilt can cause tremendous anxiety when a person assumes that he or she has done something wrong and then feels an exaggerated need to keep it secret. For instance, a person may experience anxiety about having sexual fantasies because he or she considers them immoral, unnatural, or an act of unfaithfulness to the partner and then increase the anxiety by keeping the fantasies secret. Guilt about sexual thoughts, longings, or acts can also produce physical symptoms, such as tears, headaches, or worse.

For example, during an emergency room visit, Ben, age sixty-seven, complained of a rapid heartbeat and severe chest pains. His blood pressure was high. His wife of thirty-seven years had recently died. He told the emergency room doctor, "I feel so guilty that she died first. She was only sixty years old." "Why guilty?" asked the doctor while arranging for tests to be done. "Because I was with her when she died. We made love that night, and it was always great for both of us. When I woke up the next morning, I thought she was just sleeping. Right before I left the house, I went back to the bedroom to ask her something and I realized she was dead. We were too old. We shouldn't have had sex." Was this appropriate guilt? No. But it had its effects nevertheless. The grief and regret produced by the loss of Ben's life partner were normal, but his self-blame and guilt were totally misplaced. Ben's doctor reassured him that sex had nothing to do with his wife's death and told him that his tests had come back normal. Anxiety, precipitated by guilt, had brought on Ben's chest pains.

A person can also experience guilt after betraying his or her partner in a relationship—for example, by having an extramarital affair—whether or not the partner knows about the unfaithfulness. The pain and anger the betrayal produces when the partner learns of it can only be resolved through straightforward communication, forgiveness, and the gradual rebuilding of trust over a period of time. The truthfulness of the errant partner will be tested and retested before healing can begin.

But the situation can be even thornier if the partner does not know about the infidelity. "How could I have done this?" asked Judy, a thirty-five-year-old flight attendant. "I love my family, and my husband loves me. But I don't think I realized how lonely I was. A couple of drinks, some attention and flattery, and all my defenses seemed to melt." Judy had an affair with a handsome passenger after a long flight to the Far East. She had never been unfaithful before, but because of the perceived anonymity and remoteness of the situation, she acquiesced to having a fling. Now she found herself in a serious moral crisis. Feeling shame and remorse, and suffering from bouts of insomnia, Judy came to me for individual psychotherapy.

Judy had two choices. She could tell her husband about the affair to relieve her guilt and risk destroying their relationship ("I would leave him if he cheated on me," she said) or she could live with her remorse and vow never to be unfaithful again. I could not decide for her, but I could help her decide by asking her what purpose the telling would serve. I also asked Judy to write down three pluses and three minuses of sharing the secret with her husband and then a list of three pluses and minuses of keeping silent. After completing this task, Judy decided that, even though keeping the secret would be harder and more painful for her than telling her husband, she would not divulge her secret because it would hurt him deeply. She opted for silence at the time she ended therapy.

These days, some single parents feel guilty about having sex in their own homes with a new partner because their children are around. Jay, age forty, had been divorced for three years. He and his girlfriend, Lynn, had been in an exclusive relationship for about eight months. They had sex at Lynn's apartment once or twice a week, but Jay would never stay overnight because of his two teenage sons. He was concerned about the example he would be setting for them if they suspected that he and Lynn were sleeping together without being married.

Lynn understood Jay's feelings, but thought that it would be more honest if the boys knew what was going on. Then, Jay began having sporadic erection problems, so the couple came to our clinic for help. We advised Jay to sit down with the boys and talk it out. "When I finally explained to the boys that Lynn and I loved each other and that she would be staying overnight at our house sometimes, they were amazingly nonchalant about it," said Jay. "But, boy, it was tough for me that first night Lynn stayed over, knowing that they were sleeping just down the hall."

Jay's sons accepted Lynn into their lives fairly easily and, gradually, Jay came to accept the situation as well. His erection problems had completely resolved themselves by the sixth week of sex therapy.

Sexual Trauma: Healing the Emotional Scars

Some people with sexual problems have experienced sexual trauma—sexual abuse or rape as a child, teen, or adult. Sexual trauma can cause a variety of sexual problems, including a fear of closeness or touching, a lack of interest in sex, an inability to reach orgasm, or a spasm of the vaginal muscles (vaginismus). Most victims are females, but males can also be the subjects of sexual assault. The national incidence of child sexual abuse is unknown but, in one recent national survey, 27 percent of the females and 16 percent of the males reported experiencing sexual abuse in childhood. At our sex therapy clinic, 15 percent of the women and 11 percent of the men said they were molested as children by an adult or a peer.

We live in an era of the eroticized child, but in a values vacuum. Such vehicles as X-rated cable TV have given nine year olds a sexual vocabulary unknown to thirty-nine year olds several decades ago. But too few people—including most parents—teach children how to grapple with the real issues that surround being sexually active. Not only do we neglect teaching children how to form loving, committed relationships, we also avoid discussing the prevention of sexual abuse.

The range of adult-child sexual crimes extends from fondling to rape to murder. But even when the child is not physically harmed, doctors consider adult-child sex totally unacceptable because of the physical and emotional inequality of the child in relation to the adult. The adult usually must somehow coerce the child into participating. The child's normal curiosity, sexual innocence, and respect for adults as authority figures combine to make it difficult for the child to say no. The child may even experience normal reflex arousal from the fondling or like the special attention he or she receives from the adult, especially if there are rewards, such as money or candy, for cooperating.

The severity, timing, and number of the sexual acts all determine the effects on the person. When the acts are discovered, the general panic, blame, and fighting among family members may be more traumatic to the child than the actual sexual experience. No wonder many victims generalize the overall chaotic experience so that all sex seems scary, wrong, or evil.

Mary Jane, forty-two, came to our sex therapy clinic because she lacked interest in sex. She could not be aroused sexually, would not let her husband touch her below the waist, and had never masturbated. Her father had died when Mary Jane was two years old, and her mother became a sexually promiscuous alcoholic. The family was poor, and Mary Jane's maternal uncle, Eddie, often brought them food. Her mother soon remarried. Once, when Mary Jane was five years old, Uncle Eddie undressed her, sat her on the side of the bed, and began to fondle her genitals. Her uncle was gentle, and she enjoyed the contact. He offered her money to let him touch her again. At that point, Mary Jane's older brother walked into the room, saw the exchange, grabbed the money, and ran to tell her mother and stepfather.

"All I remember was the fighting and the shouting," said Mary Jane. "My mother was screaming, and my stepfather hit Uncle Eddie. He was bleeding. I cried. I was terribly afraid and thought I had caused it. It wasn't the sex that scared me. It was the fighting. After that, my mother warned me over and over for years, 'Don't ever let anyone touch you down there.'"

I asked Mary Jane to write a letter to her dead Uncle Eddie so she could discharge any residual feelings she might still have about the incest experience. She wrote, "You're a sick man. You should have been put away years ago." This statement showed she had taken an adult perspective on the situation. "I was too small to know better," she continued, absolving herself of the blame. "I could kill you. No, I don't mean that. I understand you are sick." This last statement displayed healing forgiveness. "Don't bother me again because I'm ready to handle it all. Love, your niece, Mary Jane." She still cared for him because he had been kind to her.

Sexual abuse can have devastating effects. Extensive treatment of those effects is beyond the scope of this book. If you have unresolved feelings about being sexually abused or raped, I strongly urge you to seek professional help from a qualified therapist or counselor. Call a social worker at your local community hospital to find out what kind of help is available in your area. Don't endure the pain alone.

Divorce and changing social customs have altered the family landscape, allowing men and women to move in and out of relationships of varying stability. Most parents bring their children into the new relationships, creating a formal or informal, reconstituted, or blended stepfamily. Today's increasing numbers of stepfamilies, foster families, and live-in-lover families create new forms of kinship that have yet to be defined. Children may be upset or ambivalent about having to cope with new "relatives," who may be chosen by a parent but unwanted by the child. These changes in the structure of the family have given greater prominence to child-to-child sexual abuse or coercion. Familiarity may not always breed contempt. Sexual attraction may appear instead.

Children and teenagers who live together but are not blood relatives may feel free to approach each other for sexual favors, especially when they are unsupervised. Limited supervision in families in which both parents work provides privacy and opportunity for sexual experimentation. A strong, eroticized adolescent can threaten and terrorize a younger, weaker, or disabled one. Children can rape children and blackmail each other to keep quiet about it. If you live in a blended family, it can happen to your unsupervised children. It is not as rare as you might think. The solution lies in early training in the rights and wrongs of adolescent sexual behavior. Simply say, "Sexual feelings are strong and natural, but you can deal with them by going into your room, closing the door, and releasing your sexual tension alone and in private. You may absolutely not take advantage of your little sister. That's not experimentation. It's wrong, and it breaks the law."

If you are a parent, you must teach your children that, like stealing, forcing sex on another person or being forced to have sex is wrong. Children also need to learn that they have the right to refuse sexual advances from within the family just as they do those from outside it. Some families may have a pattern of sexual abuse that is hard to break. In blended families, the usual sexual taboos may blur or break down completely. Regardless of the circumstances, no child should feel that he or she must endure inappropriate sexual behavior from anyone, for any reason. Extra supervision, frank discussion about incest, and sex education can help prevent sexual trauma from hampering your children's normal, healthy sexual growth. If you have experienced this kind of sexual trauma, know that you are not alone and that help is available.

Just as sexual abuse traumatizes a young child, rape can completely alter a woman's normal sexual expression. Women who were once warm and open can become overly sensitive, tense, sexually withdrawn, and fearful after a rape experience. The strong feelings of violation and lack of control coupled with fear of sexually transmitted disease or pregnancy can stop a woman from engaging in a healthy sexual relationship. Lack of interest in sex and inability to reach orgasm are common in women who have been raped. Many sexually assaulted women who enter sex therapy find that the therapy helps them break the silence and discuss the rape with their partner for the first time so they can let go of the trauma and reclaim their sexual selves. Men who have been sexually abused can also benefit from this kind of therapy.

Remember that, no matter what the cause of your particular sexual problem, you are not alone. Many other people struggle with the same difficulties you face. Your sexual problem is treatable, and you should feel proud of yourself for seeking help. Using the methods I describe in this book, you can learn how to resolve your sexual problem and have a more sexually satisfying and loving relationship with your partner.

2

The Sex Education You Never Had

Lack of knowledge about sex—what I call sexual illiteracy—is an important cause of adult sexual problems. That's why the first thing I do for the patients who come to our sex therapy clinic is teach them a quick, updated course in sex education. I'm also going to give *you* a healthy dose of the same sex education in this book. I believe that sex education is the best tool we have to fight the sexual ignorance and misinformation that are still rampant today—years after the so-called sexual revolution.

How many of us can say that Mom or Dad sat us down and said, "My child, sex is good. Let me tell you about it"? Very few of us. Sexual silence at home is common. But it's not really silent at all. It says, "It upsets Mom and Dad to talk about this secret subject." Most of us learn sexual behavior the same way we learn language, by listening, watching, reading, and trying out. But just as some people do not learn the skills of reading and writing, many men and women do not learn sexual skills. Unless they are taught, they remain sexual illiterates.

The absence of sex education may be the most influential message of all. It says, "We do not or cannot talk about sex here." Sex then becomes a taboo subject, to be learned from peers, inaccurately and incompletely. Other children teach children about sex. How? In exciting, secret, forbidden, scary, often inaccurate ways—sometimes in fun and sometimes by force.

Parents who think they are the dominant influence in their child's life after the age of nine are burying their heads in the sand. Unless a radical change occurs, initiated by open-minded, concerned parents, backyard sex educators will remain our children's main source of information about the important topic of sexuality.

Children see images of sex all around them—in advertising, on TV soap operas and music videos, and even in movies without X ratings. The birth control pill has been available as a street drug in most schools for at least fifteen years, sometimes used wrongly and without a doctor's supervision. Our children are overloaded with sexual stimuli but receive little guidance in sexual matters. Today's children are not sexually innocent, but they may be entirely ignorant about sexuality, affection, relationships, and love.

Most parents know that immunization protects their children against diseases such as diphtheria. In everyday life, where sexual stimuli abound, sex education can act like immunization, protecting against the negative consequences of sexuality, such as unwanted pregnancy, sexually transmitted disease, and child sexual abuse. When will we finally educate our children? When they have their first baby at age thirteen? When they get AIDS? When they have their third abortion? Only the unwanted consequences of sexual expression produce strong moral, emotional, and political reactions.

Accurate sex education does help prevent these social problems. Just as important, it can prevent the needless anxiety and guilt that often surround healthy, normal adult sexuality. In my experience, an overwhelming number of adult sexual problems are rooted in sexual ignorance and early sexual misinformation, which often lead to deepseated sexual inhibitions.

Sexual awareness begins in infancy. We begin to explore ourselves soon after we are born. Just as we investigate our toes and fingers, we explore our genitals. It's normal. We all have a sexual self that we remember, clearly or vaguely, from our childhood. It might be very joyful. It might be very negative. Sometimes childhood sexual expression is severely punished and the experience becomes a traumatic memory. It's not only sexual abuse that's punished; parents may also punish children for normal sexual behavior, such as masturbation. The shame of discovery may remain for years. But Mom and Dad knew no better. They were taught that way too. So forgive Mom and Dad, but most important, forgive yourself. You lacked knowledge. Now it's up to you to learn all you can about your body and your sexuality.

A Lesson in Female and Male Anatomy

Because a man's penis must enter the vagina to deposit sperm, the penis is external—on the outside of the body. Because a baby develops inside a woman's uterus, a woman's reproductive organs are internal. This "invisible" structure protects the growing fetus. But it also discourages many women from learning about their bodies.

During toilet training, we teach boys to look at and touch their penises every time they urinate, just like Daddy. But many girls learn that their genitals are concealed, unpleasant, and untouchable—or they learn nothing about them at all. We often teach girls to be sexually neutral—that is, to be receptive, responsive, and passive—rather than to be active and take the initiative sexually. We sometimes tell them that they don't need to know about their bodies because their male partner will "know what to do." Worse yet, we sometimes use negative terms to refer to normal female functions. The "plague" and the "curse" are standard expressions for menstruation, for example. Most women have never even looked at their external genitals.

Now you have a chance to learn about your sexual organs and to know where each part is in relation to the others. The best way to see your genital area is to examine it with a mirror. Pick a time when you are not rushed and can have privacy. Remove your clothes and sit down on your bed or squat on the floor with your legs spread apart. It might even help to illuminate the area with a flashlight. You may feel uncomfortable about doing this self-examination, but I want you to know about your body and to explore it so you can understand and enjoy it. You have my permission to look at, touch, and know about your genitals. Pretend that I've written you a prescription to learn about your body. Just don't try to take it to the pharmacy!

If you are a woman, the first thing you will see is your pubic hair, which covers the mound of protective tissue called the mons that lies over the outer genitals (see illustration below). Under the mons are two flaps, which join at the top like an inverted "V," known as the outer lips, or labia, of a woman's genitals. Gently spread these lips open and you will see two inner lips of hairless skin that protect the urinary opening and the vagina. At the top, where the inner lips join, lies a semicircular hood over the shaft and tip of the clitoris, the primary site of sexual stimulation in a woman. You can pull the hood up a bit to see the shaft more clearly.

A woman's clitoris becomes erect (firm and swollen) during arousal

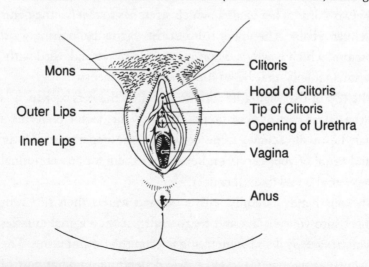

Mons
Outer Lips
Inner Lips
Clitoris
Hood of Clitoris
Tip of Clitoris
Opening of Urethra
Vagina
Anus

Female Genitals

in the same way that a man's penis does. But while a penis has three jobs—urination, procreation, and recreation—the clitoris has only one. It is the only human organ with no function other than pleasurable arousal. The clitoris is richly supplied with nerve endings and blood vessels. During sexual arousal, the clitoris throbs, swells, and becomes more sensitive. When it becomes erect, the clitoris moves up and back under the hood, not up and out like the penis. That's the reason many women and couples cannot locate it. Just below the clitoris, you will see a small slit, the urethral opening, which releases urine from your bladder. Some women mistake it for the clitoris. When the opening is rubbed roughly, it can become irritated, making urination painful.

Under the opening to the bladder lies the entrance to your vagina. The vagina is the muscular passage that leads from the uterus to the outside of your body. The lower third of the vagina is under your voluntary control. You can contract it and relax it the same way you can contract and relax the circular muscles around your eyes, mouth, and rectum. This lower third of the vagina has been called the love muscle because contracting it feels good. Some women can fantasize or watch a sexy movie and bring themselves to climax without touching themselves simply by contracting this muscle. A woman cannot contract the upper two thirds of her vagina, which stretches to receive the penis and to deliver a baby. The upper third of the vagina balloons upward during orgasm, which is why a diaphragm could move and, used without a spermicidal jelly, may be an ineffective contraceptive.

At the top of the vagina lies an organ called the cervix, which is actually the lower part of your uterus. When your doctor performs a Pap smear, he or she scrapes some cells from the upper part of your vagina and canal of your cervix and examines them for any abnormal cell changes that could foretell cancer.

Wash your hands carefully with soap and water, then slip your index finger into your vagina and try to contract the vaginal muscles around your finger, as if you were trying to stop the flow of urine. The walls of your vagina may feel wet or dry, depending on what part of your monthly menstrual cycle it is, whether you are aroused, or whether you are past menopause, when your vagina naturally becomes drier. Slide your finger deeper into your vagina and you will feel the way the vagina angles back in your body; it does not extend straight up. If you can reach in to the top of your vagina, you will feel your cervix, which is the bottom of your uterus. It may feel like the tip of a nose or chin with a small dimple, which is the opening into your uterus.

You will not be able to see or feel your uterus or the rest of your internal sexual organs (see illustrations below). Extending from the top of your uterus are the two fallopian tubes. Each month, one of your ovaries—which lie near the ends of your fallopian tubes and produce the female sex hormones estrogen and progesterone—releases an egg. One of the fallopian tubes grips the egg, which travels through the tube to the uterus. If a sperm joins with the egg and fertilization takes place, the egg may implant into the uterus, which will nourish the embryo. If fertilization does not take place, the egg dies and the lining of your uterus, which thickened in anticipation of receiving a fertilized egg, begins to shed. The sloughed-off lining passes through the small opening in the cervix and out through the vagina. This shedding of tissues and blood is what you experience as menstruation.

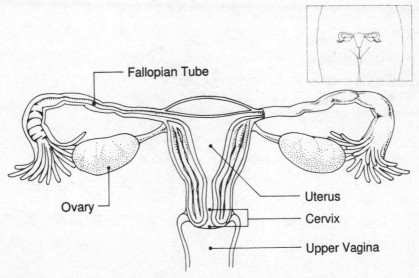

Female Reproductive Organs

A man's sexual organs (see illustration below) include the penis, through which both urine and semen pass. The testicles, which are enclosed in a pouch of skin called the scrotum, produce sperm and the male sex hormone testosterone. The sensitive testicles hang below your penis because, to make sperm, they need a slightly cooler temperature than that found inside the body. Your left testicle normally hangs lower than the one on your right to make it easier for you to cross your legs, walk, and run. Some men think they're abnormal because one of their testicles hangs lower than the other. Not true at all. Above each testicle lies an organ called the epididymis, in which your sperm mature.

A long, tiny tube called the vas deferens rises up from the back of each testicle into your lower abdomen, behind the bladder. Each tube carries sperm to a small storage pouch called the ampulla of the vas

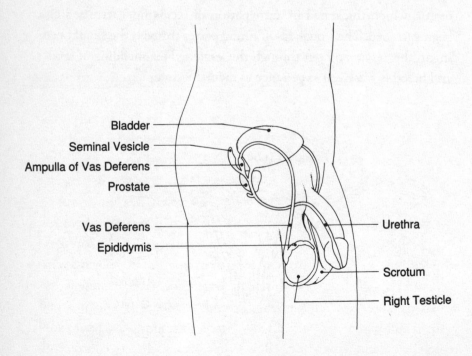

Bladder
Seminal Vesicle
Ampulla of Vas Deferens
Prostate
Vas Deferens
Epididymis
Urethra
Scrotum
Right Testicle

Male Reproductive Organs

deferens. Sperm can remain there for several months—even after a vasectomy, a simple operation in which each vas deferens is severed so that the man's semen will no longer contain sperm. That's why you may still be able to make your partner pregnant for a while after a vasectomy if you don't use birth control. Doctors always ask a man to come for a checkup eight weeks after having a vasectomy so they can examine his semen for live sperm.

Just before you ejaculate, your sperm mix with nourishing secretions from the seminal vesicles. Then, when they enter the urethra (the tube inside the penis that carries urine out of your body), they mix with secretions from the prostate gland. This mixture of sperm and secretions from the prostate gland and seminal vesicles is called semen. Semen is cream-colored, has a salty-sweet taste, and is quite harmless if swallowed, so your partner need not worry about having oral (mouth-to-genital) sex. (Although extremely rare, there have been a few isolated incidences of HIV infection from oral sex.) Although the urethra is the same tube that discharges urine from your body, you do *not* urinate into your partner during intercourse. When you are about to ejaculate, a reflex shuts the internal valve of the bladder so that your penis can release only the semen.

You begin to ejaculate semen just before your body's orgasmic contractions begin. This fact explains why withdrawal—removing the penis from the vagina before the man reaches orgasm—as a method of birth control is so ineffective. Even the very first drop of preejaculate, the clear fluid that comes out of your penis before orgasm, contains thousands of sperm—and only one sperm is needed to fertilize an egg.

The head of your penis has a thick covering, called the foreskin, which is often removed shortly after birth in a procedure known as circumcision. Studies show no significant difference in the experience of sexual pleasure between circumcised and uncircumcised men. Your penis is richly supplied with blood vessels to nourish the tissue and muscles inside it. When your penis is soft, its muscles are contracted. But when you become sexually aroused, the muscles inside the penis relax, blood rushes in, and your penis becomes swollen and erect. (Heavy smoking can cause the muscles inside your penis to contract even when you are aroused and, after a time, can damage the delicate tissue in the penis. So, if any of you are smokers, quit, guys, for the sake of your penis. It's sending up messages saying, "Don't hurt me please.")

The size of the flaccid penis varies widely among men. But an erection just about equalizes size differences. An erect penis extends about five to seven inches in length. Erection may quadruple the size of a small penis while adding only half an inch to a longer penis. Many men worry that their penis is too small but almost all erect penises are about the same size. As I tell my anxious male patients, a man whose erect penis extends five inches experiences the same degree of pleasure as a man with a seven-inch-long erect penis. Neither does a woman's pleasure depend on a man's penis size. Women, do not judge a man by his penis size. Skill and sensitivity, not size, are what's important—and not just skill with his penis, but also with his words, his hands, and his mouth.

Some women are afraid that they will hurt a man's genitals if they handle them too roughly. It's true that a man's testicles are extremely sensitive. But the penis is not fragile; it's much less sensitive than the testicles. Many men say that they would like much more stimulation of the penis than they receive. Check with your partner to find out how firmly he wants you to grip or stroke his penis. Ask him to show you exactly how he would like you to stimulate him.

In both sexes, nerves that extend from the lower spine eroticize the entire genital area. That's why it feels good when your partner caresses your upper thighs, lower back, and buttocks. It also explains why anal (penis-in-rectum) sex can be orgasmic for some people. Did you know that your skin is the largest erotic organ in your body? It has millions of nerve endings, and that's why I want you to touch and explore everywhere on your bodies. Touching is free, nonfattening, and nonsinful. It's also a great way to start the adults-only part of your evening after the kids are in bed.

Contrasting Sexual Cycles

The graph on page 36 shows the differences between the sexual response cycle of a man and that of a woman. When you have privacy and a sexually arousing and responsive partner, or exciting thoughts when you're alone, you will go through predictable stages of arousal, whether you are a man or a woman. These stages are called preliminary arousal, plateau, a point of inevitability when the arousal is no longer under voluntary control, and climax (orgasm). But, although the stages of arousal are similar for both sexes, the timing is radically different; arousal takes much longer in a woman. These differences are not wrong; they are just different. Let's go through the stages for a man and then for a woman.

When a man becomes aroused, he will have a partial and then a full erection. If you take time out to answer the phone, you may lose the erection, but it will come back when you return to sexual activity. You will then reach a plateau of arousal and stay erect. In a short time after appropriate stimulation, you will reach a point of ejaculatory inevitability, which means that you will not be able to control your level of arousal anymore. At this point, you will start to climax, even if you hear a boom of thunder or the smoke detector goes off. For these few seconds, your response is reflexive: you ejaculate and climax. The total time, from entry of the penis into the vagina or beginning of masturbation to climax, averages less than three minutes. If you're in a big hurry, you can climax even more quickly. The premature ejaculator (see page 82) may ejaculate so quickly that he doesn't reach the bed or ejaculates between his partner's thighs before he can even enter her.

After orgasm, a man cannot have another sexual cycle until a certain amount of time goes by; the length of time varies greatly. This time is called a refractory period. It is much shorter in a teenage boy or young man and is longest in a man over the age of fifty, especially if he hasn't recently been sexually active. Interestingly, a woman has no re-

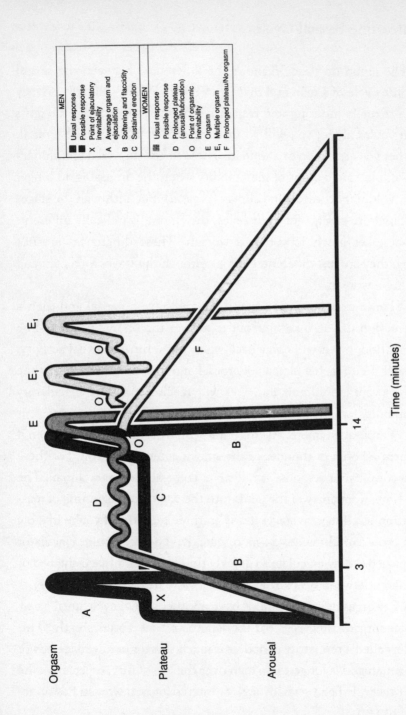

Male and Female Sexual Response Cycle

fractory period after climax. She can have many orgasms in a row without a "waiting period." Again, this difference between men and women is natural and normal.

A woman has similar phases of arousal, but her timing is completely different. As you become aroused, your clitoris will become erect and your vagina will lubricate to prepare for receiving your partner's penis. You will reach orgasmic inevitability and will climax, but your sexual cycle from start to finish usually lasts about thirteen or fourteen minutes—almost four times longer than a man's. This difference in timing explains why some women cannot reach orgasm during intercourse—their partner finishes long before they are ready. And the difference can cause needless blame, sexual incompatibility, and friction. He doesn't know about it. She doesn't know about it. He calls her frigid. She calls him Speedy Gonzales. They fight, and their relationship becomes strained over a difference that is completely normal. But, because they never learned about this natural difference, each partner thinks that there is something wrong with the other or with himself or herself. I can't tell you why this difference in timing exists, only that it does. Just do not blame yourself or each other.

"When Dr. Renshaw told us about the different timing of arousal between men and women, I felt like it explained a lot," said Charley, a forty-three-year-old high school math teacher who came to sex therapy with his wife, Karen, age forty, also a teacher. Karen had never had an orgasm during intercourse and had lost all interest in having sex. The couple had been married for eleven years.

Eight years before, during the delivery of her first child, Karen experienced an intense and pleasurable orgasm in the birthing room. This experience is not unusual, but many women feel confused and ashamed when it occurs. "I didn't know what was happening," said Karen. "And I was so embarrassed about it that I started to cry. The funny thing is, sex never felt that good with Charley, before or after it happened. I want it to, and that's why we came here."

The couple listened to our instruction about male and female anatomy and faithfully did their loveplay exercises at home (see page 116 for an explanation of home loveplay). Knowing that a woman's response time is nearly four times longer than a man's helped Charley and Karen approach their particular problem with new enthusiasm. After extensive kissing and caressing, Charley patiently stimulated Karen's clitoris with his fingers until she felt adequately aroused and ready for him to penetrate her. By the end of the seven-week sex therapy program, Karen had experienced an orgasm twice, once during intercourse and once while Charley stimulated her by hand.

Can a woman learn to climax more quickly than the norm? Yes, just as a man can learn to delay his ejaculation. Many couples adjust to the different timing together without ever having heard of sex therapy. You can learn to negotiate the difference with your partner. Maybe your partner can attend to you after he has had his orgasm. For a man with erection problems, an approach called the squeeze technique can help prolong his erection (see pages 197–198 for an explanation and illustration of the squeeze technique). As a man gets older, his plateau phase lasts longer, making it possible for him to extend his erection time. That's why some couples say that, as they get older, sex gets better.

What Happens During Orgasm?

For centuries, no one had studied or understood the phenomenon of orgasm. Ejaculation confirmed a climax for a man, but for the average woman climax remained a mystery, cloaked in misinformation and romanticized inaccuracy. Then, in 1966, Masters and Johnson published their landmark work, *Human Sexual Response*. Thanks to them, we now understand what happens during orgasm.

Physically, orgasm is a buildup of pressure in the blood vessels and tissues of the genitals that culminates in a peak of tension and sudden discharge. During the discharge phase, pleasurable muscle contractions occur in the genital area and throughout the body. Men and women can have big or little orgasms. The quality depends on your state of mind (eager anticipation or inhibition) and on the state of your body (relaxation or tension).

Four sites in the bodies of both men and women have tissue that becomes erect during arousal: the earlobes, nipples, the lining of the nose, and the genitals (penis or clitoris). As part of the total orgasmic response, every muscle in your body contracts: toes, legs, back, neck, face. But, unlike the exaggerated contortions in X-rated movies, they are small contractions. They don't make you fall off the bed. After having an orgasm, you reach total relaxation. The satisfying and relaxing way you feel after reaching orgasm is a natural sensation that you should understand and enjoy. A few people feel highly energized after having an orgasm and feel they must do some creative work before they can sleep.

When a woman reaches climax, the muscles in the lower third of her vagina contract involuntarily and repeatedly while the upper third of her vagina balloons up. The uterus also contracts rhythmically during orgasm, just as it does during the delivery of a baby. Because of these contractions, orgasm can actually relieve menstrual cramps by emptying blood from the uterus. Conversely, the final stage of delivery of a baby can cause an orgasm. Both of these responses are perfectly natural, but women vary in their awareness and acceptance of them.

Only 20 to 30 percent of women can have coital climax—that is, orgasm during intercourse. Why can these women have a coital climax while most others need manual or oral stimulation of the clitoris? Partly because of the difference in timing of a man's and a woman's sexual cycle that I explained on page 35. But this situation also goes back to the old coital versus clitoral climax controversy.

Marriage manuals once taught that an orgasm that occurred during intercourse was somehow superior to and more "mature" than an orgasm that required manipulation of the clitoris. We now know that there is only one type of female orgasm, triggered by the stimulation of the roots of the clitoris, similar to those in the penis, that attach to the front arch of the pelvic bones. Manual or oral stimulation of the clitoris will inevitably stimulate these roots and can produce climax. The friction of the penis in the vagina during intercourse, coupled with the impact of the pelvic thrusts, can also stimulate these roots.

No matter how it is produced, the climax is the same. An orgasm is an orgasm. Reaching orgasm during intercourse depends on your anatomy and your activity. In other words, certain couples fit together and move in a way that stimulates the woman's clitoris to orgasm while others do not. One woman asked me, "What's the matter with me? My first husband was alcoholic. He treated me like dirt. But I could have climaxes during intercourse with him and I can't with my current husband. Do I need to be mistreated to have an orgasm?" Nonsense! It all depends on the fit and the way you move.

Some women's genital areas tilt back, some are horizontal, some tip forward. Maybe you can find different positions for intercourse that better stimulate your clitoris. You can even slip your own hand between your bodies so you can stimulate your clitoris during intercourse. If your partner struggles to find it and hurts you, World War III could start! It's important for both of you to find out what works and tell each other about it.

A woman can attain orgasm during intercourse more readily when she is on top. Some men and women feel this position is too aggressive a position for the woman and may be a threat to the male. Maybe it's been a long time since you've discussed different positions. Couples, you need to talk to each other and develop enough trust to experiment with positions so both of you can reach orgasm. Only 36 percent of American couples prefer the woman-superior position, but there are cultures in which it is the favored position. It's a wonderful position for the reversal of many sexual symptoms, such as inability to attain orgasm or painful orgasm in women and ejaculation or erection problems in men. I recommend you browse through your local bookstore and find a book that describes different sexual positions you can try.

Many women experience cycles of arousal that reflect the hormonal changes of their monthly menstrual cycle. Some women have premenstrual swelling in the breasts and genitals that causes a peak of sexual arousal. Other women report a similar peak at midcycle, during ovulation. Still others feel more aroused during menstruation because they are free of the fear of pregnancy. These cyclical peaks of arousal are all completely normal.

When a man becomes sexually aroused, his brain sends signals to his penis by way of the nervous system. The muscles inside your penis relax, and the spaces between your muscle and connective tissue fibers fill up with blood like a sponge. Sixteen times as much blood flows into your penis as when you are resting. The pressure inside your penis rises and an erection occurs. When you reach orgasm, through intercourse or masturbation, the muscles surrounding the base of your penis contract to help expel the semen from your penis. The ejaculate amounts to only about a teaspoonful of fluid. Every time you have an orgasm, the testosterone levels in your blood go up. That's one reason why men who have not recently been sexually active may benefit from regular masturbation as a way of "jump starting" their slower testosterone metabolism.

In both sexes, blood pressure goes up, heart rate increases, and breathing speeds up during arousal and orgasm, all within generally safe limits. If you can climb one flight of twenty steps without shortness of breath or chest pain, you can usually manage an orgasm. If you are unsure about the condition of your heart, check with your doctor. Some men and women sabotage their orgasm by trying to suppress the rapid, deep breathing that starts during arousal because they worry that the heavy breathing is just too animalistic or barbaric. Such blocking interferes with the natural release of sexual tension. You have to breathe through your mouth during arousal because the tissue inside your nose swells. This is no time to worry about being proper!

Characters in romance novels routinely attain simultaneous orgasm and you may abandon common sense in your efforts to duplicate their experience. In reality, simultaneous orgasm is a joyous rarity. It should be savored as an occasional piece of good luck, not regularly and relentlessly pursued. Constant pursuit of simultaneous orgasm can backfire. When both partners become tense and self-conscious, neither may have any orgasm at all.

Masturbation:
Natural and Normal Throughout Life

Many of the women who come to our sex therapy clinic have never had an orgasm. Most of these women have never masturbated. By learning how to give yourself a climax through masturbation, you can find out what feels good to you and then communicate this information to your partner.

We have associated masturbation with madness and evil for many centuries. Prohibitions against masturbation predate Christianity. The Talmud (the authoritative book of Jewish tradition) refers to death by stoning for a man who masturbates instead of having sexual relations with his wife. The ancient Spartans forbade masturbation as part of their strict, self-disciplined existence. Later, during the Middle Ages, clergy attacked the practice as evidence of complicity with the devil. In 1758, a prestigious Swiss physician, S. A. Tissot, cited masturbation as the cause of tuberculosis, gonorrhea, epilepsy, suicide, and insanity. This association of masturbation with insanity endured throughout the 1800s. At the turn of the century, accepted "treatments" for the practice included tying a child's hands to his or her crib, a cage strapped around the genitalia, and a horrendous surgical procedure in which two holes were drilled into the foreskin of the boy or genital lips of the girl to fit a metal padlock.

As recently as the 1940s, doctors believed that masturbation caused homosexuality, premature ejaculation, and impotence. But publication of the first book by sex researcher Alfred Kinsey in 1948, which revealed the sexual practices of over five thousand men in the United States, made it clear that masturbation is a natural and universal component of human sexual expression. Ninety percent of males and 50 to 80 percent of females later surveyed reported that they masturbated.

We now know that masturbation is a completely normal activity that can begin in infancy and extend into old age. It is not a perversion.

In fact, we have found that a lack of sexual self-exploration and self-stimulation is a common feature of people seeking treatment for sexual problems. I usually prescribe masturbation, used in concert with sexual fantasy, for any woman who has problems attaining orgasm. It helps her collaborate with her partner in attaining climax, rather than placing the burden of her sexual satisfaction on him. I also recommend fantasy and masturbation for a man who has erection problems. Having good erections during masturbation builds a man's sexual self-confidence in the same way a woman becomes more confident when she learns how her body can attain orgasm.

Many people still find masturbation embarrassing and difficult because their beliefs and feelings prohibit it. I respect that. Sex and values are closely bound. You cannot go further or faster than your beliefs permit. But it may help you to know that theologians are revising their views about masturbation in light of present-day medical knowledge. Many now regard masturbation as a morally neutral activity. If you have concerns about the way masturbation conflicts with your religious beliefs, talk with your minister, priest, or rabbi to find out your religion's current teachings on the subject.

"I was raised in a strict Protestant home," said Richard, age thirty-four. "My parents never talked about sex, and I didn't learn about it at school. My friends gave me lots of misinformation about sex, but I was too afraid to touch myself or explore. It just seemed dirty." Richard's problem was premature ejaculation. He was a virgin when he married Catherine. She had little sexual experience, so she couldn't help Richard learn about his body. Catherine had never had an orgasm and, not only was she uninterested in sex, she actually found it repellent. She put up with it about twice a month only to please Richard.

We taught Richard the squeeze technique (see page 197) to help him overcome his performance anxiety and premature ejaculation. We also prescribed masturbation every other day for Catherine during the first two weeks of therapy and twice per week during the following three weeks, so she could get in touch with her neglected sexuality. Catherine refused to try masturbation at first, but reluctantly agreed to go through with it once, in week 2, after discussing her anxiety with me in private. She told me about a bit of self-discovery she'd had. "Just thinking about masturbation makes me feel so sinful," Catherine said. "But I forced myself to think about this long and hard, and I've discovered that my upbringing taught me to believe that I don't deserve to feel good because I'm a sinner. Sinners are supposed to suffer, and that's what I've done during sex—suffered through it."

This revelation helped Catherine see how her beliefs had limited her ability to show her love for Richard. She masturbated twice a week at home, in private, during the remaining weeks of sex therapy but was unable to bring herself to climax. Finally, in week 7, she experienced an orgasm while being manually stimulated by Richard. The squeeze technique helped Richard overcome his problem, and the couple continued to explore their sexual selves at home after the conclusion of therapy.

You may not believe that masturbation is wrong, but you might still be uncomfortable about doing it while you are in a relationship. Many normal married people masturbate when they are apart or in between the times they have intercourse, especially if they have different levels of sexual desire. They often do it secretly with much needless worry. It isn't wrong to masturbate during marriage, but you should also be looking for ways to increase your togetherness and intimacy. Couples, talk to each other about masturbation. Clear the air of secrets so you can gain understanding and find alternate ways, such as mutual masturbation (masturbating each other), to share your peaks of desire together at times when you don't want to have intercourse.

Masturbation does not damage the body or mind, nor does it weaken athletic performance. It does provide complete relaxation for some time after climax. Why cheat yourself? It's far healthier than alcohol or a sleeping pill, and there's no hangover!

How to Masturbate
Before you begin to masturbate, empty your bladder and get comfortable. You may find it useful to look at your whole body first in a mirror,

not critically but with curiosity. Accept and appreciate it just the way it is.

Next, begin touching your body with your hands. Try using oil or lotion; it may heighten the sensation in your skin. Explore every part of your body, especially the parts that are the most sensitive, such as your nipples and your pubic area. Certain ways of stroking, pressing, and lightly flicking may feel more arousing than others. Be patient and take your time. Closing your eyes might help you focus your mind on the sensations your body is experiencing. Try imagining a favorite sexual fantasy.

Now focus on your sexual organs. Women, place a finger on your outer genital lips. Gently pull the lips apart and slip a finger inside the outer lips. Feel the sensations that arise as you slowly move your finger around the area between your outer and inner genital lips. Move your finger up toward your clitoris and leisurely explore it. What kind of motion and pressure does your clitoris respond to most? Is this your first attempt at masturbation? You may be able to bring yourself to climax by stimulating your clitoris, but if you find you can't, don't worry. Many women cannot reach orgasm during their first experience of masturbation. Try again at another time. What's most important is that you move at your own pace.

Move your finger down to the opening of your vagina and slide it in. Remember that I said the lower third of your vagina is under your voluntary control. You can experience this by tightening the muscle that encircles your vagina around your finger a few times each day, as if you were trying to stop the flow of urine. How does this contraction feel? You can actually strengthen this muscle by contracting it often.

Be sure your genitals are lubricated to avoid discomfort. Body oil, such as coconut oil, works well. So does saliva. You may also try petroleum jelly during masturbation, but do not use it during intercourse if you are trying to avoid pregnancy or a sexually transmitted disease. (Petroleum jelly and baby oil interfere with the effectiveness of barrier contraceptives, such as condoms or diaphragms, because they can break down the latex rubber.) Do not use lotion that contains alcohol because it could irritate your genital area. Make sure you avoid any substance to which you might be allergic.

Sometimes this self-exploration of the whole body is difficult for men. Raised to be tough, many men think it's silly to be sensuous. When most men masturbate, they don't even think of becoming sensual. It's just ejaculation, amen. But it's so important to go slowly and learn how your whole body can respond sexually.

You can stimulate your genitals by hand movements or by the friction of your genitals against clothing or an object such as a pillow. Try mutual masturbation. A vibrator can provide a more intense sexual response and a quicker climax than manual masturbation because it stimulates the rich vibratory nerve endings that cluster at the base of the penis or clitoris. A hand-held pulsating shower head will provide a similar stimulus. Your vibrator will cause numbness or irritation if you use it on the tip of the penis or clitoris, so use it on the shaft of the penis or on the sides of the penis or clitoris. Of course, the bathtub is *not* the place to try out a vibrator (as one of my patients found out). You don't need to be electrocuted for an orgasm! Nor should the device be inserted into the rectum, where it might slip up beyond reach, requiring removal in the emergency room.

Oral and Anal Sex

Many couples have questions about oral (mouth-to-genital) sex and anal (penis-in-rectum) sex. "If I want oral sex, am I normal?" "Is anal sex only for perverts?" "What if my partner likes them but I think they're gross?"

Many couples engage in oral sex, both cunnilingus (when the man stimulates the woman's genital area with his mouth) and fellatio (when the woman stimulates the man's penis with her mouth). While considered immoral and deviant by some people, for others, oral sex is an accepted alternative to vaginal sex. In fact, it may be a good option for couples who cannot have intercourse because of health problems, such as arthritis, cancer, or confinement to a wheelchair. But be aware that if your partner has a sexually transmitted disease, he or she could transmit that infection to you during unprotected oral sex.

A minority of heterosexual couples and many gay couples enjoy having anal sex. Because the nerves that extend from the lower spine supply the buttocks and rectum as well as the genital area, anal sex can result in orgasm for some people, if they find the idea of anal sex acceptable. Again, it is possible to contract a sexually transmitted disease, including HIV infection, from having anal sex, just as it is possible from vaginal sex. Also, bacteria that naturally reside in the rectum can cause an infection in the penis or in the woman's vagina if the couple has vaginal sex without using a condom after having anal sex. That's why the man should always wash his penis thoroughly with soap and water right after having anal sex.

Neither oral nor anal sex is right or wrong in itself but, if one of the partners is uncomfortable with the idea of experimenting with either of these alternatives, then the other partner must not coerce the person into complying. Each partner's values must be respected. If you are interested in experimenting with oral or anal sex, begin by talking it over with your partner. But never force your partner to engage in any sexual practice in which he or she does not want to participate.

Sexual Fantasy

The most important sex organ in your body is your brain. Thinking about sexual activity is like turning the key in the ignition of your car to warm it up. Early mislearning causes many people to feel guilty about having sexual fantasies. They may be ashamed of allowing "dirty thoughts" to enter their minds. They may feel they are betraying their partner in thought if not in deed. They may even wonder if they are attempting to escape the reality of sex altogether. But most experts agree that sexual fantasy is a normal, healthy, nonneurotic way of kindling and enjoying sexual desire.

Sexual fantasy represents a safe rehearsal of affectionate or sexual activity that we are then free to explore, enjoy, or dismiss. It can act like a strong, safe, and natural mental aphrodisiac to trigger sexual arousal. Think of sexual fantasy as a special power you have to awaken your desire for your partner. Use it before or during sexual intercourse or masturbation. It's a wonderful way to spice up a marriage or long-term relationship in which sex has become routine or mechanical.

Sexual fantasy can take many forms. You could visualize sex with your partner, with someone else you know, or with a movie star. You might replay a sexy film in your mind and then add scenes of your own creation. Some people prefer to keep their fantasies private. Others tell their partner their favorite fantasies and playfully act them out. Can sexual fantasy be bad? Only when translated into action that intimidates or hurts another person.

"Before I got married, I had a very active sex fantasy life because I didn't have sex very regularly," said Brian, a thirty-five-year-old computer programmer. "But, after I married Melissa, I felt as if I shouldn't fantasize about sex anymore because I had the real thing." Brian and Melissa came to me privately for couple counseling because they were looking for ways to perk up their ten-year marriage. I suggested they both try including sex fantasy in their lovemaking, along with a few erotic surprises (see page 157) to warm up their sexual engines.

"Dr. Renshaw said it was OK to fantasize about sex before we made love," said Brian, "in fact, she encouraged it. Melissa and I confessed our secret fantasies to each other one night, and it was great. Now we're more playful with each other. It's made a big difference."

The Nightly Sexual Cycle

When you close your eyes and sleep, a tremendous amount of activity continues to occur in your brain and body. During the 1960s and 1970s, sleep researchers recorded the brain waves of sleeping volunteers with electroencephalography. The researchers found that sleeping people alternate between two different stages of sleep: nonrapid eye movement (NREM) and rapid eye movement (REM). Most remembered dreams occur during the REM stage of sleep, and 80 percent of these dreams are sexual. So these REM cycles are really sexual cycles that occur every ninety minutes, about four times a night in adults.

During these four nightly sexual cycles, such phenomena as sleep erections and wet dreams (ejaculation while asleep) occur in men and nocturnal orgasms occur in women. They are completely natural and normal. I once had a patient, a single woman in her forties, who had gone through psychoanalysis four times per week for eight years because she had sleep orgasms but could not have orgasms while awake. She thought there was something wrong with having orgasms during sleep. Back then, no one knew that the body responds sexually during sleep. Even doctors didn't know. Today we know that these nightly sexual cycles continue into old age, although, after age sixty, they occur fewer times during the night.

Remember that sleep is unconscious and uninhibited. It's good news if you are having sexual dreams. Now all you have to do is translate them from your unconscious to your conscious mind. If you remember your erotic dreams, use them as fantasy to help you become aroused.

Gene, age fifty-nine, sold advertising time for a local radio station. He lived and breathed for one thing—his job. He was at the office by 7:00 AM, made calls to prospective customers all day, and returned to the office from 6:00 to 8:00 PM "to tie up loose ends." People often told Gene he was "hyper," and he would always respond, "Being hyper is a plus in my job." He and his wife, Louise, came to our sex therapy clinic because Gene couldn't stop thinking about work and it affected their sex life together. "I even think about work during sex," said Gene.

Gene had very erotic dreams. He would dream about having sex with movie stars, his secretary, and the woman who cut his hair. Then he would awaken with an erection, but soon after he approached Louise in bed for sex, he would start to think about the things he had to get done at the office the next day and his erection would fade.

We encouraged Gene to use his sexual dreams in sexual fantasy to help him keep his mind off his job and on his loveplay. Relaxation exercises also helped Gene deliberately slow down so he could appreciate the moment at hand—whether it was at work, at home, or in bed with Louise. And finally, we encouraged Gene to pretend he was courting Louise all over again, as if they had just met. They both enjoyed Gene's silly love notes and his flurry of phone calls to Louise from work, asking for a date. "That silliness was fun," said Gene, "and it helped me enjoy things more. Not just sex, but life in general." By the end of sex therapy, Gene and Louise were having sex twice per week.

A Few Words About Aging and Sexuality

Recognition of the importance of sexuality in the lives of older people is long overdue. As we age, physical changes affect sexuality just as they affect the ability to run long distances. But love is not biological; it does not age. Aging can actually increase your desire for your partner as you become free of many anxieties (such as fear of pregnancy) and as you have more free time and privacy. Aging is a problem mainly if you are anxious about how it will affect your looks and your sex life.

After speaking about sex and the elderly on a local TV show, I received a letter from an eighty-year-old woman who had never reached climax and wanted to learn how to have an "organism." I wrote back suggesting she try to achieve orgasm by masturbating, possibly with a vibrator. I also urged her to communicate more openly with her husband so that he would know exactly where to stimulate her to arouse her fully. Older people are eager to seek help for sexual problems once they know it is available to them.

As a woman enters menopause, her vagina becomes less tight and may become dry because of decreased lubrication. The mucous membrane inside the vagina becomes thinner and drier and may cause pain or bleeding during intercourse. Some women lose their desire for sex after menopause, but others do not. Many women find that hormone replacement therapy, obtained with a doctor's prescription, will counteract the problem of vaginal dryness and other symptoms of menopause, and may restore lost desire. You can also use prescription estrogen cream specifically to treat vaginal dryness. If you are older, you should use lots of lubrication, such as an over-the-counter lubricant or saliva, during intercourse to prevent chafing from dryness.

A man past fifty may sometimes have only partial erections. With longer and stronger stimulation directly on the penis, these partial erections will grow to excellent full erections that actually last longer than a younger man's. The angle of the erect penis in an older man is less acute than in a younger man because of changes in the elasticity of the connective tissue in the penis and in the blood flow to the penis. The time a man needs between erections also increases.

But both men and women can enjoy a full, pleasurable, and affectionate sexual relationship well into old age. Touching, caressing, closeness, companionship, caring, love, and laughter are lifelong human needs that should not be neglected at any age.

3

The Six Most Common Sexual Problems

For hundreds of years, the only sexual problems people openly discussed were venereal diseases (what we now call sexually transmitted diseases, or STDs), the inability to conceive a child, or an unwanted pregnancy. People still have these problems, but now they are more willing to confront a different type of problem—their sexual performance difficulties. Women, in particular, have become bolder about seeking help to improve their sexual expression and enjoyment.

Today, even lifelong sexual problems may be resolved through sex therapy. For example, at the Loyola Sex Therapy Clinic, almost all of the men with premature ejaculation and 80 percent of the women who were unable to have an orgasm successfully reversed their symptoms within the brief, seven-week program.

But, before learning how sex therapy can resolve sexual problems, let's take a look at the six problems I have seen most frequently in sex therapy.

1. Erection Problems

The inability to have an erection, also known as impotence, is the most widespread sexual problem in the United States, affecting about 10 million men, including young men. Some men have never been able to keep an erection long enough to complete intercourse. Others, who previously had no difficulty getting and keeping an erection, begin to have problems. Sex therapy offers a high success rate (from 60 to 80 percent, depending on the cause) for reversing both kinds of erection problems.

Doctors consider a man to be impotent if he cannot have an erection adequate for penetration *and* cannot sustain the erection long enough to reach orgasm in at least 75 percent of his attempts at intercourse. An occasional episode of difficulty with erection under stress does not fall under this definition because the problem rapidly reverses when the stress subsides.

Men normally have erections when they wake up in the morning. It's the penis's way of saying "Good morning, head, I'm here! How are you up there?" A man who is impotent does not have erections in the morning or during masturbation. Physical factors cause about 35 percent of all cases of erection problems (see page 57). That's why it's so important to see a doctor who can do a thorough physical examination to detect and treat any possible physical causes of erection problems. The balance of cases are probably caused by emotional factors, drugs or alcohol, or a combination of physical and emotional problems.

When choosing a doctor to treat your erection problems, pick a urologist, a doctor who specializes in disorders of the urinary tract and male reproductive system. Some urologists even "subspecialize" in erection problems. At your doctor's office, he or she will ask you if you ever have partial or morning erections or if you are able to have erections when you masturbate. Your doctor will also ask you about your level of sexual desire and how often you have intercourse. Be sure to tell your doctor about any medical problems you might have, including heart problems, high blood pressure, diabetes, or drug or alcohol problems. Mention all medications you are taking, including over-the-counter drugs.

You can expect a thorough examination of your penis, scrotum, and rectal area. The doctor also may check your testicles and anus to make sure the nerves in the area are working properly. Your doctor will check for enlargement of your breasts and for hair loss, both signs of changes in the levels of the male hormone testosterone. The tests may include analysis of blood, urine, and hormone levels. Your doctor will not give you testosterone shots unless he or she has first tested your blood and found low levels of testosterone. Do not request such shots if your doctor does not think you need them because they can have harmful effects on your body. Too many men regard them as a quick fix for erection difficulties.

The doctor will probably ask you to undergo a simple, painless, and inexpensive procedure called a penile blood flow test. He or she will place a small blood pressure cuff around your penis and another one around your upper arm. The soft penis should have 80 percent of the blood pressure recorded in your arm. Sometimes the anxiety caused by the doctor's appointment affects a man's blood pressure readings. Some doctors also ask their patients to do a test of their nighttime erections at home while they sleep. If your doctor orders this test, you will be given a small strap that fastens around your penis. If you have an erection while you sleep, the snaps will pop open when the blood flow to your penis increases. If you have an erection at night, there's a good chance that you have no physical problems, although the test is not 100 percent reliable. Some doctors ask their patients to stay overnight in a sleep lab, where a technician monitors the person's brain waves and the flow of blood to the penis.

Common Emotional Causes of Erection Problems
Emotional factors can easily affect a man's ability to get and keep an erection because the mind and body are inseparably connected. Sex

therapy is most effective in reversing erection problems that are caused by emotional factors.

Anxiety   Anxiety—about sexual performance, pregnancy, parenting fears, contracting a sexually transmitted disease, being discovered, being criticized, or sinfulness—often causes a man to have erection difficulty. When job stress, time pressure, and fatigue accompany a person to bed, they can inhibit sexual arousal. Misconceptions about erection difficulty abound and can even make the problem worse. For example, some men see their erection problems as punishment for masturbation, for encouraging their partner to have an abortion, or for adulterous fantasies or acts. An older man can become anxious about the way aging affects his sexuality, but the normal partial erections that occur after age fifty, caused by changes in blood flow and tissue elasticity, can become full and functional with continued sexplay directly on the penis. Some men begin having erection problems when they try to conceive a child in an infertility program.

"I'm thirty-six years old and in the final year of my residency," said Scott, a young doctor. "My wife, Andrea, is an intensive-care-unit nurse. She's thirty-seven. Eight months ago, we decided to try for a baby and she went off the Pill. I thought it would be like a honeymoon again, with lots of sex," he continued. "The first few weeks we were both relaxed, but two months later, she started to worry about not getting pregnant. She began talking about her biological clock . . . then came thermometers and temperature charts. Now she insists she can feel when she ovulates and she wants to dive into bed immediately when the time is right. I've never had an erection problem in my life, but, in the past three months, much as I want to and much as I try, I simply cannot get an erection. Now Andy is accusing me of not really wanting a child. I checked with a urologist. He said I was normal, to throw away all the charts, and to call you."

Stress may affect not only a man's ability to have an erection, but also a woman's ovulation and even the chemical balance in her fallopian tubes and uterus, impeding conception. I suggested that this young couple try regular, sensuous, but nongenital thirty-minute love-making sessions throughout all stages of the menstrual cycle to take the pressure off performance on the one-and-only ovulation day. I also asked them to exchange loveplay and total-body caressing without intercourse twice every weekend to place the emphasis back on mutual affection instead of on "baby making." Within two months, Scott's erections returned and they were able to resume trying to conceive.

Depression   Depression usually causes below-half-mast erections. When depressed, a person experiences a general lowering of all appetites—for food and sleep as well as for sex. Potency and interest in sex usually return spontaneously when the depression resolves or is treated with antidepressant medications, if the depression is the only cause of the impotence.

Anger   Unresolved anger can obstruct the body's automatic arousal responses. Most men with a "mad-on" just cannot get an erection. In a fragile, hostile relationship, a man may deny outward expression of his anger—at himself or at his partner—yet experience impotence when his partner approaches him for sex. A man may also unconsciously express such passive anger by abstaining from or rationing sex as a way of exerting control over his partner. Some men deliberately control their erections when they are angry: "I can screw you by *not* screwing you." Open fighting can also dampen arousal. It is difficult to make war and make love at the same time.

Sexual Ignorance   A man who lacks knowledge about his sexuality may have long-standing but unnecessary inhibitions that lead to performance anxiety, premature ejaculation, and, ultimately, erection problems. People brought up in strict families that stress sexual control or in a religious environment that regards all sex as sinful often lack adequate information about sex. This sexual ignorance leads to many wrong ideas and unhealthy attitudes, such as the notion that sex is for procreation only or the "madonna complex" ("Sex is dirty and can only be enjoyed with loose women, not with my wife and the mother of my children"). These ideas can cause sexual problems. The idea that every woman should be able to have an orgasm during intercourse (when in fact only 20 to 30 percent of women can) may also produce anxiety and self-blame in a man—or criticism of his partner—if she does not reach orgasm during intercourse.

Common Physical Causes of Erection Problems

Numerous physical problems can affect a man's ability to have an erection. Many of them can be detected and treated to restore potency. The most common physical causes are:

Medications and Street or Over-the-Counter Drugs (Including Alcohol) Temporary periods of erection difficulty are common after excessive alcohol consumption. Other drugs, whether prescribed, over-the-counter, or bought on the street, can also cause erection problems. Examples include some high blood pressure and heart disease medications, tranquilizers and antidepressants (if taken for long periods or if the dose is too high), sleeping pills, diuretics (drugs that promote the excretion of urine) prescribed for heart disease or high blood pressure, and antihistamines (in large doses). If you stop taking the drug, your potency usually returns, suggesting that the drug was the cause. The doctor you see for your erection problem will ask how your sexual functioning was before you started taking the drug. Good previous erections strongly implicate the drug in the problem.

Never discontinue a needed medication just because you think it might be affecting your ability to have an erection. It can be very dangerous to stop taking certain drugs suddenly; check with your doctor first. Instead, try to make love at a time of day that is just before your dose. For example, wake up a little earlier, make love, then take your medication. Or ask your doctor to work with you to devise a more convenient treatment plan. He or she may be able to substitute another medication or adjust the dosage of your current one to enable you to have erections again.

Fatigue   Fatigue, caused by overwork, excessive travel, or vigorous exercise (or a combination of all three), can affect a man's ability to have an erection. The sleep deprivation a new father experiences can also cause erection problems. This erection difficulty is a normal response to surrounding circumstances. Rested loveplay in the morning can restore a robust erection. Such difficulties will pass when the underlying cause—overwork or sleep deprivation—is resolved.

Cliff, a forty-nine-year-old international banker, and his socialite wife, Helen, age forty-four, battled the effects of fatigue on their sex lives for years before they entered sex therapy. Cliff took extended business trips to Eastern Europe about five times every year. He would be tense and agitated for several weeks before each trip, leave the country for three weeks, and return exhausted. Cliff claimed he had no energy for sex and admitted he had difficulty having an erection.

"I try to initiate sex, but Cliff doesn't respond," said Helen. "He's either too tired, or he's in Eastern Europe. What am I supposed to do?" Cliff told us, "She just doesn't understand how draining these trips are. I put in long hours before I leave and, once I get there, the pace I keep takes everything out of me. I need sleep more than I need sex."

We reminded Cliff that sex can be a stress reliever and that it could help him sleep better. At first, Cliff became irritated at the idea of setting time aside for home loveplay, but, after he and Helen began doing the loveplay regularly, he found that it helped him relax. Cliff could not change his hectic schedule, but he could change the way he responded to it. I recommended he try relaxation exercises (see page 160) as a stress reliever.

In a few weeks, Cliff's interest in sex became stronger and he experienced full erections. "I've been sleeping better than I have in years," he said. "It's still hard to find time for sex, but when we do, it's worth a lot to me. Helen and I are so much closer now."

Anatomical Problems and Disorders   Anatomical problems, including deformities of the genitals, can affect the ability to have an erection. A very tight foreskin in an uncircumcised man can make erections painful. A severe deformity called chordee causes the penis to curve downward or to the side as it becomes erect. In a condition called hypospadias, the urethra does not close properly or opens on the underside of the penis. Both chordee and hypospadias can be helped by surgery. Another disorder, known as hydrocele, characterized by a collection of fluid near the testicles, can also interfere with male sexual functioning if it becomes large enough. In rare cases, testicular fibrosis, in which scar or connective tissue builds up in the testicles, can also cause impotence and infertility. A thorough physical examination is essential to detect abnormalities such as these.

Hormonal Imbalances   Hormonal imbalances can affect a man's sexual desire or his ability to have an erection or ejaculation. Such imbalances can cause a deficiency of the male hormone testosterone. Examples of such hormonal imbalances include the overproduction of human growth hormone, a rare condition that causes an abnormal enlargement of the skull, jaw, hands, and feet; a deficiency of the hormones normally produced by the adrenal glands, such as Addison's disease; overactivity of the thyroid gland, as seen in Graves' disease; or undersecretion of thyroid hormone. Tumors in the pituitary gland (which regulates many body functions) at the base of the brain can also cause a hormonal imbalance. Men who are being treated for prostate cancer also may have reduced sexual desire and difficulty getting an erection because of the medication or radiation therapy they are taking. Hormonal imbalances are rare but treatable. Your doctor must perform special blood tests to rule them out.

Inflammation and Infection   Both the prostate gland, which secretes fluids that form part of the semen, and the urethra, through which urine passes out of the body, can become inflamed from infection. So can the bladder. The inflammation produces soreness and swelling that can make urination, erection, or ejaculation painful. In some uncircumcised men, the foreskin becomes so tight over the swollen tip of the inflamed penis it cannot be drawn back. Some men neglect to clean under the foreskin, and it can become infected, sometimes seriously. Infection with the organisms that cause gonorrhea, chlamydia, or herpes can also affect a man's ability to get an erection. Concern that he might infect his partner may also inhibit erections. In a male of any age, mumps can cause inflammation of the testicles; sterility can result later.

Chronic or Long-term Illnesses   Some diseases and disorders can affect a man's ability to get an erection. The list includes hardening of the arteries, heart disease, emphysema, diabetes, cancer, a tumor of the pituitary gland, Hodgkin's disease, leukemia, anemia, and an aneurysm (ballooning of an artery). General weakness, persistent pain, and blood flow changes from any illness can also affect the ability to have and sustain an erection. If a man recovers from the illness, he may regain his potency. Prostate enlargement does not cause impotence, but prostate surgery can cause a backward, internal ejaculation called retrograde ejaculation. Radiation therapy, hormone therapy, or surgery to treat prostate cancer can cause difficulties with desire, erection, or ejaculation. A sudden illness, such as a stroke or heart attack, or major surgery is a serious life crisis that can produce severe depression. In these cases, it may be the depression (which is treatable), not the illness or surgery, that is causing erection problems. If you have a chronic disorder, your doctor can tell you how it might affect your sexuality and recommend the best treatment. See chapter 12 for a fuller discussion of the effects of long-term illness on sexuality.

Nerve Damage   If the nerves that transmit messages from the brain to the penis are damaged, the messages cannot get through and you won't be able to get an erection. Nerve damage can be caused by automobile or industrial accidents, spinal cord injury, a herniated spinal disc, pelvic surgery, the later stages of diabetes, multiple sclerosis, tumors, spina bifida (a deformity of the spine that is present from birth), and syphilis.

If the damage is permanent, it does not mean your sex life is over.

You and your partner should explore the many other ways of giving and receiving sexual and sensual pleasure that do not involve intercourse.

Medical and Surgical Treatments for Erection Problems

In addition to sex therapy, medical science has come up with several technological advances to help overcome erection problems, including external vacuum pumps, injections into the penis, and surgical implants. Some of these mechanical devices can give the man an "instant erection," exaggerating his already distorted view of himself as an erection machine. Such attitudes are unfortunate but are often promoted by the overly enthusiastic "erection industry" that exists in this country. Men have so much anxiety about erection problems that many are vulnerable to the idea of a quick cure. Today's hard-working, high-achieving men with money and power want instant repair or restoration of their erections—a "fix it or get a new one" mentality.

If you opt for medical help, tell your doctor you would like to try the least invasive and least permanent procedure first. That means the procedure that is least likely to require an "invasion" into your body, such as surgery or an injection, and one that can be easily reversed.

The following three treatments are the ones doctors most commonly prescribe for erection problems. While all three can give you an erection, none can give you the ability to have an ejaculation or an orgasm. Remember, a second opinion is always worthwhile if you are unsure about any treatment proposed by your doctor.

The Vacuum Erection Device   The vacuum erection device (VED) is probably the safest, least costly, and most reversible prescribed medical treatment available for impotence. It also has the advantage of being an external instrument that is not inserted into the body. The device consists of a ten-inch plastic cylinder that fits over a man's flaccid penis. He pumps the handle or uses a battery-powered pump attached by a thin tube to the cylinder, causing a vacuum that draws blood into the penis, creating an erection. Just before the man removes the cylinder, he slips an elastic band off the rim of the cylinder onto the base of his penis like a tourniquet to help keep the erection hard. The band must be removed after half an hour, otherwise the penis loses its blood supply and may be damaged. Some men like this treatment best because, when used properly, it is harmless, painless, and can give them instant erections as often as they want, although doctors usually advise them not to use the device more than twice in twenty-four hours.

Other men or their partners find the device awkward and become frustrated when they first try to use it. I recommend large doses of patience and humor during the first practice sessions and remind them that they will need to use the device at least ten times before they feel comfortable and skilled.

Injections Into the Penis   Today, a man can get a chemical erection by injecting himself with a prescribed drug at home, in private. The drug causes tiny muscles in the penis to relax so the penis can fill with blood, thus producing an erection. This wonder drug made headlines in the early 1980s after a British lecturer at a meeting of urologists in Las Vegas injected himself at the podium and ran up and down the aisles demonstrating his chemical erection to his American colleagues. Needless to say, the treatment met with rapid acclaim. But many men stop using it within about a year because they don't like repeatedly injecting themselves in the penis. Also, infection or scar tissue can develop. If the man does not inject himself deeply enough, he may not be able to produce an erection immediately, but one could occur unexpectedly hours later.

Implants Inside the Penis   Surgical implantation of a device inside the penis to simulate an erection has been available to men for about thirty years. There are two kinds of implants. The first consists of a simple silicone rod or flexible metal coil implanted inside the penis like a permanent internal splint that the man can just bend into a comfortable position for intercourse. The second type of internal implant has hollow cylinders connected to a tiny internal pump that the man squeezes or presses to send fluid from an internal reservoir into the cylinders. When the cylinders are full, the penis becomes erect. The man must deflate the cylinders when lovemaking is over.

Steve, a forty-three-year-old man who had had the second type of penile implant inserted surgically to treat his impotence, entered sex therapy with his second wife of four years, Pam, age forty-two. Pam had threatened divorce because Steve had approached her for sex only about once every three months since his $10,000 implant. The surgery was a success, but Steve said that Pam was so nagging and bossy that he would deliberately refuse to use his implant. He had the power to give himself an erection in his index finger, but he stubbornly refused to puff up his puffer-upper! During sex therapy, both Steve and Pam observed their own obstinate behavior, but insight does not always translate into change. The couple continued to pursue their power play and finally divorced about a year after completing therapy. This story proves that mechanical solutions are not always successful unless change also occurs in the mind and the emotions of each partner.

Penile implant surgery is very expensive; some men dislike having a foreign object in their penis; and the devices can malfunction, develop an obstruction, cause an infection, leak, or erode the skin, requiring removal. Some concern has also surfaced about the long-term effects of the silicone inside the inflatable models leaking into surrounding body tissue.

Today's new technology (almost) guarantees an erection. It is (almost) fail-safe. As reliable as an automatic door-opener, a VED, an injection, or an implant promises "instant" erections. But, unless accompanied by renewed intimacy, such devices remain mechanical at best. Men must accept the fact that secure, relaxed intimacy is not sentimental; it's a good medical strategy for symptom reversal.

Sex Partners of Men With Erection Problems

"It makes me feel cheap to have to beg him for sex. Then he says no. I feel so mad and hurt that I start crying. What I really want to do is hit him, run to a bar, and pick up a man—any man—just to prove I'm a woman," said Joanne, age twenty-eight. Her thirty-year-old husband had come into their marriage eight years earlier with a severe premature ejaculation problem. He began having erection problems two years ago and now says he is not interested in sex. Premature ejaculation is sometimes a forerunner of an inability to have an erection. The lack of sexual fulfillment created by premature ejaculation can lead to anxiety, then erection problems. To avoid facing both the premature ejaculation and erection problems, the man may lose his desire, a sexual "giving-up" syndrome.

A woman with normal sexual needs, Joanne is trying to cope with a sexless marriage while remaining faithful to her husband. Are her feelings unusual for the wife of a man with erection problems? No. She feels rejected and alone while he struggles separately with his hurt. Going outside the marriage for sex can be a tempting coping mechanism for some partners in such a situation. Partners of men with erection problems experience a wide range of emotions, including confusion, loss of confidence, self-blame, rationalization, resentment, desire for retaliation, and, finally, resignation. Some partners of men with erection problems develop sexual problems themselves, such as the inability to have an orgasm or loss of interest in sex, after the onset of the man's impotence. After years of futile struggle to initiate intercourse, a woman's feelings of rejection and unattractiveness may culminate in an avoidance of affectionate exchange altogether.

In our sex therapy clinic, I have found that many men with erection problems never try alternatives to intercourse to meet their partner's sexual needs: kissing, caressing, or stimulating her genitals by hand or mouth. The man with erection problems sometimes seems unable to leave his private island of pain, loss of prowess, performance anxiety, shame, self-blame, or projected blame long enough to see his partner's suffering and need. One of my patients, Joe, age forty-five, was a diabetic for thirty-five years who needed daily injections of insulin. His diabetes was so advanced that nerve damage was evident in his legs. It was clear to me that diabetes was causing Joe's inability to have an erection and that he had very little chance of naturally regaining his potency. He did not know or seem to care that his wife of nineteen years, Fran, had never attained orgasm.

During sex therapy, I recommended that Fran try masturbation to explore her own sexuality as a prelude to mutual genital stimulation. In week 3 of treatment, Fran masturbated to orgasm. When she told Joe about this at the clinic, he was deeply hurt. He wept and banged his fist on the table. "Why you? Why not me?" he said. This statement dramatized the one-sidedness of their relationship and his long-standing insensitivity to her sexual needs. Our therapists were more upset than Fran at this outburst from Joe. She had understood and accepted his single-minded search for his own sexual release. Fran did not reject or blame Joe (she had been taught that sex was for a man's pleasure and that women complied to have babies), and she had not sought sexual gratification outside their marriage. After Joe's display of frustration, she gently put her hand over his and told him she loved him with or without sex. By the last week of sex therapy, Joe said he enjoyed the caressing and nongenital play he and Fran had begun. He became interested in her sexual responses and was able to bring her to climax by hand.

Sometimes a man tries to blame his partner for "causing" his erection difficulty. He may describe her as too old, too fat, too critical, domineering, castrating, or sexually demanding and aggressive. The implication is that if she were younger, more slender, or more submissive, seductive, and adoring, he would not be impotent. Men also sometimes blame the increased sexual freedom and assertiveness of women and the women's movement for intimidating men. But the inability to have an erection was a prevalent problem centuries before the word "feminism" was coined.

The real emotional causes of erection problems are anxiety, anger, and sexual inhibition. The psychoanalytical approach to erection problems has kept many men on an analyst's couch for years but has only rarely been successful. Brief sex therapy, with the participation of both partners, offers an optimistic chance for symptom reversal.

2. Lack of Interest in Sex

"I'm just not interested in sex, Doctor," is a complaint that both women and men frequently make. In fact, lack of interest in sex is the second most common sexual problem. The problem includes not only a lack of desire for one's partner but also the inability to become physically aroused during sexual activity. A desire disorder often masks another sexual problem, such as a man's premature ejaculation or inability to have an erection or a woman's inability to have an orgasm.

Like erection problems, lack of sexual desire sometimes has a physical cause. If you experience a lack of interest in sex, see your doctor, who will take a complete medical history and perform a comprehensive physical examination. Fatigue, stress, hormonal imbalance, infection, anemia, pain in the genital area, and long-term illness can all reduce sexual desire. The sedative effects of heavy alcohol consumption, some medications, and other drug use can also lower sexual arousal. But emotional factors are usually present in most desire disorders.

Certain sexual situations can turn off desire. Maybe you're turned off by your partner's behavior. He or she may be hostile, critical, or drunk in the bedroom, demanding sex without affection or tenderness. Neglecting to bathe every day, gaining excessive weight, or watching TV during lovemaking may all be countererotic. Difficult as it may seem, you or your partner can learn to forgive rude behavior or smelly socks, and even drunken behavior can be changed with enough motivation. But, for some people, lack of desire does not depend on the situation. It can persist for life no matter who the partner is, especially if there is an underlying physical cause.

Loss of Interest After Childbirth

Some women feel a lack of desire after the birth of a baby. Having a baby is a demanding physical process, especially if the woman is in labor for a long time or has a cesarean section delivery. Research shows that pain from an episiotomy (a surgical cut routinely made in the tissue of the vagina to enlarge the vaginal opening for a baby's birth) can last three to four months after delivery, and, for some women, the pain in the healed scar can continue for about a year (a woman can insert a lubricated finger into her vagina from time to time to stretch the area). Women's sexual activity declines for about a year after they've given birth, according to one study. Yet some new mothers have a robust sexual appetite with abundant vaginal lubrication soon after a pregnancy.

Bleeding from the vagina can last for up to two weeks after delivery, even after a cesarean section. Abrasions in the genital area after delivery can cause stinging during bathing or urination. For these reasons, it is best to refrain from intercourse for at least two weeks after delivery (your doctor may recommend a longer period of abstinence). But caressing and kissing are not prohibited. In fact, I strongly encourage them. They strengthen the emotional bond between new parents.

Sleep loss is a common problem for both partners. It's hard to feel erotic when you're exhausted. Parents of bottle-fed babies often take turns getting up to feed and change the baby. But a woman who breastfeeds may feel chained to a pattern of nightly interruptions, resenting both her husband and the baby. As one working supermom told me, "I don't need sex. I need sleep and help." I told her to express some milk, refrigerate it, and let her husband feed the baby on alternate nights so she could catch up on some survival sleep. She also began taking a two-hour nap in the evening while her husband cared for the baby.

Some women feel uncomfortable about the normal, reflex nipple arousal that can accompany breast-feeding. A breast-feeding mother may perceive this arousal as wrong or sinful and mentally repress all feelings of arousal in the breast. Once a woman denies her eroticism in this way, all sexplay and lovemaking can provoke anxiety. Sexual detachment after breast-feeding can turn into a chronic lack of desire that lasts for years. More than thirty women who came to the Loyola Sex Therapy Clinic over the years expressed inhibited sexual desire that could be traced to conflicting feelings while breast-feeding two to twenty-four years earlier.

"I loved my baby, but it was all too new and too much for me," said Joyce, age thirty-two. "I couldn't understand why I felt aroused when I breast-fed my daughter. My mom had died two years before I had Jennifer, and I didn't have anyone else I could ask, not just about this but about a lot of other baby-related things. I even thought, 'What's the matter with me? Does it mean I'm perverted because I feel this way about my little girl?' " I assured Joyce that her sexual arousal was a completely normal reflex response to her baby's sucking.

Some couples feel disconcerted when the woman's breasts begin to leak milk during sexplay. This too is a natural occurrence and one that calls for understanding and a sense of humor.

Here are some other factors that can cause a loss of sexual desire after the baby comes:

- Avoidance of sex because of fear of another pregnancy
- Postpartum depression, which is both common and treatable
- Withholding of sex as retaliation for an unwanted pregnancy
- Physical discomfort with certain positions caused by problems such as hemorrhoids, varicose veins, constipation, and heartburn that arise during and after pregnancy
- Emotional withdrawal of the father, who feels left out of the intense mother-child bond
- Ignoring of the father by the mother, who is consumed by the mother-baby relationship
- Fear of injuring the woman's genitals after delivery
- Conflicting feelings of men who watch their baby come out of their partner's vagina and then become turned off by the idea of having sex with her or feel that they caused their partner's pain.

After having a baby, many women also struggle to accept the way their body has changed. "I couldn't wait to go to bed with Bill before the baby, but something changed," said Charlotte, a successful thirty-year-old graphic artist. "Now I wait until he's asleep before I go up to bed. I once modeled proudly for Bill's nude sketches, but after the pregnancy my body wasn't the same. I became huge. My stretch marks looked like a road map. Labor was so long and painful. I had stitches, and it burned to urinate. I hate myself now," Charlotte continued. "Bill says he still loves me, but how can he? I never had a problem with orgasms before, but now sex just does not interest me." To release her frustration, Charlotte cleaned her house until it was spotless.

Charlotte and Bill had not had sex since their one year old was born. He accepted this as being "because of the baby" and masturbated privately without pressuring or blaming Charlotte. After several discussions about self-forgiveness and some guided imagery exercises (see the section "The Fantastic Voyage" on page 167), Charlotte was able to let go of her prepregnancy body and accept her present healthy and still good-looking body. She also realized that much of her anxiety arose from the fear of another pregnancy and that the more anxious she became, the more compulsively she cleaned to avoid having sex with Bill. By the fifth week of therapy, Charlotte's desire was rekindled, after reassurance from Bill that he would be meticulous about birth control. She remains a perfectionist, but her anxiety and avoidance of sex are gone.

Once new parents resume intercourse, they should indulge in lengthy foreplay; a new mother's worry about her baby can be distracting and prevent her from becoming aroused. Men, be gentle and patient! New parents should also use lots of lubrication because decreased levels of the female hormone estrogen can make the vagina dry for twelve weeks or so after delivery. To avoid excessive pressure on tender genital areas or on the cesarean scar, the couple can try the L-shaped position (see page 263), facing each other with torsos at right angles. Or the woman could be on top or lying with her buttocks at the edge of the mattress and her legs on her partner's shoulders. A sense of humor can help you relieve tension in your fumbling attempts to experiment with new positions.

Other Causes of Decreased Desire

If you experience reduced sexual desire or arousal, ask yourself if it began after you experienced a loss or went through a difficult period.

Were you having financial problems? Did you lose your job, get a divorce, or grieve over the death of a relative or close friend? Sexual apathy for a short period of time after a painful life event is common. But sometimes the effects persist for years.

Pete, age fifty-nine, was in his second marriage. He had shown no interest in sex with his fifty-two-year-old wife Marian for about twenty years and periodically had erection problems. She masturbated in secret. He had had two daughters from his first marriage; one, Jeannie, had died suddenly at age seventeen in a traffic accident. When I mentioned Jeannie during sex therapy, Pete started sobbing so hard he couldn't speak. The floodgates of his grief had been opened. He seemed almost angry that I had brought up the subject of his daughter and said that he did not remember much about her. I suggested that he and Marian talk about Jeannie at home and tell me what happened the following week. At the next session, Pete told me he now realized that it was since Jeannie had died that he had lost interest in sex. He had scolded his daughter the day before she died for exceeding the speed limit. Delayed grieving and unresolved anger that she might have been speeding just before she died had caused Pete's sexual problems. Pete had buried his sex life when he buried his daughter.

This couple did very well in sex therapy after coming to terms with this tragic past event. Their open discussion led to increased closeness between them. Marian's gentleness and reassurance gradually sparked a new interest in sex for Pete.

Conscious or unconscious, anxiety impedes the body's normal arousal responses. Several factors can produce anxiety severe enough to extinguish interest in sex, including fear of an unwanted pregnancy. Worry about an inability to please, an inability to climax, or a failure to meet (possibly unrealistic) expectations can cause a person to avoid sex. Moral values that make the enjoyment of sex seem sinful will engender complex shame and guilt reactions. Guilt-ridden people may not perceive their own sexual needs. When they express their sexuality, they feel regret, remorse, shame, or guilt, which can lead to self-condemnation. They may rigidly control their sexual expression or deny any sexual feelings at all.

For such people, long years of social conditioning have worked all too well. "Don't look, touch, talk about, think about, or enjoy 'down there.' It's bad, dirty, and dangerous." The person becomes disconnected from the sexual aspects of the self: "I just don't think about sex." The psychological word for this kind of disconnection is dissociation. Sensation of the entire genital area may become blocked. It's as if the lower half of the body is excluded from the person's awareness: "I wish my vagina could be sewn closed. I'm sick of sex." Dissociation may also cause irrational fears (phobias) about the genitals or a variety of imaginary physical illnesses (hypochondriasis). If it persists, dissociation may require professional treatment.

Time pressure is also a factor in lowered libido (sexual drive). In today's complex, high-speed world, we often organize our lives by making long lists of things we have to do. Sex may be last on the list. Sexual enjoyment requires time and relaxation. If you are too busy, too tired, or too anxious to relax and make time for sex, you may place a low priority on lovemaking and instead avoid it altogether.

Chuck and Lois were a married couple in their mid-thirties with three children. Chuck had worked at a roofing mill for eleven years. Within one year, he was laid off from his job at the mill, landed a job as a truck driver, and got laid off again. He finally found work as an aide in a nursing home for a dollar above minimum wage, but his cut in pay forced him to take a second job as a bartender. Lois also found a job as a cashier at a local convenience store and took in ironing. With their four jobs, the kids, housework, and all the changes in their lives, Chuck and Lois were so fatigued and stressed that they both seemed to have lost all interest in sex. They were happy just to see each other one or two evenings a week, but realized that they might end up in a sexless marriage.

At a marriage-enrichment seminar, Chuck and Lois told me their story and asked for help. I gave them a simple task to do at home that would take advantage of the natural sexual cycle that occurs every night during sleep (see page 48). If fatigue is ruining your sex life, you may want to try the following exercise yourself.

When You're Too Tired for Sex

Fatigue is your body's way of telling you that you need some rest. This simple task can accommodate both your need for rest and your need for sexual expression.

Pick a night and set your alarm to ring an hour and a half after you go to bed. Then get up, shower together, and make love. The body's first sexual sleep cycle begins ninety minutes after you go to sleep, so your arousal level should be at its peak. The shower will refresh you, and the lovemaking will relax you so you can get back to sleep again.

Some people react to this advice with skepticism. "I'm not getting enough sleep now and you want me to wake up in the middle of the night to have sex?" asked one thirty-two-year-old supermom. But when they try the technique, couples find that the nap and shower have revitalized them and they're able to make love. You may be skeptical too, but try it anyway and see what happens. Another alternative is to go to bed an hour earlier than usual so you can wake up an hour earlier and make love. But many couples "cheat" by using the extra hour in the morning to jump out of bed and get a head start on the day. That's why I like the first alternative better.

Maximize the time you have together. Sleep late on the weekend, and plan vacations so you can have some relaxing time together. Many of our patients tell us they have sex more regularly on vacation, when their time is less scheduled. Vacations don't have to be expensive. You can drive to a cozy bed-and-breakfast hotel in the country or spend a weekend in an inexpensive hotel in your own hometown. Being together and having some privacy are the most important requirements.

If your fatigue is related to your parenting responsibilities, be creative in carving out some time for yourselves. One of our patients organized a baby-sitting pool so she and her partner could have one free night together every other week. "One night every two weeks may not sound like much, but, compared to zero nights together, it was wonderful," she told us. "Sometimes we went out for dinner. Other times, we just cuddled together on the sofa. It really helped bring us closer."

The Haunted Bedroom

Old "ghosts" sometimes visit your bedroom, and you need to lay them to rest so they don't haunt your current sex life. They might be previous men friends or women friends, parents, ex-husbands or ex-wives, living or dead. Why they pick the moment when you want to have sex with your partner, I don't know. Maybe because of past associations with the act of sex. Tell yourself, "This is not my ex-husband." Fight the ghost off with a little humor. Try to put a bit of fun or teasing into your lovemaking because that will defuse some of the intensity and seriousness that come up when these old ghosts appear.

A dose of lighthearted humor helped Helen confront the ghost of her ex-husband, Roger. Four years after her divorce, Helen married her second husband, Ted. Before marriage, Helen enjoyed sex with Ted, but afterward, she became less and less interested in it. During sex therapy, Helen realized that her lack of interest had something to do with the fact that, after they got married, she and Ted had moved into the house she had shared with Roger. Having sex with Ted in the same bed in which she had had sex with Roger somehow bothered her. "I feel as if Roger were still there watching us," she said.

To ward off Roger's tenacious image, Helen went home from the third session of sex therapy, stood in the bedroom, and shouted out, "Roger, if you're here, I want you to know that Ted is a better lover than you ever were!" That night, she and Ted drank a toast to Roger in bed before they turned out the lights. After that night, Helen's interest in sex slowly blossomed. She and Ted were having intercourse twice a week by the end of therapy.

Anger, Depression, and Denial

Anger is an antierotic emotion. Angry feelings may be caused by resentment from a recent slight or from a long-standing conflict. Your anger may be conscious and intense or unconscious and simmering. You may be angry at your partner or at yourself for not being more sexually skilled or more attractive. You may be angry at sex itself for not being more exciting. Denying your anger just complicates the situation. One of my patients reacted to his wife's constant ridicule in their bedroom by saying, "No, I'm not angry at her. I just get annoyed." He was out of touch with his anger—he just passively avoided sex and silently withdrew downstairs, where he slept on the couch (see page 11 for a discussion of how interpersonal conflict can affect your sex life).

Depression can also dampen libido. When a person feels deeply depressed, he or she feels little joy. Food becomes tasteless, and sleep becomes difficult. The person loses weight and has no desire for sex. Don't fight depression alone; get a professional's help. Antidepressant medication helps 80 percent of people with serious depression reverse all of these symptoms, including reduced sexual drive, within four to six weeks.

A traumatic sexual experience in childhood—from within the family or outside of it—may account for a lack of interest in sex in adulthood. Frightening and unpleasant early experiences can affect a person later, unless the person lets go of self-blame, secrecy, and anxiety about the event.

Sandy and Dan were both in their mid-forties when they sought sex therapy. They had been married for fifteen years. In that time, they had had intercourse twelve times. They slept in separate bedrooms throughout their marriage "because Dan snores," Sandy told me. Both said they lacked interest in sex. Sandy, who worked at a small printing company, was very negative, blaming, and derogatory. Dan, an actuary, was mild-mannered and passive. Typically, when Sandy went on a rampage and began badgering Dan about everything he had done wrong, Dan would quietly withdraw. Neither had sought individual or marriage counseling before.

When Sandy was six years old, one of her brothers, who was fourteen at the time, had intercourse with her several times. Later, when Sandy was thirteen, a neighbor raped her. These early experiences so deeply affected Sandy that, as a defense mechanism, she lost all interest in sex. She directed her suppressed rage about her past at Dan. They learned how to communicate with each other better during sex therapy, but Sandy needed counseling beyond the seven-week course to solve her complicated and deep-seated childhood problems.

How Often Is 'Normal'?

Some people wonder if it's OK if they have sex only infrequently. Gary and Anne Marie, both in their early forties, attended a marriage-enrichment seminar I gave. They both worked and had two young children to take care of. The couple had sex about twice a month. "We agree that it's fine for us, but we sort of wonder if we're normal," Gary confessed. "When we were dating, we couldn't keep our hands off each other and we miss that intensity." I told Gary and Anne Marie that, if the quality of their sexual relationship was good, then they shouldn't worry about the frequency. This couple was very loving and felt relieved when I confirmed that their relationship was sexually and emotionally sound.

If the frequency of your intercourse is not what it used to be or not what you think it's "supposed" to be, do not be alarmed or think that you are abnormal if the quality of your lovemaking is still good. But, if at least one of you is distressed by your lack of frequency, brief counseling could help you either make love more often or adjust to the relative infrequency of your intercourse.

After a certain amount of time together, most couples find that they make love less frequently than they used to, especially if they have many demands on their time, from such things as a job or children. Don't force yourself to conform to a sexual ideal. Just make sure you approach each lovemaking session with affection and positive feelings.

Finally, it is important to realize that, for some people, lack of interest in sex is selective. What these people are really saying is, "I'm not interested in sex *with my partner*." Some people who come to sex therapy discover that they unconsciously or impulsively chose to have a relationship with their partner not because of sexual attraction, but because it was better than being alone or because of the person's status, stability, security, money, or power. When they get to know each other better, one or both partners find that the reality of living with the other person on a day-to-day basis is different from their dreams of perfect happiness and compatibility. The couple must then do some serious soul-searching to find out how to heal their relationship or accept it as it is. Negotiation, compromise, and acceptance of each other become a lifelong task.

"I'm just not attracted to my husband," confessed Debra, a thirty-three-year-old homemaker. "I never have been, and I never will be. He's a wonderful father and he's always been good to me, but I only love him like a brother. I've been with other guys, so I know that I *can* be attracted to men. It's not me. It's me in relation to Nick."

Debra had married Nick, an executive recruiter, only eight months after breaking up with her longtime boyfriend, Wally. She knew that sex with Nick wasn't as thrilling as it had been with Wally, but assumed the thrill would grow over time. It did not. In fact, it lessened to the point where Debra could now barely tolerate Nick's touch. "What can I do to make it better?" Debra asked. "I don't want to divorce Nick because I couldn't support the kids on my own—I haven't worked since I was a department store clerk in high school."

We told Debra that there are good points in even the most negative of relationships and that she surely could find some in her relationship, which was very positive in many ways. Debra never used sexual fantasy to rev up her sex drive because it reminded her of Wally and his rejection, which hurt her. I told her, "You respect Nick, but you've deadened your body by blanking out your mind during sex. Try this. Tell Nick you're Sleeping Beauty and you're waiting to be awakened by a kiss from Prince Charming. Give yourself permission to wake up to playful, arousing sex with Nick." Debra tried this suggestion, and the change in her was striking. "You gave me permission to wake up in a fairy tale," she told me. "It gave me a chance to start over with Nick."

If you suspect that your lack of interest in sex relates exclusively to your partner, you may need more personalized help than you can find in this book. I recommend that you seek advice from a professional therapist who can guide you through the difficult circumstances surrounding your particular situation.

3. Inability to Achieve Orgasm

Many women have never experienced an orgasm—in my practice, about 15 percent of female patients have this problem. As with erection problems, the inability to have an orgasm may be lifelong or may begin at a given time.

A look at the way female sexuality was perceived in the past may help explain some of the reasons today's women have certain expectations—and problems—when it comes to having an orgasm.

In the romantic novels of Victorian times, earth tremors, falling stars, and fainting spells accompanied the heroine's lovemaking. But physicians of the time were not aware that women were even capable of achieving an orgasm. That misconception persisted into this century. Not until the 1960s did medical science begin to study the "mystique" of a woman's sexual responses. Today's popular culture challenges women to realize their full sexual potential, though at times this challenge is extreme. Magazines report female orgasms lasting thirty minutes to three hours in duration. Such bedroom Olympics are impossible for most women to achieve but create new myths with which today's women must struggle.

A woman who is a high achiever in other areas of her life may feel cheated when she doesn't live up to such impossibly high standards of sexual performance, let alone attain regular orgasm. She may feel that her partner is upset because she doesn't respond the way he thinks she should. The woman who cannot have an orgasm may become tense, experience performance anxiety, and look upon her inability to achieve orgasm as an island of failure in an otherwise successful life. Her response may be to retreat from sex and make her work or other important areas in her life her top priority, shunning even the well-intentioned concern of her partner. One hugely successful female real estate broker told me, "I get such a high when I sell a home. It's like an orgasm, and I want a cigarette after the closing. It's the only time I ever smoke!"

A woman who cannot reach orgasm may feel that sex has little to offer. She may have normal orgasms during sleep (an unconscious and uninhibited state) but be unable to have them while awake. Frustrated and ashamed, she may fake orgasms for years because this response seems easier than talking to her partner or her doctor about her lack of sexual fulfillment. Anorgasmic women are not abnormal or "frigid"; they have just not given themselves permission to be fully sexual. They may also lack adequate sexual information.

When Carrie, age thirty-two, came to the clinic, she had never experienced an orgasm. She had been married to her husband, Brett, for six years. While she was in sex therapy, Carrie had no problem talking freely about their home loveplay exercises, but she had difficulty actually initiating loveplay at home. One time when she tried to masturbate, the family dog came into the unlocked room and watched. The dog's curiosity seemed dirty and embarrassing to Carrie, and she wasn't able to continue. I told her to find a part of the house where she would find total privacy—even from the dog—and try again. With patience and persistence, Carrie overcame her inhibitions and anxieties and eventually was able to bring herself to climax through masturbation, the most reliable first step in learning about your sexual self. Then she told Brett, reluctantly at first, how to stimulate her to orgasm so they could begin to explore and enjoy their sexuality together.

The Keys to Arousal: Masturbation and Sexual Fantasy

You can learn ways to improve your sexual responsiveness. In general, you need to become more aware of your body and your own way of responding sexually. You have my permission to explore your own sexual responses. Masturbation and fantasy are natural ways to do this.

Fantasy is one of the essential keys to arousal. But while millions of women read romance novels, the very stuff of fantasy, many hesitate to fantasize during sexual activity. When I ask women what they think about during loveplay, some answer something like, "I don't know. I don't think about anything." Many women tell me that they think it is wrong to fantasize during loveplay. They're relieved to hear me say that it is completely normal to have erotic fantasies. Don't be afraid of your imagination. Remember, you are free to act on or control your fantasies. You can still control your sexual behavior in accordance with your values, just the way you have for years (see page 47 for a discussion of sexual fantasy).

For women, masturbation may yield a more intense physical experience of orgasm than intercourse because, during intercourse, each partner has to adjust to the other's reactions and expectations. Studies comparing intercourse to masturbation in the same woman show that heart rate, blood pressure, breathing, and muscle tone are a little more elevated, although of shorter duration, during masturbation than during intercourse. But women usually report that orgasm during intercourse feels more pleasurable and satisfying emotionally than during masturbation, even though the physical sensations during masturbation may be more intense (see page 44 to learn how to masturbate).

Because it is intensely stimulating, a vibrator can help a woman attain orgasm—even if she's never had one before. It is not an addictive instrument, as some women and their partners fear! A vibrator simply stimulates the sensitive nerve endings around the clitoris so that the woman and her partner can learn where she most enjoys being aroused.

Extended foreplay, such as kissing and body or breast massage, also helps a woman reach orgasm more easily because the timing of a woman's sexual cycle is longer than a man's. Remember, it takes a woman almost four times as long to reach orgasm as it does a man (see graph on page 36). Ask your partner to explore your body by giving you a full, relaxing scalp-to-toe body massage. The two of you might enjoy a warm bath or shower together before lovemaking. Whispered romantic words often act as a most powerful aphrodisiac.

As I said before, women who climax during intercourse are in the definite minority. Most couples find other ways to stimulate the woman, such as massaging of the clitoris by hand before, during, or after intercourse. The woman-on-top, sitting, or "spoon" (man's chest against woman's back) positions may offer better stimulation of a woman's clitoris than the traditional, man-on-top missionary position. Feel free to experiment with positions.

If you have never had an orgasm before, know that you can learn how to have one if you want to. If you have had one or more orgasms in the past, you can again. By following the steps outlined in this book, you will learn how to give your sexual nature its full expression.

4. Differences in Sexual Drive

People have different levels of sexual desire, and those differences are completely normal. But dissimilarities in sexual drive can cause plenty of friction, blaming, and hostility in a relationship.

"Is there something wrong with me?" asked Janet, a thirty-five-year-old management consultant. "I work out at the health club five days a week, but I can handle sex only twice a month. My husband wants intercourse every night. He told me to ask you for a booster shot of hormones or something." Janet and Ray, a stockbroker, had been married for five years, were otherwise compatible, and wanted a child soon. He worked longer hours than she did, but she needed an extra hour more of sleep than he did and her sex drive was lower than his.

This couple had dated for a year before marriage and began having sex on their third date. Janet's libido was much higher during courtship than it was now. Back then, sex was more pleasurable to her. "The chase, the newness, and the attention were a real high for me," she said. After the courtship was over, Janet's priorities changed: the wedding and honeymoon plans had to be made, then finding and decorating their new home took time. Now physical exercise and sleep had become more important than sex.

Janet compromised by giving her husband oral sex twice a week to satisfy him but preferred no such attention in return. "I need to sleep," she would say. There did not seem to be a power struggle in the bedroom. "We don't fight about sex, but I know Ray wants it more than I do." When I asked her about sexual fantasy, she responded, "I never fantasize. Maybe I'm too sleepy." Ray said he felt that sex had become a duty rather than a shared pleasure for Janet, whom he loved.

I told Janet that Ray's desire for her was a natural expression of his internal sexual drive, his response a compliment to her physical attractiveness, and his love for her. Each person's internal sexual rhythm is different. Each can learn to express or control the response. Juggling her time could allow Janet to carve out thirty minutes every other day or so for some special sexual closeness just as she had set time aside to exercise at the health club. With sufficient foreplay, even an unaroused woman can respond sexually if she relaxes and uses fantasy during the first stages of sexual activity. When Janet made time for sex and drew upon her courtship memories for fantasy, she began enjoying their sexual encounters as much as she had before their engagement. Her memory bank was a sexual treasury.

I asked Janet to be the one to approach Ray for sex every other time they made love. This tactic helped her see sex not as a burden to put up with but as an enjoyment to be savored. It also made Ray feel wanted and desired.

Differences in sexual drive are normal, but certain physical factors can lower desire. Pain anywhere in the body, but especially in the genital area, such as from inflammation or an infection, can block sexual desire. So can hormonal imbalances, produced by such causes as an underactive thyroid gland or an overactive segment of the pituitary gland. Other factors that can affect sexual drive include drinking too much alcohol or taking sleeping pills, tranquilizers, street drugs, antiseizure medications, or blood pressure medications. Recreational drugs can also affect libido. As I've mentioned, depression or severe anxiety can lower all of your appetites, including the one for sex.

In the 1990s, one of the most common physical factors that can interfere with your desire for your partner is fatigue. Janet is a good example. She spent long hours at her job and then went directly to her health club, where she worked out five days a week. No wonder she lacked the energy for sexual activity.

Naturally divergent sexual drives are not abnormal and are not a symptom of a sexual problem, although they can cause problems. They do not always need counseling to be fixed. Most couples accommodate their desire differences on their own by negotiating a compromise. For example, after finishing sex therapy, Janet and Ray decided they would have intercourse twice a week. In addition, they exchanged oral stimulation twice a week. It was fun and quicker for both. By sticking with this arrangement, Janet and Ray found sexual satisfaction through mutual agreement.

5. Premature Ejaculation

The definition of premature ejaculation is controversial. Some experts define it as a period of less than a minute between penetration and ejaculation. Others describe it as ejaculation in fewer than eight pelvic thrusts. The American Psychiatric Association defines it as "ejaculation occurring before the individual wishes it, because of recurrent and persistent absence of voluntary control of ejaculation and orgasm during sexual activity." Most untreated cases of premature ejaculation start young and last for life. But the condition can be temporary—and normal—in inexperienced men, adolescents, and men who are too highly excited or who have abstained from sex for long periods.

Why does premature ejaculation happen? Physical causes are truly uncommon. Some experts attribute it to negative early intercourse experiences, which caused high performance anxiety, made worse by severe sexual inhibitions and lack of knowledge about sex. Current thinking links the problem to incorrect learning—the man simply has never learned how to control his ejaculation. Premature ejaculation sometimes leads to impotence and then to lack of interest in sex, an unhappy progression but one that is quite reversible through sex therapy.

The most important thing that you should know about premature ejaculation is that *it is highly reversible*. In my practice, several hundred men with premature ejaculation have reversed their symptoms through brief sex therapy. The key is learning to relax and be attentive to the pleasurable sensations that your body feels during sexual activity instead of worrying about ejaculation or performance.

"I try to think of things to distract myself so I can keep from coming," said Barry, age thirty-four. "I think about my business or my car, anything to try not to ejaculate. I feel like I'm being unfair to Kathy because I can't extend our lovemaking long enough to satisfy her. Then I come. I feel so guilty about it. The more I try, the quicker I ejaculate. We never talk about it, but it's like an undercurrent in our relationship." Barry was an auto mechanic who owned a repair shop business. His first sexual experience, at age sixteen, occurred when his best friend's inebriated mother seduced him. The shame and embarrassment he felt when his friend found out about the episode colored his subsequent sexual experiences and made him feel awkward with women.

Barry learned to reverse his premature ejaculation problem during sex therapy. First, I suggested that Barry and Kathy engage in extended foreplay at home without breast or genital touching for a full two weeks (see "How to Do Your Home Loveplay" on page 117). This type of foreplay, which does not focus on intercourse, took away Barry's pressure to perform and allowed him to concentrate on his pleasurable feelings. Then I taught Kathy how to perform the squeeze technique on the tip of Barry's penis (see page 197). Masters and Johnson learned this simple technique from a urologist in the early 1960s. It has helped countless men reverse premature ejaculation.

To ensure the procedure's effectiveness, Barry had to lie passively on his back and allow Kathy to stimulate his penis until just before he felt the urge to ejaculate. He told her when to stop, and then she squeezed the tip of his penis with her thumb and index finger for fifteen seconds. This pressure lessened Barry's erection by about a third. They waited about half a minute and repeated the process. The couple performed the squeeze technique a few times each time they made love. After about twelve times, Barry noticed that he could stay erect longer and longer before he felt his ejaculation was inevitable. Barry also practiced the technique several times alone.

Couples, you can alternatively try a stop-and-start technique that involves no squeezing to reverse premature ejaculation. Engage in foreplay until the man *almost* reaches orgasm, then stop. Relax, hug, hold each other until his erection goes down about a third. Then repeat your loveplay to the same point and stop again. Such deliberate loss of the man's erection will build his sexual self-confidence because he will see that more loveplay brings the erection right back again.

If he does lose the erection completely or ejaculates too soon, accept it. Laugh about it. Joke about it. It's not the end of the world or of the evening. Take a break and try again in an hour or two. Remember, the second erection lasts longer anyway. Knowing this fact, many men with premature ejaculation masturbate in private two to four hours before having intercourse. I sometimes recommend this practice to men with premature ejaculation.

6. Vaginismus and Painful Sex

The involuntary spasm of the muscles in the lower third of a woman's vagina is called vaginismus. This condition makes intercourse impossible because the muscles surrounding the opening to the vagina become so tight the penis cannot penetrate. Many women who have vaginismus cannot even insert a tampon or their finger into their vagina. Inability to achieve orgasm is quite common in women with this disorder.

Vaginismus is an exaggeration of a simple, protective vaginal reflex, similar to the reaction of closing your eyes in a sandstorm. Temporary vaginismus sometimes accompanies a physical problem that affects the genitals, such as an abscess or severe inflammation of the vagina.

Any traumatic sexual experience, such as rape or sexual abuse as a child, can produce vaginismus, either temporarily or permanently if untreated. But in my experience, the most common emotional factors that cause vaginismus are:

- Shame, guilt, and conflict about the genitals, arising from early warnings such as "Don't touch down there"
- Faulty sexual learning, resulting from inaccurate information about sex (for example, the notion that sex is always painful) and minimal self-exploration of the genital area
- Performance panic, caused by fear of pregnancy or anticipation that sex will be painful, possibly establishing a vicious cycle of anxiety followed by spasms

Georgia, a twenty-eight-year-old homemaker, was sometimes able to attain orgasm when her husband Mark stimulated her clitoris with his finger, but she developed vaginismus every time he tried to penetrate her. The couple had been married for six years, and their relationship was strained. Georgia had let Mark enter her forcibly five or six times during their marriage, primarily when she had had a lot to drink. "I told him to force me, to do whatever he had to do," confessed Georgia. But the sex was always painful for her.

Georgia did not have a past history of sexual abuse, but her upbringing had been very restrictive. She was the only child of a fundamentalist Christian minister whose wife had died while giving birth to Georgia. When disciplining her, Georgia's father sometimes reminded her of her mother's death. As a teen, Georgia had finally burst out, "Enough already. God took Mom; I didn't."

During sex therapy, Georgia learned that, with simple exercises done at home, *vaginismus is 100 percent reversible*. The muscle spasm can be voluntarily contracted and relaxed away. If you have vaginismus, try these simple techniques at home:

- Lock the door, disconnect the phone, and lie down in a comfortable spot. Breathe very slowly and open your mouth when you exhale. Insert your finger, well lubricated with water-based lubricant or saliva, into your vagina and continue to breathe deeply. Keep your mouth open while you slowly exhale. You will feel how your vagina angles back about forty-five degrees. Relax. This is your own finger. No one is hurting you. Explore your own vagina. Breathe slowly and deeply. It's starting to feel looser already.

• Now deliberately contract the muscles in the lower third of your vagina very tightly around your finger as though you were trying to stop the flow of urine. Relax and repeat. This exercise will teach you that you can control these muscles voluntarily, both to tighten and to loosen.

• Repeat these exercises for five minutes twice every day. On the first two days, use one finger. For the next two days, insert two of your fingers into your vagina, while breathing slowly in and out with your mouth open. Don't forget to contract and relax the muscles surrounding the opening of your vagina. On the next two days, ask your partner to place one lubricated finger into your vagina while you continue your slow, open-mouthed breathing. Guide his finger into your vagina. Use plenty of sexual fantasy to keep your mind focused on your sexuality. Then, on the following two days, after an extended period of foreplay, let your partner lie passively, straddle him, and stuff his nonerect penis into your vagina. Contract and relax your vaginal muscles around his soft penis. You should soon be able to feel your partner's erect penis inside your vagina without feeling pain. If you need more time for any of these stages, don't worry. The important thing to remember is that you are in control; you set the pace.

In all of the exercises, you should be active and your partner should be passive. In this way, you will learn how to be responsible for finding a comfortable, relaxed way of inserting your finger or your partner's finger or penis into your vagina. If you feel comfortable going further after this self-exploration, try masturbating to orgasm (see page 44 to learn how to masturbate). These exercises, done at home, have effectively reversed vaginismus for many women. They can help you too.

A woman can experience painful intercourse without spasm of the vaginal muscles; it can be caused by a variety of physical factors. The pain may be in the external parts of the genitals or deep in the pelvic area. In women, causes include lack of lubrication, a vaginal or bladder infection, soreness after childbirth, endometriosis (in which uterine tissue is displaced outside the uterus), or conditions affecting the ovaries. Common causes of painful intercourse in men include a tight foreskin, sexually transmitted diseases, an infection of the prostate gland or bladder, an anatomical abnormality of the penis, or inflammation of the penis. Spermicides used for birth control can produce a chemical irritation that causes a burning sensation in both men and women.

These causes are physical, so you should see your doctor if you are having pain during intercourse that is not related to spasm of the vaginal muscles.

Now you understand the most common sexual problems. I hope it has helped you to know that you're not alone. The one thing I tell my patients again and again is that sex happens as much in your head as below the belt. You don't cure sex problems simply by making sure all the parts work. You have to rediscover—or build—the intimacy in your relationship. In the next chapter, I'll tell you about some of the factors that can create that intimacy—or inhibit it.

4

Intimacy and Intercourse

When most of us wish for good sex, we're probably not envisioning just a night of erotic fireworks. What we really want is the intimacy that comes with good sex in a loving relationship. In this chapter, I'd like to tell you how to communicate better with your partner so you can improve your relationship as well as your sex life. Sharing your feelings—not only in words but through your actions—can help to create an atmosphere in which trust and positive regard develop into loving intimacy.

Before this century, multigenerational living arrangements were common because people could not afford to live on their own. Mass urban housing did not even exist before World War II. Getting married was the only respectable alternative to living in your parents' home. Families arranged pragmatic marriages on the basis of ethnic, religious, or social compatibility. What about love, romance, happiness, and intimacy? They might "develop." If they did not, the marriage continued anyway. As far as sex was concerned, the wife was expected to "submit" to sexual intercourse, which was "demanded" by her husband. She did not even think of approaching him sexually.

Today, most people marry for love. Many marry someone they see as a dream lover, thinking that a strong, magnetic sexual attraction will guarantee they live happily ever after, just like in the movies or a fairy tale. They soon find that good sex does not necessarily ensure a good relationship. And a bad relationship may quickly lead to bad sex. Relationship problems can cause a sexual problem or make it worse.

What Is Intimacy?

Today, we seem to live in crowds. Airports, expressways, public transportation, shopping malls, and sporting events bring together large numbers of people in an overwhelming excess of noise, activity, and fellow humanity. Yet each individual in the crowd can feel lonely and struggle with the need for recognition and intimacy. What is intimacy with another person? A closeness of your minds, your emotions, and your beliefs. In a loving relationship, affection and sexual exchange are also part of that intimacy.

It may surprise you to learn that intimacy can develop on several different levels: the personal, emotional, social, intellectual, sexual, and spiritual. Two people who hold the same inner beliefs may feel they know a great deal about each other and can trust each other, even if they have just met.

At any level, intimate interaction with another person can be summed up by these seven Rs of relationship:

- Respect—Respect means having great appreciation for your partner, deferring to his or her needs for closeness or solitude and allowing him or her time to pursue interests that may differ from your own.
- Risk-taking—In a relationship, you must be willing to take chances in trying something new or telling your partner some-

thing important (even if it's as simple as "I love you") in spite of the consequences.

• Responsibility—You both have to take total responsibility for your relationship, for keeping it alive and thriving. It's not fifty-fifty. Each must give 100 percent.

• Rights—Each person has certain rights, such as the right to privacy and honesty, that you must consider.

• Regard—You and your partner need to recognize and take a protective interest in each other's worth.

• Reciprocity—Interacting means give-and-take. If she lets you go to the basketball game with your buddies, you must allow her time to see a movie with a girlfriend.

• Response—Responding to your partner means listening and acknowledging him or her. It is different from reacting, which is automatic. Take a moment and think before you blurt out that insensitive remark.

When your relationship contains these seven components, true intimacy can evolve on many levels. For example, intellectual intercourse may be profoundly important to two scientists who share ideas through letters and journals. Even though they may never meet each other, they share intellectual intimacy because they relate, reciprocate by exchanging ideas, respect each other's views, take risks in sharing information, act responsibly, and respond to each other.

Intimacy that is exclusively sexual may, in fact, be a shallow form of intimacy if it engages only the body and ignores the feelings and the mind. Sexual intimacy that does not include emotion, thoughts, and beliefs is sexmaking, not lovemaking. "My wife 'endures' intercourse," said one man. "It's like she gives her body but not her soul. Her mind is somewhere else."

Some couples begin their relationship with ecstatic erotic feelings that turn to ashes after the flames of passion are quenched by orgasm. Soon they discover that they have little regard or respect for each other's ideas or feelings. Barriers to intimacy on any level can easily develop into unresolved conflict, lying, cheating, or substance abuse. Some of these barriers include an inability to touch, ineffective communication, jealousy, anger, and poor listening skills. You can learn to break through these barriers that constrict your sexuality by depriving it of intimacy.

Learning to Touch

Intimacy arises from emotional connection, and touching is one of the most important ways couples have to express their intimate relationship. Courting couples usually cannot wait to enjoy each other's touch. But, after a time, too many couples look upon some kinds of sustained touch, such as holding hands, as being adolescent, silly, or embarrassing. Too many couples restrict their affectionate touch only to sexual intercourse, depriving themselves of the enriching closeness produced by holding and being held. One woman told me, "He complains that I just lie there during intercourse. I've often asked him to do some petting and kissing, but he says he hates kissing and that he's not a teenager who 'makes out.' I'd rather do without sex altogether because I feel like a nonperson this way."

Men often struggle against cultural stereotypes that imply that tenderness is a weakness. Indoctrinated from boyhood in the belief that it is manly to score in sex as well as in business and sports, many men focus on the physical sensations rather than the emotional feelings. Their partners feel used, and both experience frustration and disillusionment. It is often said that women use sex to get love, while men use love to get sex. When the courtship pretenses end, he demands sex while she insists on romance. With these cross-purposes, couples mate and alienate, wondering what went wrong.

Dave and Sheila were both thirty-four when they came to the sex therapy clinic. They had been married for ten years but had had sex only six times in their marriage. Both were successful in their jobs but were sexually inhibited with each other. Sheila frequently initiated sexplay but said she was tired of being rejected by Dave. Although he said he enjoyed foreplay, Dave admitted he felt vulnerable and anxious when Sheila asked for sex. He claimed that he could not ejaculate during their six attempts at intercourse. Yet his chief complaint was lack of desire.

Dave grew up in a large, troubled family in which there was no expression of affection or love. His dad and several of his siblings were alcoholics; his father beat all of the children. Dave's brother died of a cocaine overdose. Dave never received any affectionate touch in his family, so he had difficulty showing affection through touch. He was the only child of the ten who got a good education. Therefore, his family relied on him heavily. Whenever there was a family problem or a shortage of money, the family would call Dave. Being unassertive, Dave could not say no. He repeatedly rescued his troubled and troublesome relatives.

As Dave grew older, he became less and less in touch with his own body. He had never masturbated as an adolescent or as an adult. In fact, he equated masturbation with cheating on his wife. As part of his therapy, I asked Dave to masturbate at home, first in private, then in Sheila's presence. This exercise would help Dave concentrate on the strong physical sensations masturbation produces and would tell me if his erections were working. Each arousal and climax would also circulate extra testosterone through his system. Sheila also agreed to masturbate in Dave's presence at home. I told both to use sexual fantasy to enhance arousal.

Masturbation is a normal part of development and helps a person learn about his or her sexual responses. When someone represses these responses through inhibitions, as did Dave, all sexual feelings become overcontrolled. Having both partners masturbate in front of each other brings them closer together and teaches each person about the other's sexual responses.

Dave and Sheila did their home loveplay exercises diligently, and, by the fifth week of sex therapy, Dave had not only initiated foreplay, he also said he enjoyed it. Sheila said it had never felt so good. The couple had not fully progressed to intercourse by the end of therapy, but they had made good progress and were confident they would reach this goal. Dave was learning how to touch and be touched for the first time in his life.

For some families, even affectionate words or nonsexual touch is uncomfortable or threatening, so they avoid it. Men in most Western countries have been cheated out of pleasurable touch because they wrongly consider touching unmanly, except in fighting or sports. Many men and women confine their nonsexual affectionate touch to contact with infants or loved ones on their deathbeds.

A patient once told me, "He shows more affection to the dog than to me." Our culture does give greater permission to show affection to pets than to people. But pets make fewer demands and create less conflict than do people. Pets are also playful and unconditionally affectionate, while we in our work-ethic culture lose our playfulness early in life.

Most people learn affectionate touch within their birth family. But some families are less touch-oriented than others—they may care deeply but do not show it through touch. Some people never learn that touch is enjoyable because of a "no-touch" family policy. Others learn that touch is painful because they identify it with physical punishment, the only type of touch they received at home. If your partner's touch needs are different from yours, you need to understand and respect the difference and not consider it right or wrong, good or bad. Both of you may have "touch hunger" but be hesitant or ashamed to ask for what you want.

People can learn to change the way they communicate by touch. But first they have to talk about it, relax, and give it a try. The touch exercises in this book can teach you how to accept and enjoy nongenital touch as a way of restoring closeness. Home loveplay, derived from "sensate focus" exercises developed by Masters and Johnson, can help you and your partner learn how you each give and receive various ways of touching. (You will learn how to do home loveplay in the next chapter.)

Communicating With Your Partner

Just as some people come from "no-touch" families, others grow up in "speak-only-when-you're-spoken-to" families. They learn not to communicate their own everyday needs in words or to ask another person what he or she feels or wants. As adults, they cannot talk about their personal needs, especially their sexual needs, to their partner and never think to ask their partner what he or she needs sexually. Someone from a noncommunicative family often is unconsciously attracted to a complementary partner, one who is talkative, sociable, and expressive, and vice versa. But, as the relationship matures, the partners may become a "we-don't-communicate" couple for whom sex becomes an important form of positive nonverbal communication. Other noncommunicating couples withdraw from each other both sexually and verbally in a "no talk, no sex, no love" stalemate. There are literally thousands of such couples who have opted to live in a sexless marriage.

John, age fifty-six, and Mary, age fifty-four, had been married for thirty-two years when they entered sex therapy. On their wedding day, John bluntly told Mary, "I'm telling you now that I love you, and that's that. Don't nag me about repeating it. I don't believe in all the commercial stuff, like cards, gifts, and parties for Christmas, birthdays, and anniversaries. Thanksgiving is enough fuss." John and Mary abided by this "no-frills" contract throughout their married life.

John had been unable to have an erection for years. Mary's chief complaint was lack of communication. She said John was kind, quiet, hardworking, and allowed her to manage the money. He even helped her with the housework. Both had learned to read each other's nonverbal signals well. Mary knew a worried silence from a tired one. John sensed when her silence meant hurt or anger, but he never said anything to her. Instead, he would fix something around the house or help her with the chores to please her. But Mary wanted more—she wanted him to say he loved her.

John and Mary followed my instructions during the seven-week sex therapy program, although the home exercises that required touching, talking, and kissing embarrassed them both at first. Still, they persisted because, as John volunteered, "It's like castor oil. If you need it, you need it." The home loveplay soon awakened their emotions, even restoring the erections John had not had for five years. During the third week of the program, John spontaneously told Mary that he loved her, quietly adding, "Maybe I won't wait thirty-two years to say so again."

Most couples who complain about lack of communication do not start out with as rigid a "no-romance" agenda as John and Mary did. Instead, as the relationship becomes more routine, there is less talk but more assumptions about what the other person thinks, feels, wants, or would do. "I like broccoli, so Paul must too," reasoned Meg. But did he? "She should know by now that I hate broccoli," thought Paul as he ate it but said nothing, which Meg interpreted as enjoyment. When I asked Paul why he never told Meg he hated broccoli in all those years, he answered, "She never asked me." Disliking broccoli may not seem as significant as not having an erection or an orgasm, but nothing need be endured permanently.

There is as yet no TV screen on the forehead that displays human thought. But many people act as if there were. Worse yet, seeking to please or to avoid conflict, people like Paul often encourage their partner's assumptive mind reading (sometimes with barely controlled resentment).

Lack of verbal communication or nonverbal cues soon affects what happens in the bedroom. Foreplay may be the first thing to be sacrificed on the altar of the relationship. Silent, routine "intercourse only" on certain nights may become acceptable to both. For others, power play eventually replaces foreplay *and* loveplay. The two then live miserably ever after.

Jesse, a fifty-two-year-old bus driver, and his wife, Dolores, a part-time receptionist age fifty, came to sex therapy because they were bored with their sex lives. Jesse was contemplating having an affair. "We have been married for almost thirty years," said Jesse. "There is just no spark left when we have sex. I am over fifty years old, and I don't want to live the rest of my life like this." Dolores agreed that the passion had left their marriage, but was more willing to passively accept the situation. "What does he expect? Fireworks?" she asked. "We've had four kids; we're over the hill."

Had they ever talked about their boredom? No. The couple's real problem was that they could not communicate with each other about their sexual tedium. "How do I tell Dolores I'm tired of her without hurting her?" asked Jesse. I asked him if he didn't think his being unfaithful would hurt her. "She'd never find out," he answered. "I already have someone in mind who Dolores doesn't know."

Affairs are not permitted during sex therapy at our clinic, and I reminded Jesse of this restriction. In a long-term relationship, sex with new partners destroys the couple's commitment and erodes trust. Jesse and Dolores needed to rework their relationship. To illustrate how, I told them the story of the workers in the diamond mines in my native South Africa. They reworked the refuse heaps and found precious powdered gold and diamonds. If you are in a long-term relationship that has become dull, you must rework it for the gold and diamonds that are still there. Your tools are time and imagination. Make the time to explore your relationship. Use your imagination to come up with the new activities, different positions, and sexy surprises you need to put the zing back into your lovemaking.

The real solution to the problem of sexual boredom lies in transforming the mechanical, uninspired act of sex into an imaginative, sexually charged act of love. How? You will have to find your own solutions, but I'm happy to offer a few suggestions:

First, as I suggested to Jesse, use sexual fantasy (see page 47 for a fuller discussion of sexual fantasy). Try to remember your first few dates, the first times you kissed or made love, or those moments of anticipation just before you saw each other again in the old days. How did you feel back then? What was it about your partner that gave you a thrill? Talk to each other about those times and pretend that you are courting again. Send her a single red rose at work. Call him during the day to say you want to make love later that night.

Don't be afraid to enjoy sexy books or movies. Rent a romantic video or page through a sexy magazine together. If he's interested in a more explicit movie or book and she's agreeable, try one of those. It's not bad or wrong for adults to view this kind of material as long as both partners are willing. But neither partner has the right to force or coerce the other into anything he or she is not ready for.

One of the most fun ways to put spice back into your sex life is to plan an erotic surprise for your partner (see page 159 for some sexy suggestions). Only try this tactic if you are willing to do it with a sense of humor. That way, if it backfires, you can at least laugh together, which might lighten up your mood and make sex more fun.

Don't be fooled into thinking that sex always has to be as glamorous and breathless as it is in the movies. Movies are made to sell fantasy as fact. Popular culture portrays sex in ways that can make your normal, enjoyable sexual exchange seem ordinary or even boring. What's important is how it feels for both of you, not how it compares to some unrealistic ideal.

Older couples like Jesse and Dolores often have more time and discretionary income to invest in their relationship than do younger couples. Jesse and Dolores came up with the idea of a getaway weekend in Wisconsin to kick off their newfound togetherness. Their youngest child was sixteen and could take care of himself for a few days. The couple also experimented with some new positions and used more sexual fantasy. By the end of therapy, they had not only improved their lovemaking, they had also become closer emotionally. "Now some of my favorite fantasies are coming true in bed with Dolores," said Jesse.

Other partners who do communicate verbally may speak in a way that hides their feelings by avoiding eye contact. Used to relaying only factual information, such people can't find any words to describe how they feel. I tell my patients whose partners have difficulty expressing their feelings to watch their partner's eyes and mouth for signs of tension, anger, or distress. You can also use a visual reminder when you want to know how your partner feels about something. For example, you can hold up your hand, a bright yellow piece of paper, or a red scarf as a reminder to express feeling. It tells your partner, "Wait. Tell me how you *feel* about this. Or, if you can't tell me, show me by your actions." This reminder has a strong visual, nonverbal effect on a person, especially one who cannot easily put feelings into words.

Another way to encourage communication when one or both of you cannot or will not speak is to sit down and write your partner a letter, especially when either of you is angry. Formulating your words in writing gives you time to think, change your mind, and rewrite instead of automatically reacting with stinging words that cannot be unsaid. Your partner will be better able to understand in a letter what you felt and why you felt it because your written language is less colored by the emotion of the moment. Hold the letter twelve hours, reread it to make sure it says what you think *now*, then leave it where your partner will see it.

Jealousy

Jealousy is a strong human emotion that can flare up when you perceive or fear a loss of attention or love. The emotion is often irrational; it usually consumes and controls its owner. Jealousy's corrosiveness can damage both your own well-being and your partner's positive feelings for you. Blind jealousy can kill a relationship. Plus, the time and energy spent on this emotion could be more productively spent on other things.

What causes jealousy? Early normal abandonment experiences, such as when a parent goes to work, must leave a child in the hospital, or leaves the home permanently, may make a person anticipate disloyalty, deceit, or duplicity from a partner. Insecurity, feelings of inferiority, and low self-esteem can provoke anxiety, leading to suspicious behavior, such as looking through pockets for a telltale note or phone number. There are times when jealousy is evoked by a real betrayal of trust, such as an extramarital affair. Is that relationship still salvageable? Of course it is, if *both* partners are willing and able to start over and rebuild trust. More commonly, one person simply has an irrational fear of betrayal. But irrational feelings make sense when you understand what's behind them.

Art, age forty-eight, was a construction worker. His wife, Edie, the same age, was an executive secretary. Edie earned a good salary, and her position required that she wear business suits to the office every day. Art, who wore blue jeans and a flannel shirt at work and at home, begrudged Edie her "fancy" clothes and became suspicious when she had to stay late at work. He thought she was too friendly with the male executives in her office and imagined that she was having an affair with one of them. His jealousy was totally unfounded. Edie loved and was faithful to Art but could not convince him of her fidelity.

During sex therapy, Art complained of sporadic erection problems and revealed a severe lack of self-confidence that he tried to hide with bravado. He said in confidence that he didn't deserve someone like Edie and, because he wasn't good enough for her, that she must have tried to find someone else. He had projected his low self-esteem onto Edie, thinking that, in her eyes, he compared unfavorably to the men with whom she worked. After completing the role reversal exercises in week 4 (see page 204), Art was able to face his fears more openly and accept that Edie loved him as he was. By the end of the seven weeks, Art's erections became more reliable, especially after plenty of tenderness and stimulation by Edie.

Anger Education

All of us have felt anger, either inside ourselves or from the outside, directed toward us. But a great deal of ignorance about and avoidance of anger exists, so we try to ignore it. Ignorance about anger is *not* bliss. It may become an emotional booby trap that can hold your relationship hostage. We all need to become educated about anger so we can *use* it instead of being *used by* it.

Anger is a protective emotion. It protects us from the loss of our life, our property, our self-esteem, our security, and our privileges. It is a *normal* emotion that you can learn to use constructively. When you are angry, hormones circulate through your nervous system to alert your body to protect itself. This response is the "fight or flight" reaction. It gives you enormous amounts of energy that you can use either to strike out at your partner or to take a walk, wash the floor, or write a letter. Many creative people use the energy produced by anger to paint, write a song, or redecorate a room, transforming the negative energy into something positive and creative.

You can express your anger privately in your thoughts; verbally through your words; physically with destructive action; or indirectly by sulking, being sarcastic, "forgetting" chores or birthdays, developing physical symptoms, or refusing to compromise on anything from sex to squeezing the toothpaste from the end rather than from the middle. Unresolved anger can cause vague tension and irritability as well as physical symptoms, such as headaches, insomnia, or dizziness, and emotional problems, such as depression, anxiety, or panic disorder. Perhaps most important, anger can drive your partner away.

Both Al, sixty, and Roni, fifty-five, had been previously married. They had not had sex for the last four and a half years of their five-year marriage. Al was an auctioneer and edited a magazine about antiques. Roni no longer worked but had been a city planner. Al's previous wife had died seven years before, and he had had no sex life after her death until he married Roni. Roni had been friends with Al and his previous wife. In fact, Al had had an affair with Roni when he was married to his first wife.

When I saw them, they were ready to divorce each other. The anger between them was explosive. Al was a quiet man, and Roni was a nagger. The louder and longer she railed, the more Al withdrew. Roni would get so angry that she would start hitting Al. Then he would push her away. The cause of most of their arguments? Sex. "He never initiates," she would say. "I feel like we're ninety years old." "I have a sex drive," he would counter, "but I don't like her aggressive nature." It was her mouth that he was fighting. He would come around but only if she could learn to control her rage.

Roni had a hard time learning to channel her anger and express her honest feelings instead of blaming Al (see " 'I' Language," page 140). When she finally did master "I" language, it was miraculous. If she spoke calmly, saying, "I want to be close to you," he responded. They both wanted tenderness in their marriage but had repeatedly missed the mark. Roni said that the final week of therapy was the most remarkable week they had had in years. They had intercourse, and Roni was able to have more than one orgasm.

How to Listen (Not Just Hear)

Hearing sound may not mean receiving the meaning—that's listening. Can you listen and talk at the same time? Not well. Can you listen and plan your reply before your partner finishes talking? Partially. Can you listen when you're hurt, scared, or angry? Only poorly, inaccurately, or incompletely. Why listen? Because it's a way you can learn about how your partner thinks and feels. It also tells your partner that you value him or her. Being listened to feels good and can be a healing experience.

Active listening is listening *with* rather than *to* another person. Alert listening is a special gift from you to your partner that says "You count" or "I want to know you." It allows you to enter the special world of your partner's experiences. The barriers to active listening erect walls between you and your partner. These barriers include:

• Avoiding eye contact, looking around, watching TV, reading the newspaper, or falling asleep while the other is talking
• Trying to predict what your partner will say or assuming what he or she means
• Being in a hurry

- Being a passive or distracted listener or not evaluating what you hear and see
- Being critical of your partner's dress, looks, grammar, mannerisms, or accent, rather than listening to what's being said
- Overreacting to what your partner says or the way it sounds, or interrupting
- Asking "yes" or "no" questions instead of exploring your partner's meaning with open-ended queries
- Prematurely agreeing or disapproving before your partner finishes what he or she has to say
- Preaching, blaming, criticizing, or changing the subject, which tells a lot more about your intolerance or insecurity than about your partner's ability to communicate

Lou, age fifty-two, and Candy, age thirty-eight, had been married for seven years and came to our sex therapy clinic because of Lou's lack of desire. Lou was a colonel in the marines and he wouldn't listen to anybody. "I am a marine," was expressed in his very demeanor. During sex therapy his attitude toward the therapists was "I've seen combat in Vietnam and you are all a bunch of kids who can never imagine the grittiness of real life. Why should I listen to you?" Lou compensated for his lack of desire by calling Candy a nymphomaniac every time she approached him for sex. Her desires were those of a normal woman, but Lou would not accept that—he could not be wrong.

We literally had to plead with Lou to listen to Candy. Lou called Candy "Buddy" because he saw her as "one of the guys." He had been best friends with Candy's brother, who had introduced them. The three of them would go out together for a few beers, and Candy prided herself on being able to "drink them under the table." But she had always wanted to shed her tomboy image. Lou had no idea how much she resented it each time he called her Buddy. It made her feel unfeminine and unlovable.

During therapy, I persuaded Candy to tell Lou that she wanted him to stop calling her Buddy and start treating her more like a woman. When she did, Lou expressed utter surprise but was obviously touched emotionally. Candy had recently lost about ten pounds and bought some new clothes. I made a point of encouraging Lou to hold her hand and tell her how good she looked. It was a big change for Lou, whose gruff manner and foul language were appropriate for the barracks but completely inadequate to sustain his marriage.

The home loveplay exercises Lou and Candy did furthered their newfound communication. They were able to inject some interest back into their relationship by having a romantic candlelight bubble bath together (see the section "Erotic Surprises" on page 157). They had intercourse early in therapy—before they were "supposed to." Lou found he could enjoy sex more when he shed his macho image in the bedroom.

How to Listen to Your Lover

Can good, active listening be learned? Yes. Here are some tips that can help you to listen to your partner more effectively:

- Make eye contact from time to time.
- Forget grammar, tune in to your partner's meaning.
- Try to understand your partner's feelings by watching his or her eyes, face, and body.
- When you discover the main point of the conversation, highlight it in your mind or jot it down on paper so you won't lose it.
- Accept some silence to give your partner time to formulate a response, but don't deliberately use long silences to make him or her nervous.
- If you don't understand something, ask about it. Say something like, "You said that it makes you angry when I leave my clothes all over the bedroom floor. Why? I put them in the hamper in the morning. Could we talk a little more about that?"
- Don't interrupt, derail, change the subject, or be sarcastic.

• Don't trivialize what your partner says or state what you believe he or she *should* think.

You'll learn more about communication skills in chapter 5.

Forgiveness

It is difficult to achieve intimacy without forgiveness. To forgive is to open your clenched fist and let go of past hurts, resentments, and anger. Forgiveness can free you when you are ready to let go of the injury. Forgiveness does not excuse, forget, or tolerate wrongs. It faces the wrongs, the hurt, the shock, and the disappointment so you can absolve them and give you and your partner the chance to start fresh again.

When your partner has betrayed your trust or hurt you, it's difficult to believe that you can forgive. Even if you think you "should" forgive, your feelings may not allow it. Feelings feel; they don't think. But forgiveness can be an act of choice—an action arising from your will instead of a reaction coming from your emotions. *Decide* to let go. Open the clenched fist, then reach out and reconcile yourself with the person who hurt you, even if you have to do it in a letter that you do not mail. Writing the letter will help you get it out of your system.

Here is an example of a couple who forgave not only each other but themselves. Keith, forty-two, and Mary Ann, forty-five, had been married for eleven years. About seven years before they came to therapy, Mary Ann became pregnant and had an abortion without telling Keith beforehand about her decision. When Keith found out, he was very upset, especially since she could not explain why she did not want the baby. He had wanted a child. But he never disclosed his feelings to Mary Ann. Instead, after the secret emerged, he moved into a separate bedroom. They had not had sex since the abortion. In therapy, Mary Ann said it was because she feared pregnancy, childbirth, and potential birth defects, especially now, at age forty-five.

Keith came from an average family with reasonably good relationships. But Mary Ann was an only child who grew up in a disruptive family environment. Her father was a troubled man who verbally abused Mary Ann, her mother, and her maternal grandmother, who lived with them. When Mary Ann was a teenager, her father once fondled her breasts in front of her mother. Mary Ann's mother was too meek to confront the father and could not protect Mary Ann from him. At age eighteen, Mary Ann moved out of the house and has not seen her father since.

During therapy, Mary Ann revealed that her decision to abort her baby sprang from a fear that she would be as bad a parent as her own parents had been. Her self-esteem was so low she assumed she would fail as a mother. "I don't want to screw up another generation," she said during therapy. I asked Mary Ann to write a letter to her parents (one that would never be sent) to discharge her negative feelings about them. "You should never have had children," she wrote. "I should never have been born." She saw that she had projected those feelings further when she uttered her own wish never to have a child.

Keith and Mary Ann had completely blocked out the abortion episode from their lives and had suppressed their sexuality in the process. Only after these revelations surfaced did Keith realize how terrified Mary Ann was of having a child. He understood her motivation and recognized that her action had not been directed at him. When Mary Ann discovered that Keith had wanted a child all this time, she understood why he had left their marital bed. Their mutual understanding led to mutual forgiveness. Although their lack of interest in sex did not reverse during the seven weeks of sex therapy, the couple's relationship improved. They now slept in the same bed and were optimistic that their affection would turn into arousal "within the next year."

Forgiving your partner gives you freedom, self-respect, and self-healing. It can be difficult, and it requires repeated attempts. But it prevents you from becoming a prisoner of an ongoing cycle of hurt and hate.

How Sex Therapy Can Affect Your Relationship

The sex therapy exercises in this book will profoundly affect not only your sex life but also your relationship because they force you and your partner to do some deep emotional "root canal" work. This frightens some couples. "Help us but don't change us," they sometimes say. But if you didn't want to change something about your relationship, you would not have read this far. Change is inevitable—it will happen anyway. Why not try to influence things to change for the better?

Don't involve your family or friends—however well meaning they might be—when trying to change your relationship. Respect each other's privacy and confidentiality. The responsibility for change rests exclusively with you and your partner. Even if you work with a therapist, he or she must not be allowed to impose a solution upon you because this tactic will promote dependency rather than growth. You must talk to each other. If you can't talk, then write to each other. Try to come up with at least two possible solutions to the issues that are causing conflict, and ask your partner to do the same. From these suggested solutions, your task will be to find a workable resolution or compromise to your problems on your own. Here's how one couple did it.

Molly was a thirty-three-year-old woman who had a fourteen-year-old son, Jason, from a previous marriage. Jason was continuously in trouble with the police for shoplifting, vandalism, and drinking. Molly's current husband, Kyle, age thirty-six, could not establish a good relationship with Jason; they argued all the time. Although this problem did not cause the intermittent impotence and lack of interest in sex that brought Molly and Kyle to sex therapy, it affected their sex life and their entire relationship adversely. They constantly quarreled about Jason.

At my request, Molly and Kyle sat down and came up with their own suggestions for dealing with Jason's unacceptable behavior. They decided they would take Jason to a therapist who specialized in counseling adolescents. They also resolved to involve him in a summer ac-

tivity that would both fill his idle time and give him some money he could use to buy the things he wanted. Kyle teamed up with Jason to begin a small-scale yard-work business. Jason responded reluctantly at first, but when he saw how willingly the neighbors paid him to weed their gardens and mow their lawns, his interest blossomed.

During his individual counseling sessions, Jason later revealed that he resented his own father's desertion and his mother's new relationship. His delinquent behavior was the only way he knew to get his mother's attention back. This insight helped the family work through their problems while Jason's behavior slowly improved. The hope of solving their family problems made it easier for Molly and Kyle to overcome their sex problems during sex therapy.

As you both do the exercises in this book, you will learn many techniques that can improve your relationship. But if you fail to make a meaningful step forward and your relationship seems unworkable, you will eventually have to make a decision about whether or not to stay in the relationship. Here is an exercise that I use with couples who feel they are at the end of the line.

Is It the End of the Line?

Before you think about ending your relationship, try this. Make a list of three positives and three negatives about your relationship. Limit the list to no more than three each so you can focus on items that are truly important. Have your partner do the same. You may share your list with your partner unless you think he or she will be upset or overly sensitive to its contents. But the main reason for doing this exercise is to find out for yourself if the positives outweigh the negatives and whether the negatives can be overcome. Do you want to keep your relationship with your partner going or not? Write down three positives and three negatives about a divorce or breakup and see if the positives outweigh the negatives.

Do the lists show that you and your partner have the same values?

Interests? Goals? *Disparities are not necessarily incompatibilities.* Are you keeping the relationship going primarily because you are dependent on your partner economically? Socially? Emotionally? Is this a good enough reason to stay in an unsatisfying relationship? You cannot change your partner; you can only change yourself. Are you willing to try? You'll find out a lot about yourself and your partner by doing this exercise, and you will both gain perspective on your relationship as a whole.

If you both agree that your relationship is worth saving, take the next step. Turn to page 111 and begin week 1 of your sex therapy at home.

Part 2

Seven Weeks to a Better Sex Life

5

Week 1: Give Yourself a Joy Break

Starting Out

Sex can be fun. Not only playful fun but special, serious fun. But it can become frustrating when you can't seem to "get it right." If you strike out in a baseball game or miss the hoop in a basketball game, you can usually just shrug it off; you know your luck will change and you'll play better another day. But sex is supposed to be one of the supreme joys of life, so when it doesn't go right, it can be devastating. You might feel ashamed, discouraged, and defeated. Of course, you can try to ignore your sexual feelings and say to yourself, "Sex really isn't that important." For some people it may not be. They compensate by throwing themselves into other activities, such as work, sports, or exercise. A few know deep down that they are fooling themselves. They lose some of their zest for life, and their relationship may become hostile, distant, or bitter. But there is no need to tell you all of this. You know it already—

111

that's why you bought this book and why you've read this far. Help is on the way.

Sex therapy offers no magic formulas. But it can work magic. How? By increasing your knowledge of your sexual self and by teaching you how to use your own experience to overcome your sexual problems. Practicing the exercises in this book can also improve communication between you and your partner and enrich your relationship. Seven weeks is a short time, but you can change a lot, even if your problems are long-standing. Therapy for a sexual problem can be a challenge because change is difficult and painful, but you will be taking giant steps toward resolving your problem simply by reading this book and doing the recommended exercises.

As I said before, the first thing that you should do before beginning sex therapy at home is get a complete physical examination by your doctor, including an examination of your genitals. Your sexual problem may have a physical cause (see chapter 3), and it is important to rule out this possibility. When you meet with your doctor, tell him or her that you are reading this book and that you intend to practice the exercises in it.

Reading the book is not enough. Each week, you will have "homework" (loveplay exercises) that you and your partner should do in the privacy of your own home. This homework is the most important part of your therapy. Make a commitment to your loveplay exercises. When you do, you'll be reaffirming your commitment to your relationship, to the discovery (or rediscovery) of your sexual self, and to the joy of loving each other.

The real learning, the real improvement, and the real benefit will come from doing the loveplay at home. The outlook for reversal of your sexual symptoms is excellent, but *success directly corresponds to the number of times per week that you and your partner do your home assignments*. No one can do your home loveplay for you. Make it a regular part of your schedule, like an important appointment. The first few times may be awkward, but they will be well worth the effort in the long run.

You probably want to know what to expect and what you will get out of this therapy. The most important benefit is that you and your partner will begin to understand your sexual selves. Here are some other things that my patients have told me they have gotten out of sex therapy:

"The ability to reach out and talk to and touch my husband again. To learn to accept him and myself as we are, not as I would like us to be."

"A release from my mental jail, a granting of permission, both externally from you and internally from myself, to enjoy my sexuality."

"I have a better feeling of us as a couple. I learned how each of us has to share our needs so we can better satisfy each other, not only sexually, but emotionally. I also have a better understanding of my own feelings and emotions. I thought I already knew all this, but we keep changing."

"A new sense of direction—now I understand that we don't always have to have intercourse to have love, that touching is a big part of loving."

"My best friend is back! Thank you for the insights, the guidance, and the warm, caring approach to healing our relationship."

"I have learned things about myself—physical and emotional— that I never really knew before. I can tell my husband what I want or like openly now."

"I understand better how our relationship drifted and got to this point. We took each other for granted and lived separate lives in the same condo. Now we know what needs to be done to help change it."

"The joy of experiencing sex again and knowing it will continue."

"I'm less embarrassed about talking with Mike about sex and saying what I want and don't want. I can talk about sex as well as have sex, and I like my imperfect body better."

"I discovered the difference between sex and intimacy."

"Sex therapy reduced the level of blaming and hurt between us. It also alerted me to some of the things Peggy needs before she can respond to me. I learned how to verbalize my feelings."

Getting Through Week 1

You may be wondering how you and your partner will live through the first week of intensive sex therapy at home. You may be thinking, "My sex life is a mess. How can I just jump into these sexual homework assignments?" or "I couldn't possibly do the things you're asking me to." Be assured that no one has died of embarrassment yet. Both of you will survive. But you will go through a certain amount of anxiety and uncertainty before you attain the intimacy you're working toward.

Everyone in sex therapy feels some hesitancy at first. Here are some common difficulties people have encountered during sex therapy:

1. *The first attempts at home loveplay seem awkward or mechanical.* Expect to be rusty if it's been years since you kissed and caressed each other lovingly. Try to have a sense of humor during your first attempts at loveplay. After a few tries, it will feel more natural. Remember, this is not a contest and no one is judging you. These exercises are for you and you alone, so don't worry if they look or feel funny at first.

2. *One or both of you may be so relaxed or fatigued that you fall asleep*

during loveplay. Some of the exercises will call for you to lie still and relax while your partner caresses you. If you fall asleep during loveplay, take advantage of your natural body rhythms by napping for an hour and a half (see exercise on page 72). Then get up, shower, and begin again when you are relaxed and refreshed. If your partner falls asleep while you are caressing him or her, don't take it personally. You're not doing it wrong. Your partner's need for sleep at that moment is no reflection on you. After ninety minutes, wake him or her with a kiss and a body rub.

3. *Your partner refuses to cooperate.* Avoid accusing your partner of being uncooperative. Say in "I" language (see page 140), "I would enjoy doing the home loveplay exercises tonight." If your partner still resists or makes excuses, try asking half an hour later, or ask when a better time would be. Explain why committing yourselves to the loveplay is important to you.

4. *Career, family, or financial problems get in the way.* When doing your home loveplay or other sex therapy exercises, try to put other problems on the back burner. Pretend you and your partner are on your own desert island. Plan for your time together, and don't let anything else take you away from it. Lock the door, take the phone off the hook, get a baby-sitter for the kids—anything to help you make your own private corner of time and place. It might seem impossible to shelve your other cares temporarily, especially if you have small children. You may have put yourself on the bottom of your list of priorities for so long that you've forgotten you have your own relationship to nurture. For the next seven weeks at least, commit to putting yourselves at the top of the list.

5. *You are unable to refrain from having sex during your home loveplay exercises.* During the first few weeks of sex therapy, I want you to postpone intercourse so you can focus instead on sensuality rather than sexuality. But erections and vaginal lubrication are

normal responses to loveplay. Understand and enjoy these responses. Stop and hold each other for a while until they subside. No one has died of an unused erection or unfulfilled arousal yet.

My patients have encountered all of these problems, and they still have benefited from sex therapy. You can too.

Your Home Loveplay Exercises

The home loveplay exercises in this book are designed to help you focus on the bodily sensations you feel while being touched by your partner so you won't be distracted by thoughts like "How am I doing?" "Will I have an orgasm?" "Am I stimulating him (or her) enough?" "What if I ejaculate too soon?" Home loveplay allows both of you to feel physically comfortable with each other again without worrying about attaining orgasm. Without the pressure to "perform," you can discover—or rediscover—the joy of intimacy.

Make four or five half-hour dates per week with each other for your home loveplay. Not times when you are dead tired or when you only have a few minutes. Instead, pick times when you can reduce distractions, when the kids are not underfoot, when you can relax for that precious private half hour together. To find the time, you may have to trim your schedule for a few weeks so that you can plan time together. Think of it as a time investment in your relationship savings account. The greater your investment, the greater the funds you'll have to draw on later when you need them.

Some couples worry that such planning will take the spontaneity out of sex. Perhaps. But unless you schedule parties or vacations, they might not happen either. The busier you are, the harder it is to make time. You have to set your priorities. It's like needing gasoline. You had better fill the relationship tank or you'll run dry and get stuck. Making time for each other says, "I value us highest of all." You always have to make time in life for things that are important. What could be more important than improving your sexual relationship? Playing volleyball? The sacrifice will be worth it. Again, look at it as an investment in each other that will pay rich dividends. Improving your sexual relationship has a ripple effect—it will improve your overall relationship as well.

The methods presented in this book have helped thousands. You can benefit too, *if* you keep your end of the bargain by doing your home loveplay exercises several times each week. The changes will surprise you. Regular participation in the home exercises can improve your love life *and* your sex life—maybe for the *rest* of your life. I get letters from patients I saw many years ago that verify this fact.

Your home loveplay exercises will teach you how to be both sexual and sensual, and they will show you the difference between the two. Many people, especially men, have not learned the difference. The loveplay you do at home will help you discover the sights, sounds, touches, tastes, and smells that you find most sensual, arousing, and pleasing so you can learn to relax and enjoy them before progressing to intercourse.

Your loveplay is literally a *re-creation* of your relationship—a starting over. During each of your loveplay sessions this first week, feel free to touch your partner lovingly anywhere on his or her body except for the breasts and genitals. *No intercourse yet!* Even if you have the best erection or the best lubrication since you were sweet sixteen! You need to relax and avoid any pressure and performance anxiety about having intercourse. Look at your loveplay as a "joy break" that will relax and refresh you. It will also help you become physically comfortable with each other again.

How to Do Your Home Loveplay

First, take the phone off the hook or turn on the answering machine and lock the door. Take off your clothes and shower—together or solo. Soften the lights and play soothing music. Sit on the bed facing each other and begin by exploring your partner's face with your fingertips and your lips for about five minutes (see illustration on page 118).

Then enjoy being the receiver as your partner does the same for you. Both of you can use your favorite fantasy to heighten arousal.

Be creative and playful. Put a sheepskin rug on the floor in front of the fireplace, decorate the room with fresh flowers—anything to bring a little fun into your loveplay. Use different strokes with your fingers, lips, and tongue—light, firm, brushing, feathering, whatever comes to mind.

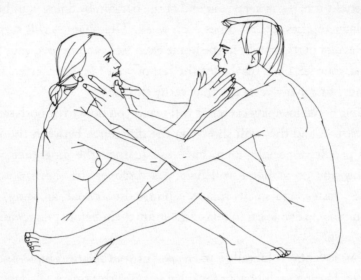

Face-to-Face Home Loveplay

Next, sit back-to-chest (see illustration on page 119) and explore every inch of each other's bodies, except the breasts or genitals. Stroke, massage, caress, and kiss the areas that your partner tells you have the most sensation on the back, arms, chest, abdomen, and legs. You'll be surprised at your self-discovery. As one man said, "I had no idea I had such strong sensations in my fingertips. I'll do this loveplay the rest of my life." Take turns. Guide each other's hands—with words or silently—to the places where each of you wants to be touched.

You can also try lying passively on your back or stomach as if you were getting a massage. Your partner can sit or kneel next to you while exploring your body. Tell your partner how it feels. Breathe slowly, and use fantasy to enhance your pleasure. Now switch places.

Back-to-Chest Home Loveplay

Avoid the breast and genital areas, and *do not* have intercourse yet. If arousal or an erection occurs, simply stop, hug, and let the arousal subside naturally. Then start to play again. Refraining from intercourse places the emphasis on your sensual self, not on your sexual self. It connects the two selves and builds sexual self-confidence.

Be aware of your feelings—as a giver and as a receiver. Express your reactions with smiles, words, and sounds. Telling your partner that you enjoy what he or she is doing is a wonderful gift you can give. Many men and women do not realize how much their partners appreciate such loving feedback.

The next day, savor the special fun you both had. Plan what to do at your next home loveplay session. It's yours to repeat, and it's free. Just add surprises and laughter.

If you and your partner do not engage in very much loveplay during this week, regard it as a danger sign. Why haven't you followed through? It may be time for a heart-to-heart, hand-holding fifteen-minute talk with your partner to find out why you are setting up roadblocks to intimacy.

Remember, making sex (body only) is different from making love (body plus feelings). This book will give you much information about the former. To attain the latter, you must add the following ingredients: caring, sharing, and commitment.

What Is Your Sexual History?

Remember when I said back in the introduction that sex therapy works on the whole person—body, mind, and feelings? The home loveplay I just described is the part of sex therapy that works on your physical body. Now I'll tell you how you can work on your mind, that is, your attitudes, thoughts, and beliefs about sex. (You'll work on your feelings later when you begin doing your role-playing and guided imagery exercises.) To find out what you think and believe about sex, I've included some questionnaires in this book—the same questionnaires completed by the couples in our clinic. By filling out the questionnaires and carefully considering your answers, you will uncover many ideas you have about sex in general, and your relationship in particular, that you forgot or never knew you had. The insights you gain about your attitudes and beliefs about sex will help you better understand why your sexual problems have developed and how you can solve them. The first questionnaire I've included is about your sexual history.

When your doctor gives you a physical examination, he or she asks you a series of questions about your past health, the health history of your parents, and any current medical or emotional problems you might have. Doctors call this interview "taking a medical history." As your own sex therapist, you can employ a similar technique and apply it to your sex life—by taking your own sexual history. Your partner can do the same.

The form below contains a series of questions about your past sexual experience, including the sexual relationship between you and your present partner. In private, read the questions carefully and answer them honestly. When you have completed the questionnaire, you will have a thorough overview of your sexual experience. At our clinic, patients have the benefit of sharing the questionnaires with professional therapists. You may want to take yours to your doctor at your next visit if your sexual problem is troublesome enough, especially if it has a physical cause. But this questionnaire alone will help you place your sexual history in a broader context. You may recognize patterns of behavior or incidents or attitudes that triggered current problems. You're not out to judge yourself, just recognize yourself.

There is no need to show your questionnaire to your partner unless you are sure he or she will not be upset. An old skeleton in the closet may be your private burden to bear. On the other hand, your partner may understand and accept you, secret and all. It's for you to decide. At any rate, reread your sexual history two days from now to gain even more self-awareness.

Make photocopies of these pages, or write your answers down on a separate piece of paper so you both can complete the sexual history.

YOUR SEXUAL HISTORY QUESTIONNAIRE

I. Personal Sexual History

How old were you when you first remember sexual feelings? Describe the circumstances.

How old were you when you first masturbated? Were you discovered? Describe the circumstances.

How old were you when you first had intercourse?

How would you describe it (joyful, shameful, painful)?

What is your preferred position for intercourse? Does your partner like it or just cooperate?

When was your first climax? Describe the circumstances.

Have you ever had a sexually transmitted disease (chlamydia, gonorrhea, herpes, other)?

Have you ever been raped? Describe the circumstances.

Have you ever been the victim of sexual abuse as a child?

Describe your experience. Did you know the person? Did you tell anyone? What was the outcome?

Have you ever had sexual contact with a member of your own family? Describe your experience (exploration with a sibling or cousin, intercourse with a parent or other family member). Did you tell anyone at the time? What was the outcome? How have you coped?

Have you ever had any sexual experience with someone of the same sex? How do you feel about it?

Does your partner know about it?

Has your partner ever had any sexual experience with someone of the same sex? How do you know? How do you feel about it?

Has either of you been tested for HIV, the virus that causes AIDS? What were the results?

II. Your Current Relationship

How does your partner feel about participating in sex therapy at home?

How do you feel about it?

Which of you suggested it?

How do you think sex therapy can best help you?

How can it help your partner?

How can it help your relationship?

How long have you been in this relationship?

What first attracted you to your partner?

What did you like best about him or her?

What do you now like least? (Is it similar to what once attracted you?)

How did you meet your partner?

Are there any children from this relationship?

Names: Ages:

Have there been any abortions in this relationship?

Have you had infertility problems in this relationship?

How would you describe this relationship (close, distant, hostile, warm, equal, unequal)?

Are you committed to this relationship? What does commitment mean to you? What do you think it means to your partner?

Is your partner committed to this relationship?

Has there been a change in your relationship? Describe it.

What do you think caused the change?

If you *wanted* to change one thing about your relationship, what would it be?

What would you change about your partner if you could?

What would you change about yourself if you could?

What are the recurrent issues of conflict in this relationship?

Have you talked about breaking up? Seriously? Only as a threat?

Have you taken any action on it?

What do you see as your own biggest problem?

What is the single biggest difference between you (religion, relatives, money, social status)?

Have you had therapy before? What kind (individual, couple, family)? Did it help?

How does your sexual problem affect your partner's sexual function or vice versa?

How have you as a couple tried to handle the sexual problem so far (sex manuals, alcohol, other partners)?

Have you or your partner been married previously?

How would you describe the past marriage sexually? Financially?

Does either of you have any children from a previous marriage or relationship?

Names: Ages: Any problems with them?

Who filed for divorce, you or your spouse?

What effect has that marriage had on this relationship?

Do you think a woman should approach a man for sex?

Should a man always be the sexual initiator?

What is your concept of the proper role of a man:

in bed?

financially?

with children?

What is your concept of the proper role of a woman:

in bed?

financially?

with children?

How often do you and your partner express affection each week?

How often do you have intercourse?

Do you reach orgasm?

(For men) Do you have erection difficulty?

Do you have morning erections? Do you have erections with masturbation? Do you have sleep erections?

Did your first episode of erection difficulty involve alcohol, anxiety, or anger?

Did anything sexually upsetting ever happen to you? Your age?

Who did you tell? What was the outcome?

Do you and your partner engage in foreplay before intercourse?

Who initiates?

Do you masturbate? How frequently per month? How do you feel about it?

Does your partner know about it?

What is your partner's favorite position for intercourse? Do you like it or just cooperate?

Does your partner masturbate? How do you feel about it?

Do you and your partner ever engage in oral sex? How often?

Do you and your partner ever have anal sex? How often?

When you have sex with your partner, do you:

completely remove your clothes	never	sometimes	always
turn off all the lights	never	sometimes	always
shower/bathe together first	never	sometimes	always
touch your own genitals	never	sometimes	always
touch your partner's genitals	never	sometimes	always
try new positions	never	sometimes	always
talk about sex	never	sometimes	always
ever feel guilty	never	sometimes	always
experience anxiety	never	sometimes	always
have resentment	never	sometimes	always
feel ashamed or confused about sex	never	sometimes	always
enjoy sexplay	never	sometimes	always
enjoy intercourse itself	never	sometimes	always
masturbate before or after	never	sometimes	always
have sexual fantasies	never	sometimes	always

How are the following things handled in this relationship?

	Self	Spouse
communication		
finances		
in-laws		
arguments		
affection		
control		
suspicions		

trust

faithfulness

religion

leisure time

social activities

cooking

Have you ever had an affair during this relationship?

Does your partner know?

Has your partner had an affair during this relationship? How do you know?

III. Medical History

What is your present state of health (excellent, good, fair, poor)?

When was your last complete physical examination?

Do you have any serious medical illnesses?

Have you ever been hospitalized? What for?

Have you ever had surgery? What for?

What kind of medications are you taking (over-the-counter, prescription)?

Do you smoke? How much each day?

Do you drink alcohol? How many drinks per day?

Do you take recreational drugs? Which ones?

Have you ever been treated for a psychiatric illness?

Have you or your partner ever attempted suicide? Has a relative of yours?

Have you or your partner ever used physical violence to resolve conflict? Give the details.

IV. Family Sexual History

Your father:

Age: Occupation: Education: Cultural background:

Illnesses (alcohol, drug, psychiatric problems):

What kind of relationship did he have with your mother?

What kind of relationship did he have with you as a child? How about now?

What was his attitude toward sex?

Your mother:

Age: Occupation: Education: Cultural background:

Illnesses (alcohol, drug, psychiatric problems):

What kind of relationship did she have with you as a child? How about now?

What was her attitude toward sex?

Did you receive sex education at home? How would you describe it?

Was contraception discussed?

Do you have any brothers and sisters?

Names: Ages:

What kind of relationship did you have with them as a child (good, fair, poor)? How about now?

Which sibling was closest to you as a child?

How would you describe your family in a few words?

Did anything about your family trouble you as a child or teenager?

How would you describe your childhood (happy, sad, average, lonely)?

How did your parents handle discipline?

Did they use physical punishment?

Did you engage in any sexual exploration or sexplay? At what age? Was it fun, exciting, traumatic? Were you discovered? What happened?

(For women) At what age did you begin menstruating? What were your parents' attitudes toward it? Did they give you help or instructions about it?

V. Your Present Family

What kind of family life do you have now?

Do you have any children from your present relationship?

Names: Ages:

What kind of relationship do you have with them (good, fair, poor)?

What kind of parent do you think you are?

What kind of parent do you think your partner is?

How do you handle discipline? How does your partner?

How do you handle sex education for your own children?

Describe your relationship with your in-laws. Do they accept you?

Describe your partner's relationship with your parents. Do they accept him or her?

How does your job affect your family?

How does your partner's job affect your family?

VI. Your Emotional Life

Have you ever experienced any of the following emotions or problems? How pervasive were/are they? How long have you had them?

feelings of inferiority	never	sometimes	always
oversensitivity	never	sometimes	always
anxiety	never	sometimes	always
depression	never	sometimes	always
appetite loss	never	sometimes	always
eating disorders (anorexia, bulimia)	never	sometimes	always
weight loss	never	sometimes	always
sleep problems	never	sometimes	always
lack of self-confidence	never	sometimes	always
suicidal thoughts	never	sometimes	always

The My Body Questionnaire

In your home loveplay, you'll be concentrating on the physical sensations you feel in your body. You'll also be using your body to communicate with your partner nonverbally. During this week, when you begin your loveplay, I also want you to start thinking about your body. What ideas and beliefs do you have about it? Are they negative? "I'm too fat." "My muscles are flabby." Where did you get these ideas? "My first girlfriend told me I was a wimp." "My mother always told me I had thick ankles." Are these ideas about your body accurate or distorted? "I won't be attractive unless I lose fifteen pounds." "Men only like big-breasted women." "Women don't find bald men attractive."

The My Body Questionnaire will help you gain insight about the way you think about your body. You will learn how you compare your body to your physical ideal and how your external looks affect your inner person and vice versa. You'll also see who, over the years, influenced your body image. See if these questions trigger any emotions in you, and try to explore these emotions. Thinking and feeling are closely related.

MY BODY QUESTIONNAIRE

I would say that my body is: (circle one)

healthy	neutral	unhealthy
functioning	neutral	disabled
active	neutral	passive
warm	neutral	cool
young	neutral	old
soft	neutral	rough

firm	neutral	flabby
slim	neutral	plump
dry	neutral	sweaty
pretty	neutral	plain
strong	neutral	weak
fragrant	neutral	smelly
relaxed	neutral	tense
lovable	neutral	unlovable
touchable	neutral	untouchable
responsive	neutral	unresponsive
affectionate	neutral	unaffectionate
sexual	neutral	nonsexual
energetic	neutral	fatigued
enjoyable	neutral	unenjoyable
acceptable	neutral	unacceptable
useful	neutral	useless
hardworking	neutral	lazy

My partner would say my body is:

healthy	neutral	unhealthy
functioning	neutral	disabled
active	neutral	passive
warm	neutral	cool
young	neutral	old
soft	neutral	rough
firm	neutral	flabby
slim	neutral	plump
dry	neutral	sweaty
pretty	neutral	plain

strong	neutral	weak
fragrant	neutral	smelly
relaxed	neutral	tense
lovable	neutral	unlovable
touchable	neutral	untouchable
responsive	neutral	unresponsive
affectionate	neutral	unaffectionate
sexual	neutral	nonsexual
energetic	neutral	fatigued
enjoyable	neutral	unenjoyable
acceptable	neutral	unacceptable
useful	neutral	useless
hardworking	neutral	lazy

I would say my partner's body is:

healthy	neutral	unhealthy
functioning	neutral	disabled
active	neutral	passive
warm	neutral	cool
young	neutral	old
soft	neutral	rough
firm	neutral	flabby
slim	neutral	plump
dry	neutral	sweaty
pretty	neutral	plain
strong	neutral	weak
fragrant	neutral	smelly
relaxed	neutral	tense
lovable	neutral	unlovable

touchable	neutral	untouchable
responsive	neutral	unresponsive
affectionate	neutral	unaffectionate
sexual	neutral	nonsexual
energetic	neutral	fatigued
enjoyable	neutral	unenjoyable
acceptable	neutral	unacceptable
useful	neutral	useless
hardworking	neutral	lazy

My partner would say his or her body is:

healthy	neutral	unhealthy
functioning	neutral	disabled
active	neutral	passive
warm	neutral	cool
young	neutral	old
soft	neutral	rough
firm	neutral	flabby
slim	neutral	plump
dry	neutral	sweaty
pretty	neutral	plain
strong	neutral	weak
fragrant	neutral	smelly
relaxed	neutral	tense
lovable	neutral	unlovable
touchable	neutral	untouchable
responsive	neutral	unresponsive
affectionate	neutral	unaffectionate
sexual	neutral	nonsexual

energetic	neutral	fatigued
enjoyable	neutral	unenjoyable
acceptable	neutral	unacceptable
useful	neutral	useless
hardworking	neutral	lazy

If your mother completed this questionnaire about your body, would her answers resemble yours or your partner's?

If your father completed this questionnaire about your body, would his answers resemble yours or your partner's?

If your partner's mother completed this questionnaire about your partner's body, would her answers resemble yours or your partner's?

If your partner's father completed this questionnaire about your partner's body, would his answers resemble yours or your partner's?

Who was most influential in forming your body image? (circle one)
   mother   father   peers   boyfriends or girlfriends   teachers
   yourself   popular culture   other _____

Who was most influential in forming your partner's body image?
   mother   father   peers   boyfriends or girlfriends   teachers
   him- or herself   popular culture   other _____

If you could change one thing about your body, what would it be?

Who was most influential in forming your attitude toward touching?
   mother   father   peers   boyfriends or girlfriends   teachers
   yourself   popular culture   religion   other _____

133

Who was most influential in forming your attitude toward masturbation?

mother   father   peers   boyfriends or girlfriends   teachers
religion   yourself   popular culture   other _____

Who was most influential in forming your attitude about sex?

mother   father   peers   boyfriends or girlfriends   teachers
popular culture   religion   yourself   other _____

Who was most influential in forming your attitude about pleasure in general?

mother   father   peers   boyfriends or girlfriends   teachers
religion   yourself   other _____

Who was most influential in forming your self-confidence and general attitude toward yourself?

mother   father   peers   boyfriends or girlfriends   teachers
yourself   other _____

Do you think you have been fair to yourself in completing this questionnaire?

Do you think you have been fair to your partner in completing this questionnaire?

Do you think you have been fair to your own body in completing this questionnaire?

What do you think you have to do to accept your body or change your body image?

Barbara was a twenty-nine-year-old mother of two who came to sex therapy with her husband, Tom, because she had lost interest in sex. Barb was about twenty pounds overweight and was very self-conscious about her large thighs and plump calves. She exaggerated her physical faults and lacked self-confidence in her ability to please Tom sexually.

Her self-esteem was further eroded by Tom's habit of comparing the way she looked to other women. He constantly teased her about her physical appearance.

She filled out the My Body Questionnaire during week 1 and went over her answers with her cotherapists. The therapists pointed out that Barb had circled words like "flabby," "plump," "plain," and "unlovable" to describe her own body. And the words she chose to indicate how Tom would describe her body included "untouchable," "unresponsive," "unenjoyable," and "unacceptable." When the questionnaire asked who was most influential in forming her body image, Barb circled "father." (She told the therapists that her father used to call her "Tubby" when she was a teenager.) The therapists concluded that Barb felt so insecure about her appearance that she was afraid Tom was no longer attracted to her and would leave her. She had lost interest in sex as a defense mechanism.

With Tom's consent, the cotherapists told Barb that the words Tom had circled to describe her body on the questionnaire were far less negative than her own. He said he enjoyed teasing Barb about her chubby legs because it obviously provoked her, but that he didn't realize she took it so seriously. He seemed completely insensitive to her feelings.

The therapists suspected that Barb's body image problems began in her adolescence, when her father made fun of her awkwardness and her weight. Barb transferred her insecurities to her boyfriends and ultimately to Tom. Now, her self-image depended on his attitude toward her appearance.

Slowly, over the weeks of sex therapy, Barb learned to accept her body for what it was. She and Tom talked about his insensitive comments and he apologized and promised to mend his ways. "Just knowing that he really doesn't mind the way I look helped a lot," she said. "In fact, last night he told me I had a great body!" The couple did their home loveplay faithfully. By week 5, Barb's interest in sex had returned and they had satisfying intercourse.

Fighting Fairly

Many couples who want help with their sexual problems have differences, resentments, or deeper conflicts that are driving them apart. Sex is as much in your mind as in your body. That's why we teach the couples who come to our clinic how to fight fairly during the first week of sex therapy.

During a boxing match, a referee will penalize a boxer who hits an opponent below the belt and the crowd will boo. Nobody enjoys seeing someone take a cheap shot. But many people hit below the belt without batting an eye when they fight verbally with their partner at home. Somehow it seems OK to say cruel things to your partner—things that you would never express to a friend. You often take it for granted that your partner will take your verbal abuse yet always be there when the fight is over. But you aren't willing to give your partner—the person you chose for a special relationship—the same respect and polite consideration you would give to a neighbor, friend, or stranger. Are you repeating a history of fighting between your parents? Or misdirecting anger at another problem—work, your finances, child rearing—at your partner?

The dominant way of relating for too many couples is fighting. Some couples even make preintercourse blowups a habit. Both partners are willing to repeat the fight because the conflict may be the only excitement in an otherwise dull existence. They often defeat all attempts to stop their sparring. For such couples, the fight is the prize, not winning the argument. The fighting serves a definite purpose: it affirms that "You care enough about me to get angry with me." It also confirms that "You'll be there to fight again tomorrow."

It takes two to make war but only one to make peace. If your fighting serves to clarify issues, solve problems, and bring you closer, then it has been constructive. But if your fighting is destructive, you may need instruction in the art of fighting fairly. Here are some ground rules:

1. Don't fight in bed. Your bed should be a special place of closeness and good feelings, not a boxing ring.
2. Never resort to physical violence.
3. Set a limit on the duration of the fight. Set an alarm to ring after fifteen minutes so you don't drag it out.
4. Stick to the subject at hand. Don't dredge up past issues or resentments about friends or family that have nothing to do with the issue at hand like "Your sister never gave us a wedding present in 1977."
5. Use neutral "I" language (see page 140), rather than blaming "you" language.
6. Stick to one topic at a time, and talk it out. Try using paper and pencil to keep an agenda. Record and date the points about which you both agree to give dignity and importance to each issue you are discussing.

Lucy and Glenn fought constantly. They had years of experience; they had fought over which movie to see on their first date. Each tried to find the other's weak spots to attack. "Your overprotective mother called again last night," she would say. "Have you gained back those five pounds you lost?" he would fire back. Their favorite place to fight was in the bedroom—the worst place in which to put each other down. What purpose did this serve? Avoidance. Lucy and Glenn could avoid sex by having a big fight right before bedtime. The strategy had worked well—they had not had sex at all in two years.

For the first two weeks of sex therapy, Lucy and Glenn refused to do their home loveplay exercises. They fought instead. We tried to convince them that they were wasting valuable time, but they were too antagonistic to reconcile. They ignored my advice to make the bedroom a demilitarized zone by giving each other nonverbal massage in bed. Finally, in the third week, Glenn began to feel remorse. "I realized that we were throwing away the first chance we had of changing our relationship," he said. "So, in spite of my anger, I told Lucy I wanted to try what Dr. Renshaw suggested, to make peace for a few weeks and do the loveplay exercises at home." Lucy reluctantly agreed.

To relieve the couple's self-reproach at having lost two whole weeks of home loveplay, we asked them to do a special exercise. We told Lucy and Glenn to sit facing each other, holding hands (see illustration below), and to say in turn what they would do differently if they could magically have the past two weeks to do over again. Both said they would have stopped fighting sooner. Unfortunately, their actions did not mirror their intentions in the following weeks.

Lucy and Glenn made little progress in their home loveplay because their hostility level remained so high. When this happens, we sometimes ask the partners to write each other a "farewell forever" letter. Instead of yelling, blaming, or withdrawing into angry silence, each person writes a letter expressing how he or she would feel if the partner died or left forever.

If-I-Could-Do-It-Over Exercise

The Farewell Forever Letter

A "farewell forever" letter is a wonderful exercise. It brings to the surface all the ambivalence surrounding the relationship: the love and anger, the hurt and dependence, the rejection and longing, and the guilt and blame. It also reinforces the positive feelings each person has for the other. Reading the partner's letter can be highly therapeutic when one person realizes how many good feelings the other has for him or her. It also highlights areas that can help to resolve conflict.

Here's the letter that Glenn wrote to Lucy:

Dear Lucy,

When I thought about life without you, I went numb. Our relationship has been so strained these last few years and I see that it's largely because of my own inflated ego. I always have to have everything my way at home because I can't have it that way on the job. I'm a fool because, with you gone, I would face a huge void. I never told you that I want my way because I'm insecure and afraid that everything I have will be taken away from me. I don't know why I feel this way. Maybe it has something to do with my upbringing. But that's not important now. Having you gone puts everything in perspective. I realize that the thing I fear losing most is you. I really love you and I want us to have a good life together.
Glenn

Lucy's letter to Glenn went like this:

Dear Glenn,

When I visualized you gone, I started to cry. My emotions are right at the surface. Why do we fight so much? I just feel so hurt and angry when you insist on having things your way that it makes me want to hurt you as badly as I can. So I say things that I don't really mean or I exaggerate them all out of proportion. Now I'm trying to imagine life

without you and it's a huge black hole. Maybe if we could stop fighting, our relationship could be the way we thought it would be. What would I do without my "other half"? I'd only be half a person. I love you.
Lucy

"We were always manipulating each other by threatening divorce," said Glenn after writing his letter. "My letter forced me to face the reality of being alone." This insight helped Lucy and Glenn progress in sex therapy with new resolve. They grew much closer.

You and your partner will learn how to write each other a farewell forever letter in chapter 8 on page 207.

"I" Language

One of the most effective ways to communicate—to get your point across without blaming your partner—is to use "I" language. "I" language is simply using the first person when telling your partner *how you feel* instead of blaming him or her. It's saying, "I feel angry when you come home late" rather than "You make me so mad when you come home late." "I want us to talk more" instead of "You never tell me anything." "I would like you to touch me more gently" not "You don't know how to handle a woman." "I" language is inherently neutral because it does not accuse anyone of anything. It simply states how *you* feel, and nobody can argue with that. Using "I" language means taking full responsibility for your honest feelings. When you tell your partner something using "I" language, he or she won't have any reason to feel blamed and become defensive.

One of our patients was a woman who constantly told her husband he was a klutz in bed. Because of her repeated criticism and rejection, he was afraid to touch her. She simply couldn't understand the idea of "I" language. When we asked her to say what she felt about her husband in "I" language, she looked at him and said in exasperation, "I still feel you're a klutz!"

Further questioning revealed that a long time ago her husband had grabbed her breasts so roughly that it hurt. The therapists found out that she enjoyed breast play if it was done lightly. We suspected that what she really wanted to tell her husband was "I would love it if you fondled my breasts gently." She finally expressed her needs to her husband without animosity, and he felt comfortable in approaching her once again. They were able to resolve a major obstacle to their sexual relationship through "I" language.

It may sound ironic, but using "I" language allows you to be selfish in a good way. You are telling your partner how you feel and asking him or her to do things the way you want, without pointing a finger. When you use "I" language, you will be able to express your feelings, needs, and desires but not have to blame your partner for anything. So, by using "I" language, you get what you want without hurting your partner.

How to Use "I" Language

Couples say a lot of gruff things to each other because they take each other for granted. "I" language can help you express yourself freely and honestly while being sensitive to your partner's feelings. Look inside yourself and observe how you are feeling. Try to find out what you really want from your partner, for instance, "I'm always the one who asks for sex. I'd like you to make the first move once in a while." Tell your partner how you feel or what you would like him or her to do. Use the first person; say "I." Do not accuse him or her of "making you" feel upset, hurt, angry, or unloved. Here are some examples of "I" language and their parallel statements in ordinary conversation:

Ordinary Language	"I" Language
"You're always late."	"I worry when you're late."
"You don't love me."	"When you forget our anniversary, I feel unloved."

"All you do is nag."   "I'd like to talk about this and
                                   resolve it."

"Why can't you pay more   "I'm feeling neglected."
attention to me?"

Beginning with this week, make a conscious effort to fight fairly and communicate without blaming.

How One Couple Got Through Week 1

Nat and Phyllis were in their late fifties. They came to our sex therapy clinic because they felt their sex life had gone sour and they wanted a fresh start. They were both enthusiastic when they first heard about the home loveplay exercises, but when they began doing their loveplay, they discovered the exercises were more difficult than they had imagined.

"I couldn't get over how awkward I felt those first few times," said Phyllis. "I always wear a flannel nightgown to bed, and I felt very self-conscious about lying there naked next to Nat. He was embarrassed too. We both fumbled around for a few minutes and then stopped. After the third try, Nat said he was giving up," she continued. "I knew it was because he felt clumsy, but he was too proud to admit it."

Phyllis confronted her own discomfort and decided to proceed. "I'm the type of person who can do something—even something un-pleasant—when I've made up my mind. I looked at the home loveplay as homework and decided I just had to do it. It was my responsibility. That gave me the motivation to go on," said Phyllis. "It was an act of will."

"At first, it seemed odd that we had to schedule time together. It didn't seem romantic," Nat confessed. "I felt as if, because we had to schedule time together, there must really be something wrong. But when we thought about it, it made a lot of sense because people like us are very busy nowadays. It was sort of like making a date again."

Nat and Phyllis persisted and, by the third week, became more playful. "Our home exercises started to become a habit," said Phyllis. "And then it became sort of cute because we expected it of one another. Nat would say, 'OK, it's time for your half hour,' and it was kind of fun. In the third week, we really wanted to have sex, but we didn't cheat."

This couple did very well in sex therapy. They progressed to intercourse in the fifth week. Both were very aroused. Nat had an orgasm during intercourse, but it took Phyllis longer to reach climax, with stimulation by hand from Nat. This timing difference is quite common and normal.

"Our communication grew a thousandfold," commented Nat. He learned to use "I" language to ask for what he wanted. "I told Phyllis I'd love to try lovemaking in the shower, and she agreed. The shower was small and we splashed a lot, but I felt good about asking for what I wanted," said Nat.

Your Assignments for Week 1

1. Do home loveplay exercises for half an hour at least four or five times this week (see page 116).
2. If you argue, fight fairly (see page 136).
3. Use "I" language when telling your partner how you feel or what you want (see page 140).

6

Week 2: Erotic Surprise

This Week's Goals

Last week, I introduced you to the idea of home loveplay and tried to make you more aware of the beliefs you hold about your body in the My Body Questionnaire. I also taught you how to fight fairly and to use "I" language when communicating with your partner. So you worked on yourself and your relationship. This week, I want you to learn more about your sexual anatomy—and your partner's—firsthand. Then you'll find out how to inject the element of erotic surprise into your relationship.

The Sexological Examination

Back in chapter 5, I advised you to get a thorough physical examination before beginning sex therapy at home. During the second week of sex therapy, my patients undergo a very thorough top-to-toe physical examination that includes their sexual anatomy, but their exam takes place right in the clinic. The genital part of this examination is done *in the presence of their partner* and is called a sexological examination. I want to explain how we do it so you can understand why we ask our patients to go through it. Later in this chapter, I will ask you and your partner to do your own sexological examination, that is, to look at and learn about your own sexual anatomy and that of your partner.

Patients often tell me that this examination is the most difficult part of the program for them. They usually feel embarrassed, shameful, angry, or afraid, especially if they think the problem is not theirs but their partner's. But I ask them to go through the examination in spite of their apprehension because it is one of the most important parts of the entire sex therapy program for two reasons. First, the exam allows the therapists to learn about any physical problems the person might have that may be causing his or her sexual problems. And second, during the exam, both partners learn in detail about their own sexual anatomy and that of their partner. They get permission to look at, understand, and touch their own and their partner's genitals.

Why should each person learn more about his or her sexual organs? Why do they also have to learn about their partner's sexual anatomy? Remember, I said back in chapter 1 that, even in this day and age, many people still lack the most fundamental knowledge about their own bodies. The sexological exam teaches people exactly where the different parts of their sexual anatomy are and how they work. Lack of knowledge about sex cannot be a barrier to sexual enjoyment for people who are educated about their sexual selves.

The sexological exam also serves as an important bonding experience for two partners in a committed relationship. This bonding extends to the therapists too; they bond with the couple and the couple with the therapists. Finally, the exam is a test of how each partner reacts and relates under stress.

As I explained earlier, our sex therapy program teams a couple with a male and a female therapist. One of the two therapists in the team is a physician; he or she does both the physical and the genital exam. The doctor checks the patient's external genitals for any abnormality or sign of disease. Then, if the patient is a woman, the doctor performs a Pap smear (a test that can detect any abnormal cells in the cervix) and does an internal pelvic examination in the presence of her partner. The doctor then places a mirror in front of the woman's genital area so she can clearly see her own sexual anatomy.

When the patient is a man, the doctor points out to both partners the different parts of the man's sexual anatomy, including where a vasectomy is done. When the person being examined is a woman, the doctor shows both partners the location of her clitoris and asks the woman to place her index finger on her own clitoris. For about 20 percent of our patients, this is a new experience because neither partner has identified it before.

Then the woman guides her partner's index finger onto her clitoris so he can see and feel exactly where it is. We show all couples where the clitoris is. Overteaching is better than no teaching.

Then the doctor asks both the woman and the man, in turn, to place their index fingers inside the lower part of the woman's vagina and instructs the woman to contract tightly the muscles there, as if she were trying to suddenly stop the flow of urine. It is important for both partners to feel these vaginal contractions so they realize that the contractions are voluntary, especially if the woman experiences the involuntary vaginal spasms known as vaginismus, which can make penetration by the penis painful (see page 84). Last, the doctor answers any questions the couple might have before concluding the exam.

Now it's time for you and your partner to learn about one another's sexual anatomy. Go back to chapter 2 and reread the section "A Lesson in Female and Male Anatomy." Using a mirror, examine your own genitals, referring to the anatomical drawings on pages 29 and 32. Then sit with your partner in a private place and look at each other's genitals. Teach each other about what is there. Women, do some voluntary vaginal muscle contracting with your finger inside your vagina, then with your partner's finger inside. If either of you feels unsure of the location of any part of your sexual anatomy, talk to your doctor. Knowledge about your sexual anatomy is essential before you proceed with sex therapy.

It's important not only to learn about your physical parts, but also to find out how they work. That's why I encourage you to masturbate with sexual fantasy this week. Masturbation will teach you exactly what kind of physical stimulation you need to become sexually aroused. Then you will be better able to tell your partner what you would like him or her to do when you are making love together. Masturbation is not only for women in sex therapy; it's for men too. Refer to page 44 in chapter 2 for instructions on how to masturbate.

While one partner in the clinic undergoes the nongenital part of the examination, the other completes the Sexual Sentence-Completion and the Relationship Crisscross Questionnaires (see following pages). Both help to focus each person's attention on issues that may have been unconscious or taken for granted. Now it's time for you to complete these same questionnaires at home.

After you have completed the questionnaires, I would like you to show them to your partner. But certain questions are very sensitive. If you think divulging your secret skeletons will cause conflict within your relationship, delay showing your partner the answers to those particular questions until a more trusting time, or don't show them at all. Be sure to explain why you'd rather not divulge your answers to avoid making your partner feel slighted.

After you have shared your questionnaires, talk about your answers—how they differ, what surprises you. Ask each other about things you don't understand. This is a wonderful opportunity to get to know yourself and your partner better. Don't forget to make photocopies of these pages or write your answers down on a separate piece of paper so both of you can complete the questionnaires.

The Sexual Sentence-Completion Questionnaire

The purpose of this exercise is to enhance your sexual self-awareness. As you do this exercise, work quickly and write down your first, most spontaneous thoughts. Try to be as relaxed and open as possible as you answer these questions. There are no right or wrong answers.

————

SEXUAL SENTENCE-COMPLETION QUESTIONNAIRE

My very first memory of being a person is _____
_____.

I was _____ years old. _____ was with me.

This is what happened: _____
_____.

I felt _____.

My earliest memory of sex is _____
_____.

I was _____ years old. I felt _____.

I think women are _____.

I think men are _____.

I like women who _____.

I like men who _____.

Darkness is _____.

Shame is _____.

Sex is _____.

Intimacy means _____.

Love means _____.

Fun is _____.

Pain is _____.

It makes me angry when _____.

I'm ashamed of _____.

I feel guilty about _____.

I think it is sinful to _____.

Marriage is _____.

Divorce is _____.

My greatest problem is _____.

The anus is _____.

Obscenity is _____.

Touch is _____.

Comfort is _____.

My face is _____.

My body is _____.

My mind is _____.

I wish I could change _____.

My good points are _____.

My weaknesses are _____.

My ideal is _____.

Maybe it will help you understand this questionnaire better if I give you an example of how one of our patients filled it out. Gloria, age thirty-five, was a vice president at a large public relations agency. She had a confident and forthright personality and was known as a person who could get the job done. Her husband, Matt, age thirty-seven, was a professional photographer.

Gloria and Matt sought help because of a difficult and unsatisfying pattern of bedroom behavior. The two would fight, and then Gloria

149

would deliberately withhold sex for a few days to get back at Matt for disagreeing with her. As time passed, Gloria began withholding sex for longer and longer periods.

Here's how Gloria answered the first few questions of the Sexual Sentence-Completion Questionnaire:

> My very first memory of being a person is: It was cold outside and I was playing with a dish of water. I was three years old. My Aunt Monica was with me. This is what happened: My mother came out of the house and scolded me for playing with water when it was so cold because she said I would get sick. My Aunt Monica answered, "No, she won't." Then I repeated, "No, I won't!" I felt defiant. Mom smiled as if she thought it was cute.

> My earliest memory of sex is: kissing my schoolmate, Freddie Parkerton, on the playground. He got afraid and ran away like a baby. I was eleven years old. He was twelve. I didn't care if he told the teacher or his mother. I felt defiant.

A few questions later, Gloria completed the following sentence. "It makes me angry when: people stand in my way."

As she went over her answers with her cotherapy team, Gloria saw for the first time that the feelings of defiance she had learned in her childhood were still with her as an adult. She realized that she now expressed her defiance of Matt by withholding sex from him. She wanted him to fight with her about it. She would wait for days, but he would never take the bait. That realization helped Gloria see how a pattern of defiant behavior that might have been useful in childhood now prevented her from having a satisfying relationship with the man she loved.

The Relationship Crisscross Questionnaire

This exercise will help your unconscious, inner perceptions of your relationship to surface. It will also help you explore whether your assumptions about your partner's point of view are accurate. Circle the answer that best matches your feelings. Ask your partner to do the same. When you have completed the questionnaire, look over your answers once more. Then show your answers to each other to gain insight into each other's perceptions about the relationship. Remember that differences are neither right nor wrong. They are normal and expected. You'll be surprised at what you read.

RELATIONSHIP CRISSCROSS QUESTIONNAIRE

I think our relationship is:
very happy   happy   unhappy   very unhappy

My partner thinks our relationship is:
very happy   happy   unhappy   very unhappy

When disagreements arise, I think:
I usually give in   my partner usually gives in   we mutually agree

When disagreements arise, my partner thinks:
I usually give in   my partner usually gives in   we mutually agree

When it comes to social activities and recreation, I think:
we do too much   we do just enough   we should do more

When it comes to social activities and recreation, my partner thinks:
we do too much   we do just enough   we should do more

(For married couples)
I wish I had not married:
always   frequently   sometimes   never

(For married couples)
I think my partner wishes he or she had not married:
always   frequently   sometimes   never

(For married couples)
If I could live my life over, I would marry:
the same person   a different person   not at all

(For married couples)
If my partner could live his or her life over, I think he or she would marry:
me   a different person   not at all

I want my partner to be a certain kind of person:
always   frequently   sometimes   never   Details _____
_____

My partner wants me to be a certain kind of person:
always   frequently   sometimes   never   Details _____
_____

I feel that we confide in or confront each other about:

finances	always	frequently	sometimes	never
angry feelings	always	frequently	sometimes	never
sexual fantasies	always	frequently	sometimes	never
appreciation of thoughtfulness	always	frequently	sometimes	never
holding a grudge	always	frequently	sometimes	never

I think my partner feels that we confide in or confront each other about:

finances	always	frequently	sometimes	never
angry feelings	always	frequently	sometimes	never
sexual fantasies	always	frequently	sometimes	never
appreciation of thoughtfulness	always	frequently	sometimes	never
holding a grudge	always	frequently	sometimes	never

During arguments, do you think you fight fairly:
always   frequently   sometimes   never

Do you think your partner thinks you fight fairly:
always   frequently   sometimes   never

Do you think your partner fights fairly:
always   frequently   sometimes   never

Do you think your partner thinks he or she fights fairly:
always   frequently   sometimes   never

I can be critical of my partner without being upset myself:
always   frequently   sometimes   never

My partner can be critical of me without *my* becoming upset:
always   frequently   sometimes   never

I think my partner disapproves of me:
always   frequently   sometimes   never

I disapprove of my partner:
always   frequently   sometimes   never

I think my partner does not like me the way I am:
always   frequently   sometimes   never

I don't like my partner the way he or she is now:
always   frequently   sometimes   never

I think my partner's outward response to me is different from what he
or she is feeling inside:
always   frequently   sometimes   never

My outward response to my partner is different from what I am feeling
inside:
always   frequently   sometimes   never

I feel a risk in being open and honest with my partner about my inner
feelings:
always   frequently   sometimes   never

I think my partner feels a risk in being open and honest with me about
his or her inner feelings:
always   frequently   sometimes   never

What other people think of me affects the way my partner feels about
me:
always   frequently   sometimes   never

What other people think of my partner affects the way I feel about him
or her:
always   frequently   sometimes   never

When I'm honest with my partner about my feelings, he or she gets
upset or withdraws:
always   frequently   sometimes   never

When my partner is honest with me about his or her feelings, I get
upset or withdraw:
always   frequently   sometimes   never

I get uneasy when my partner talks about _____
_____.

My partner gets uneasy when I talk about _____
_____.

Here's an example of one couple's approach to this questionnaire. Stacey and Craig were in their late twenties and had been married for four years. Their main problem was a disagreement over how to initiate sex. Stacey felt that Craig was insensitive because he would playfully grab her right after he came home from work most nights hoping they could immediately have sex. Craig thought Stacey was overly sensitive and moody. "You expect me to jump into bed with you—just like that—as soon as you get home," she charged. "Can't you be a little more subtle and gentle?" "You're such a wet blanket, Stacey, lighten up," Craig responded. Stacey would walk off steaming.

In the Relationship Crisscross Questionnaire, Craig's answers showed that he viewed the marriage as a basically happy one with few problems. He was completely oblivious to Stacey's discomfort with his rather crude way of initiating sex. Stacey's answers were different. When the questionnaire stated, "I disapprove of my partner," Stacey circled "frequently." She circled the same response when the questionnaire stated, "When I'm honest with my partner about my feelings, he or she gets upset or withdraws."

Solving this couple's problems was straightforward. They needed to learn how to communicate better, using "I" language. We encouraged Stacey to be direct with Craig, saying, "I want you to caress me, not grab me," and "I'd like to wait to have sex until we've had dinner and relaxed a little so I can get in the mood." Slowly, Craig got Stacey's message. During week 5, he even came home with a single yellow rose and a note that said, "Sorry I've been such an oaf. I want to be your Prince Charming again. Love, Craig."

Your Home Loveplay Exercises

I'm going to ask you to avoid intercourse for one more week but to pursue sensuality. Continue with your loving mutual touching this week, but refrain from breast or genital touching. And no intercourse! Remember, the goals of your home loveplay sessions are to relax you, to remove any pressure to perform, and to help you focus on the sensations you are learning and feeling while you are caressing each other. If all the caressing, massaging, and kissing makes you feel aroused, savor your excitement, but stop, hug, and hold each other until your arousal subsides a little.

Most couples find this nongenital loveplay novel and truly enjoy it. Some feel relieved of the pressure to perform the sex act. But other couples have difficulty doing these "petting preliminaries." They say things like "It was boring," "It didn't turn me on," "We did that as teenagers," or "What's the point?" Some men, in particular, find it uncomfortable to be on the receiving end of prolonged affectionate loveplay. "Let's reach climax and be done already," they say.

I remember a young couple, Neal and Cheryl, who came to sex therapy because Neal was having sporadic erection problems and Cheryl was unable to have an orgasm. When they began doing their home loveplay exercises, Neal became annoyed at having to passively accept Cheryl's strokes and caresses. He had always been the one to take the initiative in their sexplay, a stereotypical masculine posture.

I reassured him that he didn't have to remain passive for life, only for the seven weeks of therapy, on alternate nights. Letting Cheryl initiate their home loveplay every other night would teach her to be less inhibited. I told him to enjoy the luxury of being courted. Because it was their secret, none of his macho friends needed to know about Cheryl's sexual assertiveness (although many might envy him). Neal finally accepted this aspect of sex therapy. He cooperated with Cheryl and his erection problems improved significantly.

Some rigid, compulsive, or perfectionist people focus on the mechanics of "doing" the home loveplay rather than on the sensations they are feeling. Their emotional response is to resist change. Don't think that you are alone if you feel this way too. "In the beginning, I tried too hard to get the home loveplay exercises 'right.' I thought about it too much. Do you know what I mean?" asked Doug, a thirty-five-year-old accountant. "I tried to take a step-by-step approach, like I do when I conduct an audit or something. I was up there in my head instead of feeling my body. So the loveplay became routine very quickly, and the whole idea began to irritate me," he said. "But I felt like I didn't have a choice. I had to go back to the clinic the next week and it's embarrassing not to have your homework done, so I went through with the loveplay. When I met with the cotherapists, I described how I was approaching the loveplay and they chuckled. They said I should stop trying to do perfect A+ exercises and start enjoying them instead. I wouldn't be graded on them," he said.

"They suggested I lie passively and let Suzanne massage my body before each session so I could concentrate on the sensations I was feeling. I was supposed to just relax and breathe very slowly. Once I fell asleep, but Sue tickled me and I tickled her back. We laughed so much I felt thirteen years old again. That loosened us both up. Tickling is now a sort of presex code for us," Doug explained.

Many hard workers have a problem with pleasure and playfulness. They don't know what to do when they're not earning, learning, or succeeding. *What makes you successful at the office can program you for failure in the bedroom, namely, "working hard" at sex.* On the other hand, relaxation and laughter can enhance your sexual enjoyment. That's why I have devised a simple tactic that can inject a little fun and unpredictability back into your loveplay: the erotic surprise.

Erotic Surprises

This week, I want both of you to plan a little "sexy surprise" for each other, something unexpected that can be funny and sexy. Don't make it competitive. Each of you plan your own surprise, but don't get mad or nag if your partner neglects to surprise you. Instead, try telling your partner, "I'm surprising you because I want to do all I can to make our relationship better. Won't you try too?" If your partner keeps refusing to play along, you can always treat yourself to a nonsexy surprise. Buy a funny book or promise yourself a day at a health spa or at the ball game.

If you feel disappointed because you concocted a special surprise for your partner but he or she won't play along or reacted indifferently, don't lose your enthusiasm. Instead, talk to your partner to find out why he or she won't cooperate. Is your partner too tired, too busy, or too distracted to come up with a sexy surprise right now? Ask him or her to table the idea for now, but surprise you later. Does he or she think the whole idea is silly? If so, remind your partner why I recommend this exercise: to rekindle that spark you both felt when you met and to bring you closer together. Is that a silly goal?

Another tactic is to use your negotiating skills. Tell your partner that if he or she cooperates in this area, you'll give in about something else, such as letting him have the guys over for a poker game or allowing her to buy that new sofa for the family room. We all know that a carrot works better than a stick. Be creative in your response to your partner's obstinacy.

Or try looking at it another way. You are planning a sexy surprise for you and your partner to enjoy, not because you want something in return. Do you remember when I said earlier that each partner in a relationship has to give 100 percent, not fifty-fifty? Make sure you are giving your 100 percent, and don't worry about your partner's contribution. Many times it happens that when your partner sees that you are giving without thought of return, he or she will be touched and will then do the same.

Anyway, there's fun in the secrecy and planning. Just remember that the best plans may hit a snag or not turn out the way you had hoped. Take the risk that it might flop and add a large dose of laughter. That's life. Call it a learning experience. But please risk doing it.

Many of our couples surprise themselves (and us) by what they dream up. You may feel inspired by some of the sexy surprises that our patients have come up with:

- Use a scarf, feather, comb, or soft toothbrush for mutual total-body stimulation.
- Spread whipped cream, chocolate syrup, or strawberry jam on the "good parts" (but not until week 3!).
- Soften the lights, put on some music, and dance in the nude.
- Decorate your penis or breasts with Christmas ornaments, Valentine's Day hearts, or Halloween candy.
- Place an ad to your partner in the personal section of your local newspaper, using your secret pet names for each other.
- Give each other a scented oil rubdown.
- Have a sexy breakfast or dinner in bed.
- Stay in a hotel or, if funds are low, use an absent friend's home or apartment for a romantic getaway weekend, then return the favor.
- Shop for and use a vibrator together.
- Deliver a rose or some sexy underwear to your partner at work with a note that says "For tonight."
- Drop fresh rose petals into a candlelit tub for two.
- Use a blow dryer all over each other on a cold night.
- Spray shaving cream on each other, spread it with a brush, and rinse it off together in the shower.
- Write "I love you" in masking tape on a hairy chest. When the tape is cut away, the message remains.

Consider these suggestions a starting point and go from there. Let your imagination run from the ordinary to the exotic. Take a cue from a man named Ross who arranged an elaborate evening for his wife, Yvonne. "I took a day off of work and stripped the living room of all its furniture and carpets," he began. "Then I brought in a load of sand, pinned travel posters to the wall, and put beach towels on the floor. When Yvonne got home from work, she couldn't believe what I had done. Her first question was 'Who's going to clean this up?' But she was laughing when she said it, so I knew she really liked my surprise. I cooked some steaks on our indoor barbecue grill and played Hawaiian music on the stereo," Ross said. "It was so relaxing that we . . . well, I think you get the picture." The dinner was a leisurely prelude to a romantic evening on their homemade beach.

Several of my patients have come back to the clinic wearing conspiratorial smiles after a fun erotic surprise but would not tell anyone what they and their partner did at home. Their secret brought them close, and keeping it from us brought them even closer in a positive, cheerful way. This us-two-against-the-world attitude is healthy and highly therapeutic.

You can reinforce the positive results you gained from your erotic surprise this way: write down what you did on a piece of paper and put it in your nightstand drawer. Take out the paper and read it on a bad or bumpy day: "December 4, 1995. Vicki became a Christmas tree for me to turn on. What a surprise!" Repeat your sexy surprise, or come up with a new one to make the day brighter. Intimacy is enhanced by sharing fun, laughter, and love. Erotic surprises can lighten up a difficult day, bringing the two of you closer together.

Self-Relaxation

Many patients tell me that they find the home loveplay exercises difficult because they cannot relax. I usually tell them to try some self-relaxation exercises just before they begin their home loveplay to unwind and loosen up. Self-relaxation exercises promote self-understanding, self-control, and self-growth. They also cause your body to release some especially good natural substances, such as enkephalins and endorphins—the so-called "happiness hormones"—that act as everyday pain relievers and mood enhancers. And finally, body control helps thought control; when you learn how to control one of your faculties, it becomes easier to manage another. So relaxation exercises can actually help you combat the negative thinking I will talk about in chapter 9.

I recommend that you practice self-relaxation exercises briefly, for about ten minutes at a time each day. You can do the exercises sitting or lying down. If you decide to sit, place your hands loosely in your lap. Sit up straight with your legs relaxed and your feet flat on the floor. If you feel more comfortable lying down, lie with your legs uncrossed, don't use a pillow, and keep your arms loose at your sides. Now follow these two steps.

Step 1. Breathing

Become aware of your breathing. Breathe very slowly and very deeply. Expand your abdomen and rib cage as you breathe in. Fill your lungs. Hold your breath in as you mentally count to four. Now slowly breathe out for four slow counts. Repeat these long breaths four more times, slowly, in and out. Maintain this slow, relaxed breathing during your active muscle contraction and relaxation session in step 2.

Step 2. Progressive Muscle Relaxation

Curl your toes under tightly. Lift both heels, and hold your feet tense in this position for as long as it takes to breathe in for two counts. Relax these muscles as you slowly breathe out and count to two.

Now press your heels down. Lift your feet off the floor, and tense your calf muscles on your "in" breath for two counts. Lower your heels and relax now on your "out" breath, counting to two.

Tighten and tense your thigh muscles as you breathe in, counting to two. Relax the thigh muscles and breathe out as you count to two.

Tighten your buttock muscles on your in breath and release them on your out breath, each to the count of two.

Move up to your genital muscles. Tighten them as you count to two and breathe in. Loosen them as you slowly breathe out for two counts.

Now tense your stomach muscles while you breathe in for two counts. Relax them on your out breath for two counts. Do the same with your chest muscles, deeply breathing in for two counts, then slowly out for two.

Tighten your hands into fists as you breathe in, counting one, two. Release the tension in your hands as you slowly breathe out: one, two.

Tense the muscles in your lower arms by lifting and bending them at the elbows for two counts as you inhale. Relax them as you exhale for two counts. Tighten your upper arms as you make a fist with your hands and inhale for two counts. Then exhale, count to two, and relax your hands.

Inhale as you lift and tighten your shoulders in a shrug, counting to two. Drop your shoulders and exhale to a count of two.

With your chin on your chest, tense the muscles in the back of your neck for two counts as you inhale. Relax those muscles and breathe out for two counts.

Raise your chin high with your head back to stretch the muscles in the front of your neck. Breathe in and count to two. Exhale and relax the tension for two counts.

Clench your jaw muscles as if you were gritting your teeth and inhale, counting to two. Release, exhale, and count to two. Contract the muscles around your mouth and those around your eyes as you count to two, then relax as you count to two. Lift your eyebrows up high to tighten the muscles in your forehead, inhale, count to two. Release the tension and exhale for two counts.

Now tighten all the muscles in your body. Inhale and count to four slowly. Relax your whole body as you slowly exhale. Say to yourself, "I'm like a big rag doll." One, two, three, four. How does this "letting go" feel?

Now imagine any scene that fills you with peace: a sunset; a soft, sandy beach; a white rose on a black velvet cloth. Feel it. Enjoy it. It's your private relaxation scene on your own inner thought screen.

Once you've practiced this self-relaxation technique, you can do it anywhere, at any time, in your mind. Do it while you're waiting in line, in a traffic jam, on the bus, at work, or in bed before you fall asleep. Become aware of your breathing, and take four long, slow breaths.

Then mentally go through your body, searching for areas of tension. When you've located tight spots, tighten them even more. Then relax those muscles, telling them to loosen up and be soft.

"The relaxation exercises meant the difference between doing the home loveplay and not doing it," said Kurt, a thirty-two-year-old insurance salesman who had premature ejaculation problems. "I would get so wound up during the day at work that I couldn't relax when we tried the loveplay," he explained. "So I tried the relaxation exercises. They really helped me pay attention to what I was doing during the loveplay, instead of worrying about something at work and then wondering if I would ejaculate too quickly. I felt less tense too. Now I do them every evening when I get home from work, whether or not we're going to have sex later. I'm much more calm since I've been doing the exercises." Kurt reversed his premature ejaculation with the squeeze technique, which I describe on pages 197–198. And he reduced his work-related stress through relaxation exercises.

How One Couple Got Through Week 2

"When I found out that there was going to be a gynecological exam for both of us—well, whatever you call it for men—I was horrified that we would be examined in front of each other by the doctor that was in our team," said Colleen, age thirty-two. "They told us that the doctor and the social worker who were assigned as our therapists would both be present, and even worse than that, that Tony would be present at my examination and that I would be present at his. It was shocking. I was just flabbergasted."

So you see that, while you may have been uncomfortable learning about each other's sexual anatomy, "real patients" have a difficult time of it too. How did Colleen get through it? "It was like—I don't know—there are a lot of things in life you have to live through. You just, you know, go ahead with it," she continued. "I wasn't *happy* about it. But I've been through things before that I had to grit my teeth and do. And that's how it was with this. I actually think it was more embarrassing for Tony than it was for me."

Colleen and Tony came to my sex therapy clinic because Colleen had lost interest in sex. The couple had been together for six years. They were content and close, but Colleen had been under a lot of pressure at work lately. She had a new boss whose management style was difficult. On top of that, her mother had become chronically ill and had moved in with Colleen and Tony after a recent hospitalization. Sex was the last thing on Colleen's mind. "I'm really stressed out right now," said Colleen during the first week. "My sex drive is nonexistent at this point in my life."

We reassured Colleen that her feelings were not unusual under the circumstances. The loss of sexual drive is common at times of crisis or chaos but bounces back in a few months. Colleen and Tony had not had sex or even cuddled for eighteen months—a long time at age twenty-eight and twenty-nine (although both admitted they had masturbated once in a while, which is perfectly normal and natural). I told Colleen to view Tony's embrace as a safe harbor in the rough emotional seas she was experiencing.

Tony sent roses to Colleen's office during week 2 of sex therapy. Colleen devised a modest erotic surprise. "Nothing fancy," she said. "We couldn't afford it, and I wouldn't have had time. So I just got a sitter for Mom one evening so we could go out for a drive. We drove to the forest preserve that was our make-out place in high school, and we talked and watched the stars. Then we kissed and touched each other for a while, you know, like the loveplay exercises, only in the car. When we got home, we lit some candles in the bedroom and shared a bottle of wine. It was so relaxing and Tony was so sweet that I got all emotional and started to cry. It's been a long time since we were alone together like that," she admitted.

Your Assignments for Week 2

1. Continue to do your home loveplay exercises for half an hour (see page 156). Try for five times this week, but remember, *no intercourse*.

2. Do your own sexological exam with your partner (see page 144).

3. Complete the Sexual Sentence-Completion Questionnaire (see page 148) and the Relationship Crisscross Questionnaire (see page 151) and share them with each other.

4. Each plan and carry out one erotic surprise (see page 157).

5. Try the self-relaxation exercises (see page 160).

7

Week 3: Fantastic Voyage

Look Back

Before you embark on this week's journey into your sexual self, review what you and your partner did last week. Did you masturbate? Did you have any erections? How did your erotic surprise go? Tell each other how you feel about your progress: "That first attempt at loveplay made me tense," "I enjoyed your sexy surprise," or "I didn't realize I was still angry about that time you wrecked the car." You're not out to embarrass or blame; you're sharing your feelings. Honesty only enhances your intimacy.

If you feel comfortable doing it, exchange the My Body Questionnaire that you did in week 1 with your partner so you can see each other's responses. Talk about what each of you learned about yourself and the other person from the questionnaire. Maybe there are a few answers that you'd rather not show your partner because they're too embarrassing or sensitive. It's OK if you don't want to share the whole questionnaire; try to exchange at least a part of it.

Now I want you to do an exercise that will tap your powers of imagination while bringing suppressed anxieties to the surface. Fasten your emotional seat belt and get ready for a fantastic voyage.

The Fantastic Voyage

The purpose of this solo exercise is to explore yourself and your past from the inside. Think of it as the "little" you going into the "big" you. At first, you may think it's silly, but give it a try. It can be very revealing. Each of you should set aside about an hour for this exercise when you can be alone and undisturbed. Prepare yourself for an adventure. I wish you a bon voyage!

Dim the lights. Take the phone off the hook or turn on the answering machine. Lock the door. You can take your clothes off or leave them on, but choose a loose gown or shirt so you can be comfortable. Remove your shoes. Stand or sit in front of a full-length mirror. Take a long, deep breath and slowly exhale to relax your body. Close your eyes. You may wonder what you're supposed to find. Just accept whatever memories surface and let yourself go into yourself. Maybe you will remember scenes from your childhood or teenage years. Set your imagination free and be totally absorbed.

As you begin to go into your body, ask yourself the following questions. Then answer yourself, either internally or quietly out loud: What do you like most about your body? What do you like least about your body? Is there anything you want to say about the outside of your body? Anything about your face? About any other part of your body?

Now pretend that you are able to become tiny and that you can enter your own body for a tour of your inside parts. Pick a place to go into yourself. How do you enter your body? Through your ear? Your navel? Do you seep in through the skin? What is it like inside yourself?

Let your little you tell your big you how it *feels*. Describe the colors and textures you see in each place.

Find your love center. Where is it? What does it look like? Can you describe it to yourself? Now go to your sex center. Where is that? What does that look like? Tell yourself about it. Make a phone call to your genitals. What do you want to tell them? How do they feel when you're tense? When you're relaxed? How do they feel when you're happy? How about when you're angry? How do they feel when you're feeling sexy? Where is your pleasure center? Where is your inhibition center? Your embarrassment center?

Keep going. Where are you now? Where is your scared center? What does that look like? Where is your anger center? Your grudge-holding center? Your tension center? Find your control center. Your hurt-storage center. Now where in your body is your letting-go center? Can you open the hatch to let your hurts and tensions out?

Now move to your brain. Someone's knocking at the door of your brain. Look through the peephole. Who is it? Is it someone from your present or your past? Your mother, father, brother, sister, spouse, kids, mother-in-law, ex-spouse, old lover? Is there anything you want to tell that person? If so, say it now. What do you do with the person? Ask him or her to come in? Pretend you're not home? Tell the person to leave? How do you feel about him or her? Tense, sad, scared, worried, critical, angry? Affectionate, happy, sexy? Does the little you feel different than the big you about the person?

Now come out of your brain and check your breasts, heart, chest, anus, bladder. Check your penis. What would an erection feel like there? Check your vagina, clitoris, and uterus. How would an orgasm feel there? What would it be like if your partner's penis or vagina was there? What would it be like if your partner were not interested in sex? Do you want to check out anything else in your body?

Now let your little self come out of your body. Where do you come out? Why did you choose that place? For fun? Convenience? No particular reason?

This exercise can bring up strong buried emotions. If you feel you have tapped some feelings that you cannot handle well enough on your own, you may want to make an appointment with a therapist to talk about them.

Maybe examples of how some of my patients did the Fantastic Voyage will help you understand this exercise a little better.

Vince was a thirty-nine-year-old bricklayer who had sporadic erection problems. His live-in girlfriend, Connie, had persuaded him to come to our clinic because she wanted to get married, but was afraid Vince's sex problem would affect their ability to have children.

For a man who projected a tough, no-nonsense, macho image, Vince proved to be very creative during his Fantastic Voyage. He began by telling the therapists his best feature was his muscular arms and his worst his paunch. Then Vince entered his body through his ear and began an amazing journey through his internal fantasyland.

"My lungs look like a car wash!" he exclaimed as he bounded from one organ to the next. "I'd like to go into my stomach, but I'm afraid of my stomach acids," he said. "Can I have a boat? Not a raft, a sturdy motorboat so I can feel safe." When someone knocked on the door of his brain, he peered out the peephole to see his girlfriend. "Come on in, honey," he said. "It's funny and weird in here." When Vince was finished with the exercise, he came up with a novel mode of exiting. "I exploded through my chest," he announced. A fitting finish for our imaginative friend.

What did Vince learn from his Fantastic Voyage? He learned what was causing his erection problems. Vince had told us that he felt constricted by Connie's demands that they get married. He'd had a bad first marriage and did not want to rush into another one just yet. Also, the idea of having children terrified Vince. He felt as though he were being squeezed by the impending decisions he had to make about marrying Connie and starting a family. He unconsciously expressed this feeling of tightness and compression by having erection problems.

During his Fantastic Voyage, Vince said the journey through his body made him feel "Released! I felt like I broke out of my bonds. I realized how much I loved Connie when she knocked on the door of my brain. Now I know that getting married is not something I should be scared of; it's something I can look forward to. Connie is not my first wife. She's a completely different person."

This couple was easy to treat because, in spite of their sexual problems, they loved and trusted each other. They did very well in therapy, and Vince's erection problems improved dramatically. Vince and Connie announced their engagement on the last night of therapy and were married six months later.

Bridget, age forty-five, and Derek, forty-two, were both high school teachers who sought help because Bridget felt they didn't have foreplay long enough for her to become completely aroused. After only two or three minutes of foreplay, Bridget would submit to having sex with Derek, who was aroused and ready to enter her. Afterward, she would feel resentful. She had tried to explain how she felt to Derek, but he would typically reply something like, "We've been married for fifteen years. Do we still have to act like we're teenagers necking in the backseat of my first car?"

During the Fantastic Voyage, Bridget entered her body through her mouth. She imagined that she slid down her throat and fell into an open space in the middle of her chest. When the therapist asked, "Where is your love center?" Bridget floated over to her heart and saw that it was healthy and had a wreath of flowers around it. "My heart is full of love," she said. Then the therapist told Bridget to go to her brain. She entered her bloodstream and rode the tide upward.

When Bridget arrived at her brain, someone was knocking at her door. She looked out a peephole and saw it was her father. "What do you want to say to him?" asked the therapist. "Daddy, Mom and I needed your affection. You left too soon," Bridget said. (Her father had died when Bridget was a teen.) "Mom was happy when you were together. I wanted you to know."

Bridget's Fantastic Voyage took her on a tour of her entire body. She found her pleasure center in her inner thighs and her sex center in her vagina. When the therapist instructed her to go to her scared center, Bridget went to her solar plexus (a network of nerves located behind the stomach). "It looks like a clump of muscles all tied up in a knot," she said. When Bridget had completed her voyage, she left her body the same way she had entered—through her mouth.

Because of her Fantastic Voyage experience, Bridget learned how important it was for her to make Derek understand that he needed to take enough time to stimulate her before penetration. She specifically wanted to tell Derek to stimulate her thighs (her pleasure center) and her vagina (her sex center) during foreplay. Bridget saw that her inability to communicate this information was tying up her emotions in a knot, the image she had seen in her solar plexus.

Bridget uncovered some residual sadness about her father's death when he "visited" her during the Fantastic Voyage, but she realized that her parents' marriage had been a good one. The happy home life she'd had as a child had set the stage for her own good relationship with Derek. Now, all she had to do was clear up their sexual problem by communicating her needs to Derek.

Overall, Bridget's Fantastic Voyage was a positive experience. We taught Bridget how to use "I" language to ask for more extended foreplay. And we told Derek to allow time for long, mutual full-body massages that would both relax him and help him focus on the pleasurable sensations his body was capable of having. "I had no idea how relaxing and exciting the feeling of Bridget's hands on my body could be," Derek said in week 3. At the end of sex therapy, Bridget and Derek had learned how to extend their foreplay so that Bridget could share Derek's enjoyment of their sexual encounters together.

Here's still another example of a person's Fantastic Voyage experience. Arlene was a thirty-four-year-old secretary in her second marriage. She and her husband, Sid, had serious communication problems. After dinner, they would routinely watch TV in separate rooms. Their diagnosis was a mutual lack of interest in sex. During the Fantastic Voyage, Arlene entered her body through the back of her neck, where she felt a lot of tension. She found her love center in her hands. "I love touching. I project love through my fingertips," she said. When Arlene journeyed to her vagina, she found that "it was overcast and raining," an image that reflected the negative state of her and Sid's sex life.

A self-massage technique helped Arlene relieve some of the tension in the muscles at the back of her neck. You might benefit from it too. Put your fingers on your shoulder muscles and firmly roll them forward toward your collarbone, then release them. Do the exercise several times. Or, with your arms crossed behind your head, rub your thumbs down the back of your neck. These exercises are easy stress relievers you can do anywhere, at any time. They feel wonderfully relaxing, and you don't have to pay a masseuse! I'd like you to try them so you can soothe and enjoy your body.

Of course, the most important thing Arlene and Sid could do was massage *each other*. Arlene had discovered that she loved touching, and she could use that impulse to touch Sid lovingly. If they wouldn't talk, they could communicate through touch. The home loveplay exercises were key for this couple in particular because they served as a nonverbal means of communicating their wants and needs. Arlene and Sid became much closer emotionally—and physically—during the seven weeks of sex therapy.

After doing the Fantastic Voyage, go immediately into your Gestalt exercise.

The Gestalt Exercise

Gestalt is a German word that literally means shape or form. The word was applied to a school of psychology, started early in this century, that emphasized viewing an emotional state as a whole, rather than as a series of segmented responses. Gestalt therapy encourages people to be in the here and now, to stop living in the past or future, and to experience what is really happening to them at this very moment. It helps people increase their self-awareness by looking at all aspects of themselves in their total environment. The Gestalt exercise that follows can help you see your own self in a larger context. It can also help you try and change yourself or a situation you are in by rehearsing it in private.

Sit facing an empty chair. Imagine that someone or something important to you is sitting in that chair. It can be a person, such as a close relative, or a thing, even an intangible thing, such as divorce, your father's temper, your partner's drinking, or your own passivity. Now have a conversation with whatever it is you have put in the chair. For example, try putting your job in the chair. Talk to your job. Tell it what's good about it or wrong with it and what it means to you. Then get up and go sit in the empty chair. Be the job and answer yourself: "You're lucky to have me. The airlines cut five hundred jobs last week. You could make me better by coming up with some fresh ideas." You'll be surprised at what you hear your job tell you.

Maybe your job is taking care of your children and you feel trapped because you're stuck at home and the kids' needs are so great. Put your kids in the chair. Tell them how you feel. Ask them to be good and let you have some time for yourself. Now go sit in the other chair and be your kids, answering you. "We are little and need you. We constantly ask you for things because we trust you and love you. Who else have we got?"

What do *you* want to put in that chair? A future baby? Is it a boy or a girl? Tell yourself about the baby. How do you feel about him or her? Tell yourself what the pregnancy would be like. How would you be as a mother or father? This exercise is an experiential rehearsal that can help you respond more effectively when the someone or something in the chair confronts you in reality.

Now I'd like you to put your sexuality in the chair. Talk to it. One patient said, "I'm sorry I suffocated you for so long. I wish I'd learned about you years ago." Another declared, "You have caused me endless trouble. I've had two abortions and was forced to get married because I was pregnant. You even gave me herpes." A third said, "I wish you didn't control my life. I could do so much more if I wasn't constantly thinking about you." Then this patient, a thirty-five-year-old man, moved to the empty chair, became his own sexuality, and said, "I'm a normal part of you. I'm with you from birth to death. Even when you sleep, I'm in your dreams. Make peace with me. We are one. We can become companions most of the time. We are not enemies."

"The Gestalt was very traumatic for me to go through," said Wanda, a forty-five-year-old laboratory technician who had never experienced an orgasm. "I was not prepared for becoming emotional at all. I put my father in the chair, and there was a lot of stuff that I remembered from when I was little that blew me away," she explained. "I don't even think I dented the surface. It would have been too much for me. I have too many walls there."

Wanda needed to gain perspective on her father. "My dad was uneducated, depressed, and drank too much. My mother was very dependent on him, but could not confront him about his problems. I see now that I was not to blame. I forgive them for being wounded parents, and I'm glad I've coped as well as I did," Wanda said.

What do you do at home if you hit a wall as Wanda did? Or if you encounter feelings so strong they overwhelm you? I recommend you consult a local therapist who can talk you through your feelings so you can learn how to handle them better.

Chris was a city government employee. He and his wife, Maureen, who worked for the telephone company, were in their early thirties, and both lacked sexual desire. They had been married for five years and sex was just not as exciting as it had been when they were dating. During sex therapy, Chris revealed a lot of anger toward his parents, especially his mother. He also said repeatedly that he saw his mother in his wife, which Maureen greatly resented.

During the Gestalt exercise, the therapists asked Chris to put his mother in the chair and talk to her. Chris's anger rose so fiercely that his face turned dark red. "If you put my mother in that chair, I'm going to break every piece of furniture in this room," he screamed. At that point, the unsettled therapists asked me to come into the room.

Chris's face was now purple. I went for the jugular. "Who was mom's favorite?" I asked. "Me," Chris said. "They say I look like her, even laugh like her." "Do you still love your mom?" I pressed. "Yes," he said. "But I hate her more, and I haven't seen or spoken to her in two years." "What about Maureen reminds you of your mother?" I asked. Chris broke down in tears. "I can't do anything to please either one of them, and I hate myself for it," he sobbed.

Chris loathed what he saw of his mother in himself and in Maureen: criticism and lack of appreciation. This revelation allowed him to accept his mother for what she was—critical and demanding—and he began to heal. He saw that the struggle for perfection he engaged in to please his mother had actually helped him on his job. Also, he had always misperceived Maureen's disagreement with him as criticism. By the end of week 5, Chris and Maureen were more affectionate and tried sincerely to make love (which is different from making sex, remember?).

The Gestalt can become a highly emotional exercise, and you might find yourself in tears, as Chris did. Tears are normal, protective, and healing. You may feel drained emotionally after doing this exercise because of the memories that come up, but doing it can enhance your sensitivity to your feelings. Be assured that it is making you more whole.

Rehearsing Your Relationship

While you are still sitting in the Gestalt chair, try rehearsing some dialogue with your partner. Switching chairs briefly to converse with your partner allows you to "jump into your partner's skin" so you can see how he or she feels about areas in which you disagree in your relationship. You could pretend to tell your partner how you would like to start your home loveplay this week. "Let's take a shower together. We can finish the dishes later." Then be your partner and reply. Now tell your partner where on your body you would like to have a massage. Ask him or her to go to the movies with you. Or rehearse how you would decline an invitation from your partner. Try this exercise mentally when you have a few extra moments, such as in a traffic jam or while waiting at the supermarket checkout counter. Use a point of contention between you and your partner. It could be balancing the checkbook, a problem with your child, a nosy in-law, or leaving a party. Whatever the problem is, mental rehearsal can help you find a better way to reach a solution by becoming aware of the other's point of view.

These exercises may also bring up a lot of stored emotional residue—hurt, anger, fear. Can you stay with the feeling? Get in touch with it. Talk to it. Can you remember when the feeling started? Why is it bothering you now? When will it be gone? What is the feeling stopping you from doing? What *power* does it give you over others? Don't be afraid that the emotion will overwhelm you. You have survived it in the past and will survive it again now.

Your Emotional Needs and Desires Questionnaire

Another exercise I would like you to do at home this week is what I call the "Your Emotional Needs and Desires Questionnaire." This questionnaire will not only help you identify some of your emotional needs and desires, it will also show you how your needs match or contradict your partner's needs. I want you to read each of the following statements and see how it applies to your relationship as it is now. After each question, circle the response that most closely matches what is true for you right now. The statements purposely swing from one point to another. There are no grades, just your feelings.

YOUR EMOTIONAL NEEDS AND DESIRES
QUESTIONNAIRE

I feel insecure without my partner:

always   nearly always   sometimes   rarely   never   not applicable

My partner feels my untidiness is a problem:

always   nearly always   sometimes   rarely   never   not applicable

When I'm upset, it comforts me to be held by my partner:

always   nearly always   sometimes   rarely   never   not applicable

I think my partner's interest in me is at least as great as my interest in him or her:

always   nearly always   sometimes   rarely   never   not applicable

I believe in the sincerity of my partner:

always   nearly always   sometimes   rarely   never   not applicable

I depend on my partner, although I have negative feelings about being dependent:

always   nearly always   sometimes   rarely   never   not applicable

For me, sensual touch is the same as sexual touch:

always   nearly always   sometimes   rarely   never   not applicable

Children are a source of conflict:

always   nearly always   sometimes   rarely   never   not applicable

I hold back from displaying my feelings with my partner:

always   nearly always   sometimes   rarely   never   not applicable

I am eager to see my partner:

always   nearly always   sometimes   rarely   never   not applicable

Meals together at home are enjoyable:

always   nearly always   sometimes   rarely   never   not applicable

When I'm depressed, it helps to have my partner hold me:

always   nearly always   sometimes   rarely   never   not applicable

When I'm upset, it comforts me to have my partner talk to me:

always   nearly always   sometimes   rarely   never   not applicable

I want to be in love or have love as security:

always   nearly always   sometimes   rarely   never   not applicable

Home repairs are a source of conflict:

always   nearly always   sometimes   rarely   never   not applicable

I feel we are compatible:

always   nearly always   sometimes   rarely   never   not applicable

I try to control the relationship, but feel I have lost control:

always   nearly always   sometimes   rarely   never   not applicable

I feel my partner's poor hygiene is a problem:

always   nearly always   sometimes   rarely   never   not applicable

I am prepared to "give all" for love:

always   nearly always   sometimes   rarely   never   not applicable

I am discontented with life:

always   nearly always   sometimes   rarely   never   not applicable

We laugh together at home:

always   nearly always   sometimes   rarely   never   not applicable

When I yell, it upsets my partner:

always   nearly always   sometimes   rarely   never   not applicable

When I'm upset, it upsets me more to hear my partner yell:

    always   nearly always   sometimes   rarely   never   not applicable

I blame myself for the difficulties in our relationship:

    always   nearly always   sometimes   rarely   never   not applicable

I believe my family loves me:

    always   nearly always   sometimes   rarely   never   not applicable

TV is a source of conflict:

    always   nearly always   sometimes   rarely   never   not applicable

I think my childhood was less happy than average:

    always   nearly always   sometimes   rarely   never   not applicable

My partner feels we have major in-law problems:

    always   nearly always   sometimes   rarely   never   not applicable

When I'm upset, it comforts me to drink alcohol:

    always   nearly always   sometimes   rarely   never   not applicable

Tender words are important to me:

    always   nearly always   sometimes   rarely   never   not applicable

I am able to be the one to end this relationship:

    always   nearly always   sometimes   rarely   never   not applicable

I think of divorce as the immediate solution to all our problems:

    always   nearly always   sometimes   rarely   never   not applicable

I analyze our relationship and weigh it in my mind:

    always   nearly always   sometimes   rarely   never   not applicable

I dislike any type of touch:

    always   nearly always   sometimes   rarely   never   not applicable

I consider separation a solution to our conflict:

always   nearly always   sometimes   rarely   never   not applicable

Friends are a source of conflict:

always   nearly always   sometimes   rarely   never   not applicable

Wanting to be held and to hold is frightening:

always   nearly always   sometimes   rarely   never   not applicable

When I'm upset, it comforts me to use marijuana:

always   nearly always   sometimes   rarely   never   not applicable

We fight before having sex:

always   nearly always   sometimes   rarely   never   not applicable

I feel depressed for as long as ten days at a time:

always   nearly always   sometimes   rarely   never   not applicable

I feel I am worthy of love:

always   nearly always   sometimes   rarely   never   not applicable

I believe my friends love me:

always   nearly always   sometimes   rarely   never   not applicable

I feel my partner's untidiness is a problem:

always   nearly always   sometimes   rarely   never   not applicable

I hold back on discussing my feelings with my partner:

always   nearly always   sometimes   rarely   never   not applicable

I think my partner sees divorce as an immediate solution to our problem:

always   nearly always   sometimes   rarely   never   not applicable

My partner feels my poor hygiene is a problem:

always   nearly always   sometimes   rarely   never   not applicable

I like to talk before having sex:

always   nearly always   sometimes   rarely   never   not applicable

Work is a source of conflict for me:

always   nearly always   sometimes   rarely   never   not applicable

Work is a source of conflict for my partner:

always   nearly always   sometimes   rarely   never   not applicable

Work is a source of conflict for both of us:

always   nearly always   sometimes   rarely   never   not applicable

When I'm upset, it comforts me to smoke cigarettes:

always   nearly always   sometimes   rarely   never   not applicable

When I want closeness and can't hold my partner, I feel sad:

always   nearly always   sometimes   rarely   never   not applicable

I'm jealous and possessive but not to the point of provoking angry conflict:

always   nearly always   sometimes   rarely   never   not applicable

Housekeeping is a source of conflict:

always   nearly always   sometimes   rarely   never   not applicable

My partner likes to relax, laugh, and have fun:

always   nearly always   sometimes   rarely   never   not applicable

I discuss a wide range of topics and experiences with my partner:

always   nearly always   sometimes   rarely   never   not applicable

I consider the quality of our sex to be a test of love:
> always   nearly always   sometimes   rarely   never   not applicable

I love myself:
> always   nearly always   sometimes   rarely   never   not applicable

I like to sleep after having sex:
> always   nearly always   sometimes   rarely   never   not applicable

I blame my partner for the difficulties in our relationship:
> always   nearly always   sometimes   rarely   never   not applicable

When I have trouble falling asleep, it helps me to take pills:
> always   nearly always   sometimes   rarely   never   not applicable

Meals are a source of conflict:
> always   nearly always   sometimes   rarely   never   not applicable

When I want closeness and can't hold my partner, I feel nothing:
> always   nearly always   sometimes   rarely   never   not applicable

I dislike holding children:
> always   nearly always   sometimes   rarely   never   not applicable

Being held is relaxing and tension-relieving:
> always   nearly always   sometimes   rarely   never   not applicable

I have tried to work out our sex problems and improve my technique:
> always   nearly always   sometimes   rarely   never   not applicable

When I want closeness and can't hold my partner, I feel tense:
> always   nearly always   sometimes   rarely   never   not applicable

If I want to have sex, I ask directly:

always   nearly always   sometimes   rarely   never   not applicable

When I have trouble falling asleep, it helps to hold my partner:

always   nearly always   sometimes   rarely   never   not applicable

I am preoccupied with thoughts about my partner:

always   nearly always   sometimes   rarely   never   not applicable

When I want closeness and can't hold my partner, I feel hurt:

always   nearly always   sometimes   rarely   never   not applicable

Affectionate touch is very important to me:

always   nearly always   sometimes   rarely   never   not applicable

I consider sex to be essential for me:

always   nearly always   sometimes   rarely   never   not applicable

I am willing to suffer abuse, even ridicule, from my partner:

always   nearly always   sometimes   rarely   never   not applicable

To enjoy being held is mature:

always   nearly always   sometimes   rarely   never   not applicable

Weight (mine or my partner's) is a source of conflict:

always   nearly always   sometimes   rarely   never   not applicable

To me, appearances are more important than feelings:

always   nearly always   sometimes   rarely   never   not applicable

Free time is a source of conflict:

always   nearly always   sometimes   rarely   never   not applicable

I have problems controlling what I say when I'm angry:

always   nearly always   sometimes   rarely   never   not applicable

I love my partner:

always   nearly always   sometimes   rarely   never   not applicable

I'm jealous to the point of conflict (scenes, threats):

always   nearly always   sometimes   rarely   never   not applicable

I like to kiss before having sex:

always   nearly always   sometimes   rarely   never   not applicable

I see warning signs of trouble between us but I ignore them:

always   nearly always   sometimes   rarely   never   not applicable

I prefer that my partner make decisions:

always   nearly always   sometimes   rarely   never   not applicable

To enjoy being held is a weakness:

always   nearly always   sometimes   rarely   never   not applicable

Being held is important to me:

always   nearly always   sometimes   rarely   never   not applicable

When I want closeness and am not held, I feel angry:

always   nearly always   sometimes   rarely   never   not applicable

Money is a source of conflict:

always   nearly always   sometimes   rarely   never   not applicable

I dislike being held:

always   nearly always   sometimes   rarely   never   not applicable

When I'm upset, it comforts me to hold my partner:

always   nearly always   sometimes   rarely   never   not applicable

I like to hold my partner after having sex:

always   nearly always   sometimes   rarely   never   not applicable

My partner fits my ideal image:

    always   nearly always   sometimes   rarely   never   not applicable

I use sex to keep my partner with me:

    always   nearly always   sometimes   rarely   never   not applicable

To enjoy being held is loving:

    always   nearly always   sometimes   rarely   never   not applicable

Laughter is fun and helps relax me:

    always   nearly always   sometimes   rarely   never   not applicable

When I have trouble falling asleep, it helps me to sleep in another bed/room:

    always   nearly always   sometimes   rarely   never   not applicable

I like to kiss after having sex:

    always   nearly always   sometimes   rarely   never   not applicable

I consider divorce to be a solution to our conflict:

    always   nearly always   sometimes   rarely   never   not applicable

I can laugh over some of our differences:

    always   nearly always   sometimes   rarely   never   not applicable

To enjoy being held is natural:

    always   nearly always   sometimes   rarely   never   not applicable

I use sarcasm or laugh at my partner to put him or her down:

    always   nearly always   sometimes   rarely   never   not applicable

I declare my love first, before my partner:

    always   nearly always   sometimes   rarely   never   not applicable

I like to laugh after having sex:

always   nearly always   sometimes   rarely   never   not applicable

I have trouble falling asleep:

always   nearly always   sometimes   rarely   never   not applicable

I discuss future plans with my partner:

always   nearly always   sometimes   rarely   never   not applicable

I dislike holding adults:

always   nearly always   sometimes   rarely   never   not applicable

When I have trouble falling asleep, it helps to be held by my partner:

always   nearly always   sometimes   rarely   never   not applicable

Our relationship is marked by frequent conflicts and tension:

always   nearly always   sometimes   rarely   never   not applicable

I can share grief or fear with my partner:

always   nearly always   sometimes   rarely   never   not applicable

Lack of trust is a source of conflict:

always   nearly always   sometimes   rarely   never   not applicable

I just like to roll over and go to sleep after having sex:

always   nearly always   sometimes   rarely   never   not applicable

I consider affection important to me, even essential:

always   nearly always   sometimes   rarely   never   not applicable

To enjoy being held is shameful:

always   nearly always   sometimes   rarely   never   not applicable

I use threats to get sex:

    always   nearly always   sometimes   rarely   never   not applicable

I like to be alone after having sex:

    always   nearly always   sometimes   rarely   never   not applicable

Alcohol is a source of conflict:

    always   nearly always   sometimes   rarely   never   not applicable

I like to be held before having sex:

    always   nearly always   sometimes   rarely   never   not applicable

My desire to be held is higher when I'm pregnant:

    always   nearly always   sometimes   rarely   never   not applicable

My desire to be held is higher when I have my period:

    always   nearly always   sometimes   rarely   never   not applicable

When I want closeness and can't hold my partner, I feel angry:

    always   nearly always   sometimes   rarely   never   not applicable

I like to laugh before having sex:

    always   nearly always   sometimes   rarely   never   not applicable

I think we have major in-law or other family problems:

    always   nearly always   sometimes   rarely   never   not applicable

I think that to enjoy being held is for women only:

    always   nearly always   sometimes   rarely   never   not applicable

I like to be stroked before having sex:

    always   nearly always   sometimes   rarely   never   not applicable

When I'm upset, it comforts me to talk to my partner:

    always   nearly always   sometimes   rarely   never   not applicable

I think that to enjoy being held is childish:

    always   nearly always   sometimes   rarely   never   not applicable

I enjoy sensual touch more than sexual touch:

    always   nearly always   sometimes   rarely   never   not applicable

I cry after having sex:

    always   nearly always   sometimes   rarely   never   not applicable

I try to force my partner to show more feeling and commitment:

    always   nearly always   sometimes   rarely   never   not applicable

When I'm upset, I want to hurt myself or my partner:

    always   nearly always   sometimes   rarely   never   not applicable

I have needed medication for depression:

    always   nearly always   sometimes   rarely   never   not applicable

I deliberately restrict the frequency of contact with my partner:

    always   nearly always   sometimes   rarely   never   not applicable

I prefer to make decisions on my own:

    always   nearly always   sometimes   rarely   never   not applicable

I like to talk after having sex:

    always   nearly always   sometimes   rarely   never   not applicable

When I have trouble falling asleep, it helps to hold a pillow or other object:

    always   nearly always   sometimes   rarely   never   not applicable

I use direct persuasion to get sex:

    always   nearly always   sometimes   rarely   never   not applicable

My partner uses sarcasm or laughs at me to put me down:
  always   nearly always   sometimes   rarely   never   not applicable

I use sex to get my partner to hold me:
  always   nearly always   sometimes   rarely   never   not applicable

I like to be held after having sex:
  always   nearly always   sometimes   rarely   never   not applicable

I feel no hope that our conflict will be resolved:
  always   nearly always   sometimes   rarely   never   not applicable

Cuddling and hugging feel good:
  always   nearly always   sometimes   rarely   never   not applicable

It can be difficult to distinguish true needs from desires because they are not the same for everyone. For Irene, hugging before sex may be very important, while for her partner, Hank, it means little. Hugging is probably a need for Irene but not one for Hank. This couple will have to negotiate and compromise so the needs of both partners are met.

You may have noticed that some of the statements in this questionnaire are repeated, although phrased a little differently. I did that on purpose to see if respondents would react the same way twice. Look back over your responses and see whether you circled the word "always" to similar-sounding statements. If you did, that issue is probably a need for you. For example, if you responded "always" to the statements "affectionate touch is very important to me," and "I consider affection important to me, even essential," then you probably have a strong need for affection, which you must communicate to your partner—he or she may not be aware of this need or understand its importance to you.

On the other hand, you may circle "always" in response to the statement "affectionate touch is very important to me," but then later circle "rarely" in response to "I like to be held after having sex." What does this mean for you? That you think of yourself as being affectionate but that your actions say otherwise? Look for these double messages.

Be on the lookout for statements that begin with the words "I like to" or "I dislike." They usually indicate desires instead of needs. It's OK to have desires, but you shouldn't demand that your partner fulfill them. For example, you may agree strongly with the statement "I like to kiss before having sex," but liking to kiss is not a basic need. On the other hand, it's not wrong to want to be kissed, especially if it makes you feel closer to your partner. Once again, this is an opportunity to learn how to communicate better. Maybe your partner doesn't know how important kissing before having sex is to you. Tell your partner! He or she might be more than willing to cooperate. If not, explain why it's so important to you. Talk it over; don't hold your feelings in. But remember to phrase them in "I" language.

The Emotional Roll Call Questionnaire

Now I want you to complete another test so you can gain further awareness of your emotions and the physical symptoms they can cause. I call this test the "Emotional Roll Call"; it's adapted from the Hamilton Depression Scale, a standard depression test used by many therapists. For each of the items, circle the response that best describes your feelings. The object is not to see how you "score" on this test. The reward is to be aware of how you feel.

EMOTIONAL ROLL CALL QUESTIONNAIRE

Depressed mood (sadness,
   hopelessness, worthlessness)

Absent
These feelings occur spontaneously
I cry only when I feel sad
I feel depressed all the time

Guilt feelings

Absent
I feel I have let people down
I mull over past errors and deeds
I'm being punished for wrongdoing
I hear voices telling me I'm bad

Suicidal thoughts

Absent
Life is not worth living
I wish I were dead
I have suicidal thoughts and plans
I have attempted suicide

Insomnia early in night

I have no difficulty falling asleep
I have occasional trouble falling
   asleep
I have nightly trouble falling
   asleep
I use a sleeping pill

Insomnia in middle of night

None
I'm restless during the night
I wake regularly during the night
   but go back to sleep
I wake regularly during the night
   and can't go back to sleep

Insomnia in early morning

None

I wake early but go back to sleep

I wake early and can't go back to sleep

Work and leisure activities

No difficulty

I feel fatigued or apathetic, but I push myself

I've lost interest

I spend little time at these activities

I've stopped working due to depression

Slowing of thought and speech, can't concentrate, impaired motor skills

None

I've slowed down a little

I've slowed down a lot

I just sit and stare all day

I stay in bed all day

Agitation

None

My hands and feet are restless

My hands shake, I pull my hair, I bite my lips and nails

Anxiety

None

I'm tense and irritable

I worry about minor things

I'm often anxious

I feel fearful all the time

Physical symptoms of anxiety (tremors, sweating, dry mouth, indigestion, diarrhea, cramps, sighing, crying, palpitations, tension headaches, backaches)	None Mild Moderate Severe Incapacitating
Abdominal symptoms	None I've lost my appetite, I have a heavy feeling I have difficulty eating or need laxatives
Sexual symptoms	None I have a mild loss of desire I have a severe loss of desire, I no longer have erections/orgasm
Health concerns	None I'm preoccupied with my health I make frequent complaints, requests for help, visits to doctors I'm sure I have some severe sickness, but the doctors are missing it
Loss of weight	None Probably, I haven't weighed myself I've lost ____ pounds
Insight	I know I'm depressed and anxious I'm depressed and anxious, but it's from bad food, climate, overwork, need of rest I deny having a problem

193

Time variation	My symptoms are not tied to any time of day
	My symptoms are worse in the AM/PM
Feelings of unreality	None
	Mild
	Moderate
	Severe
	Incapacitating
Feelings of persecution	None
	I suspect others are making trouble for me
	I think there are people who are against me
	Others look strangely at me
	I'm sure someone is out to get me
Perfectionism	Absent, I am easygoing
	I don't like errors but can cope with them
	Errors upset me very much
Birth-family conflicts	None or mild
	We're OK as long as we keep our distance
	Within twelve hours of a visit, we fight
	We rarely contact each other
In-law conflicts	None or mild
	We're OK as long as we keep our distance
	Within twelve hours of a visit, we fight
	We rarely contact each other

Child-rearing conflicts

None
Mild
Moderate
Severe

Stepfamily conflicts

None
Mild
Moderate
Severe

Housekeeping or mealtime conflicts

None
Mild
Moderate
Severe

Social activity conflicts

None
Mild
Moderate
Severe

Feelings of jealousy

None
Mild, we tease each other about it
I need reassurance and cause
    arguments about it
I do not trust my partner

Time conflicts

None
Mild
Moderate
Severe

Alcohol or drug conflicts	None
	Mild
	Moderate
	Severe
Money conflicts	None
	Mild
	Moderate
	Severe
Trust conflicts	None
	Mild
	Moderate
	Severe
Sex fantasy conflicts	I'm comfortable with my sex thoughts
	I worry vaguely
	I worry, "Am I abnormal?"
	I think I must be crazy

Again, I want you to go over your answers carefully. They will reveal the overall condition of your emotional state. How do you think your partner would react if he or she read your responses? Consider trading questionnaire answers and talking them over. Disclosing your inner thoughts and feelings to your partner in this way can be a bridge to greater intimacy.

If your answers show that you have frequent feelings of depression, severe physical problems caused by anxiety, or suicidal thoughts, I urge you to seek help from a professional *immediately*. These feelings are treatable. Talk to your doctor, who can refer you to a local psychiatrist for counseling and treatment. Please take these feelings seriously and get the help you need right away.

Your Home Loveplay

This week, I want you to continue your loving touch, but *now you can include the breasts and genitals*. Feel free to stroke, caress, and kiss each other's bodies everywhere. You can bring each other to orgasm through mutual masturbation if you want to, but please refrain from intercourse for one more week. Don't rush to "do it." Enjoy the journey on the way to intercourse.

Make your goal skilled lovemaking, not just mechanical sexmaking. Taking the time together for relaxed loveplay will heal old resentments. It's like courting again. Giving and receiving pleasure through caring touch are special gifts to each other. Tell your partner that you enjoy and appreciate it. The positive emotions that arise will pave the path toward an enjoyable experience next week, when I'll be giving you "permission" to have intercourse if you want.

Now I have some special information especially for men who have a problem with premature ejaculation. This sexual problem is easily curable! All you have to do is learn a skill called the squeeze technique.

The Squeeze Technique

This technique reverses premature ejaculation by teaching you how to control the timing of your ejaculation. But even if you do not ejaculate prematurely, you can use the squeeze technique to learn how to keep your erection longer so you and your partner can enjoy extended lovemaking.

After some relaxed loveplay, let your partner stimulate your penis to a point just before you feel you are about to ejaculate. Then, place your thumb and index finger around the tip or midshaft of your penis and squeeze very firmly for fifteen seconds (see illustration on following page). Let your partner caress you all over your body as you squeeze. Or have her take over and squeeze the tip of your penis very firmly for

The Squeeze Technique

fifteen seconds as you lie flat on your back and relax. Be sure to relax the muscles of your buttocks and legs. Your penis will lose some of its erection.

Wait for thirty seconds after the squeeze and then ask your partner to begin stimulating your penis again in your favorite way. Just before you feel the urge to ejaculate, again squeeze the penis for fifteen seconds. Wait thirty seconds and start all over again. Repeat the process four or five times altogether.

After you do the squeeze technique during several sessions, you will notice that you can learn to control your erection and ejaculation. It will last longer the more faithfully you do the squeeze technique. Soon, the muscle relaxation and pause in your lovemaking will become automatic and may be all you need to delay ejaculation. As you progress, thinking of the delay may be all you need to sustain your erection.

Some men with severe anxiety may benefit from a small dose of a prescription antidepressant medication. If you are extremely anxious, your doctor will decide whether an antidepressant can help you.

Another Erotic Surprise

Plan to delight your partner with another surprise from your erotic goody bag. I never tire of recommending this technique because I think it is an excellent way to bring you and your partner closer together. It spices up your sex life by creating something unexpected. It brings laughter, which lightens the moment. It makes your partner feel good. And you will feel good too when you realize that you are using your own imagination to make your relationship better. Get those creative juices flowing!

How One Couple Got Through Week 3

Brenda and Jim, both age forty, entered sex therapy to work on Jim's periodic erection problems and because "sex has just become routine and stale for us." The couple worked together in the family furniture business. Their relationship, which had once been close and romantic, grew strained as they began to disagree about the way the business should be run. Jim had had an affair, but it fizzled because of his erection problems. Brenda wanted to keep the marriage together in spite of Jim's infidelity.

"In the first two weeks, our home loveplay was awkward," said Jim. "Brenda was so mad at me about the affair and after arguing at work about the business all day, it seemed silly to come home and try to be affectionate," he explained. Our therapists knew that, unless the family business issues were resolved, the couple's relationship would not improve, so they suggested that Brenda and Jim hire an outside consultant to work out their business problems. This strategy would free the couple to focus on their relationship.

"For a while, we argued about that too," confessed Brenda. "I didn't want to spend the money on a consultant and resented an intrusion from an outsider. But during the Gestalt exercise, I put our business in the empty chair and it told me I was putting it—the business I mean—before our relationship and it should be the other way around. That knocked me out," she said. "I finally understood that the most important thing to me was us."

"After we made the decision to hire a consultant, the loveplay became more natural," said Jim. "At the end of the third week, Brenda stimulated me to climax and it was so exciting. I was surprised. That showed me there was still something left between us. We're both interested in keeping that something alive and helping it grow."

Your Assignments for Week 3

1. Do the Fantastic Voyage (see page 167), Gestalt (see page 172), and rehearsal (see page 175) exercises.
2. Complete the Your Emotional Needs and Desires Questionnaire (see page 176) and the Emotional Roll Call Questionnaire (see page 190).
3. Include breast and genital play in your home loveplay exercises (see page 197).
4. Do the squeeze technique to learn how to keep your erection longer (see page 197).
5. Plan another erotic surprise for each other (see page 198).

8

Week 4: Show Me

Your Progress So Far

You are in the middle of the most emotionally demanding part of your sex therapy program. The Fantastic Voyage has taken you on an imaginary inner tour of your body, but it may also have brought many emotions to the surface—some positive, some conflicting, some painful. This week, you will do two additional exercises that may summon even more emotions: the miming exercise and more Gestalt exercises. I also want you to write each other a special letter that is sure to evoke strong feelings. Don't be afraid of your emotions. They are waiting to help you grow closer to each other.

The Miming Exercise

The miming exercise is not new. Therapists have been using it for years to help their patients communicate better. I call it the miming exercise because participants must act out their thoughts and feelings without words, using body movements only. The exercise teaches you how to communicate nonverbally with your partner. Both of you will learn how to express in movement what you may not be able to say in words. Sometimes words can distance you from your partner when you most want to be close. In these cases, it's easier to show your partner what you are feeling by your actions, rather than by your words, because you can read each other's expressions and posture. You often do this unconsciously, for instance, when you agree to something verbally while sitting with mouth tight, arms crossed, and eyes averted (saying "no" with your body).

The miming exercise will also show you your partner's side of the story because you'll experience how he or she feels about things. You and your partner can act like human mirrors for each other, to reflect your nonverbal cues and messages.

When you are ready to begin the miming exercise together at home, dim the lights and take off your shoes. You can stand up or sit down, whatever is most comfortable. In our clinic, the therapists give each participant instructions about what kinds of ideas to express nonverbally, for example, "I feel exhausted." At home, I'd like each of you, in turn, to whisper the instructions I've outlined below. Then I want the other to respond with body language. Then switch. In other words, when you are finished responding in body language to the instructions given by your partner, then you whisper the same instructions so he or she can respond. Remember not to answer verbally. You're not playing charades and trying to guess what your partner is acting out; you're trying to learn to listen to your partner's body messages. Here are the instructions to use during the miming exercise. If a certain part is too difficult to do, it's OK to signal "I cannot."

- Touch the part of me you like best. Now show me in body language why you like it best. (Now your partner asks you and you respond with body language.)
- Show me how you would like me to greet you when I get home

from work. (Now your partner gives you the same instruction and so on.)

• Show me how you usually say good-bye in the morning.

• How would you like me to behave when we are getting ready for bed?

• How do you think I would like you to behave when we are getting ready for bed?

• Show me how you felt about last week's Fantastic Voyage (see page 167).

• Show me how you felt about the sexological examination we did in week 2.

• Show me how you felt about my erotic surprise.

• Show me how you feel about having your body stroked at home.

• Express how you feel about having me join you in sex therapy at home.

• Show me with your body what you think is your biggest problem.

• Show me with your body what you think is your biggest asset.

• Show me how you'd like me to react to you when you feel angry.

• Show me how you'd like me to react to you when you feel sad.

• Show me how you'd like me to react to you when you feel loving.

• With your whole body, express how you feel about our future together as a couple.

• With your hands only, express your feelings about this past week.

• Express your feelings about the worst part of this past week.

• With your head only, express your feelings about the best part of this week.

• With your whole body, express how you feel right now, at this moment.

• Imagine we are alone at home. The doorbell rings. It's (name a significant person). React.

• Express warmth with your body.

• Express affection with your body.

• Say "I love you" nonverbally.

• Say "I'm mad at you" nonverbally.

- Say "I hate you" nonverbally.
- Say "I'm sorry" nonverbally.
- Say "farewell" nonverbally before a six-month trip.
- Say "farewell" nonverbally after we break up.
- Say "farewell" nonverbally to me on my deathbed.
- Greet me after a long separation.
- Are there any other special nonverbal messages you want to send?

Now I'd like the person who has given the last instruction to act out nonverbally a message of his or her choice, such as "Please be more romantic," "I feel hurt when you forget to kiss me good night," or "I love you." Then the other responds to this message nonverbally. Now the person who responded acts out a nonverbal message and the partner acts out a response.

Next I want you to look over the questionnaires you completed last week and pick out an area of conflict, such as child-rearing practices or spending money. Then use your body to act out your feelings about the issue in silence. Try not to talk or ask or answer questions even if you feel awkward or silly—talking breaks the mood, as well as the silence.

Now let's use the miming technique to do a little role-reversal exercise. Here's how it works: Say Patti's partner, Bill, has a habit of tuning her out when she tries to talk to him. He buries his face in the newspaper or faces the TV with his eyes glazed over. I would say, "Patti, you be Bill, and Bill, you are Patti trying to get Bill to listen to you. Act it out for me." Patti sits pretending to read a newspaper. Bill struggles to get Patti's attention by waving to her, clapping his hands, and tapping her on the shoulder. When Bill realizes how frustrating and hurtful his own behavior is, he can begin to feel how Patti feels. Each learns his or her impact on the other.

Take turns selecting an area of conflict for your role reversal and announce the message before acting it out. Something like, "Mary, you be me when we go shopping, and I'll be you making me wait while you can't make up your mind and then end up not buying anything," or

"John, you be me cleaning the kitchen floor on my hands and knees, and I'll be you walking through with muddy shoes."

Finally, give each other a nonverbal message showing what this miming session has meant to you. Was it upsetting? Sad? Funny?

What did the miming exercise bring up for you? Did you learn anything new from your partner that he or she never told you in words? Maybe you saw something that your partner has been trying to tell you for years, but only now do you understand. Are there some things that you find easier to express with actions than with words? Did this exercise teach you how to convey your feelings better to your partner from now on?

The Gestalt Revisited

Now, as soon as you complete the miming exercise, I want you to do a Gestalt session together, just like the one you did alone last week. Keep the lights low, place an empty chair in front of you, sit across from it, and pick something significant to put in the chair. It could be religion, finances, a family member, your boss, your job, your looks, aging, anger, passivity, your sexuality, your relationship, or a breakup. If you get mad, you can even put *me*, Dr. Renshaw, in the chair and tell me off. I can take it. Maybe it will be something that came up during last week's Fantastic Voyage. Whatever it is, pretend it's in that empty chair and talk to it. Then put yourself in the chair and respond as that issue. Next have your partner pick something, put it in the empty chair, and then respond as that issue while you watch.

Let's say Jane puts her partner George's penis in the chair. She tells it, "You ignore me. You're drifting away from me. Work always comes first." Then she takes a turn in the other chair and responds as the penis, "Jane, you know you hate to touch me when I get messy. You'd rather do the laundry or anything else than play sexually." You get the idea. Then George picks something that causes problems for him and puts it in the chair so he can deal with it once and for all.

I remember one couple's story that vividly illustrates the purpose of doing the Gestalt following the miming exercise. See if you can learn from their lives. Carl and Kim got married when they were both nineteen because Kim was pregnant. Now, at age thirty-two and with three children, they entered sex therapy because of Carl's sporadic erection problems and Kim's increasing lack of interest in sex. During the miming exercise session, the therapists asked Kim to express "I love you" nonverbally. She hugged Carl with one arm around his neck and the other crossed in front of her chest with the palm facing out, as if she were trying to block him or push him away. This position sent a mixed nonverbal message, saying both "Come closer" and "Go away."

Later, during the Gestalt exercise, Kim put Carl in the chair. The therapists discovered that Kim had very ambivalent feelings toward him, just as the miming exercise had indicated. On the one hand, she valued his strength and ability to provide for the family. But on the other hand, Kim felt that she had been trapped by the pregnancy into becoming a homemaker with no skills to offer an employer. "I'm afraid that, if we break up, I won't be able to support the kids and we'll have to go on welfare," she told Carl in the chair. She also revealed how deeply she hated his binge drinking. "I resent the way you just go off with the guys every month or so and disappear for a weekend. You come back blind drunk and useless," she said. Recognizing the mixed messages her body was sending helped Kim appreciate the mixed feelings she had for Carl. Perhaps you can take what you learn about body language in the miming exercise and use it to plumb deeper feelings in this week's Gestalt exercise.

In later discussions, Carl claimed he didn't know that his binge drinking meant that he had a drinking problem. We suspected that it was causing his sporadic impotence, at least in part, and recommended that he seek help for his alcohol problem. He reluctantly agreed. The couple progressed very well in therapy after Carl got help and Kim confronted her anger and her fears.

Farewell Forever Letter

It is during this week that we ask patients to write the "farewell forever" letter that I talked about in chapter 5 (see page 139). Feelings often run high after the miming and Gestalt exercises. These are the feelings that I want you to capture in your own farewell letters: the true, deep-down feelings you have for your partner.

Dick and Ellie were a middle-aged couple who experienced many stepfamily problems that directly affected their sex life. Dick had been previously married, and, although the children from his first marriage did not live with him, they would stay overnight at his house for a week at a time, blaring the radio and watching TV until late at night. Dick's teenage kids constantly took advantage of him by asking for money, gifts, and time. They manipulated him by making him feel guilty, saying things like, "Mom gave me a leather jacket; why can't you give me a new stereo system?"

At first, Dick would say no to their requests, but then he always changed his mind and gave in. His relationship with Ellie was becoming strained. They only had sex about once every three or four months because Dick wasn't very interested in making love.

"Dick never sides with me against the kids," said Ellie. "He just caves in and gives them whatever they want. And they want a lot." Both Dick and his ex-wife felt guilt and regret over their divorce, so they competed with each other in giving the kids more and more material things to compensate for the trauma of the breakup. Ellie hadn't known she would "inherit" all of that divorce residue when she married Dick. "We spend our weekends handling crises caused by the kids," Ellie complained. "There's no time to be alone together."

The miming exercise helped Dick get in touch with his conflicting emotions, so he could express them in his farewell forever letter. During the miming exercise, the therapists asked Dick to show them with his body what he thought was his biggest problem. Dick nonverbally expressed his frustration with his children by wringing his hands and pulling at his clothes. Then he began gesturing as if he were pulling something out of his chest, hand over hand, as if to say, "I'm giving you everything I have." Then later, when asked to express with his whole body how he felt about his and Ellie's future together, Dick calmed down and his facial expression changed from anguished to peaceful. He smiled and moved his open hands apart, to suggest a long time.

When Ellie did the Gestalt exercise, she put Dick's kids in the chair. She told them that she recognized their need for attention, but that her and Dick's relationship came first. Then she said that, when they were older and found someone to have a relationship with, they would understand her and Dick's position. Ellie told us that being able to "talk" freely to Dick's children really did help her to understand where they were coming from and made her less angry. The Gestalt also brought many emotions to the surface, which she expressed later in her farewell forever letter to Dick.

During therapy, we taught Dick to be more assertive and gave Ellie permission to support him in saying "no" to his children and ex-wife. This couple needed to present a united front to Dick's kids and to assert themselves as the primary unit of authority in the household so the kids knew what their limits were. Ellie and Dick decided to go away together for the weekend, without the kids. This was a first for Dick, who began to see how he was being manipulated to provide negative attention. The couple made a rule that the kids could visit only every other weekend, and the kids obeyed. Dick and Ellie did surprisingly well after they stood firm, as a couple, and gained respect from Dick's children.

This couple's farewell forever letters helped them focus on the preciousness of each day. They planned weekend getaways and secluded evenings as they had during their courtship and honeymoon. This "alone time" gave a needed jump start to their stressed relationship. Here are their letters:

Dear Dick,

I will never see you again after today. There are some things I want to say.

I will miss many things about you: your sweetness and your toughness, and the way you always protected me. I'll miss your face, the sound of your voice, and the way you always tug at your ear when you're nervous. We've been through some pretty rough times together, but I'd like to remember the good things, like that week we spent at the beach house in Florida. I wish we had gone away together more often. I think what I will remember most is the way you suffered because you felt torn between me and your kids. Maybe now you will find some peace. Be strong and remember you have the right to say "no." I'm so filled with emotion, I want to cry. Good-bye. I love you.
Ellie

Dear Ellie,

I will never see you again after today. There are some things I want to say.

Just thinking about not seeing you again makes me feel all choked up. I can't help but feel that it's all my fault, our having to separate. If only things had been different. If only I had been different. But life is what it is and I just have to accept it.

Remember the day we met? You were wearing that light blue dress and your hair was short, the way it is now. I fell in love at first sight.

I came to this marriage with a lot of baggage—three teenage kids who wouldn't let us alone. Now that our marriage is over, I know that you have the strength to face whatever life brings. I hope you find fulfillment. Be happy.
Love, Dick

Now it's time for you to write your partner a farewell forever letter. I want you to sit down and do it right now, with your emotions still fresh from the miming exercise and Gestalt. You don't have to show your letter to your partner right away; its contents can be healing and revealing for you yourself. And it could transform some of the negative feelings you have about your partner and your relationship into positive, caring ones. Losses always shape lives after they happen. Use the threat of loss to shape your attitude and behavior *now*, so you can improve the quality of your relationship.

Before you begin writing, imagine that you will never see your partner again. You don't have to envision any awful circumstances under which you had to split up or he or she died. Just pretend that your partner is gone. You never got to say all the things you were too embarrassed, mad, proud, shy, or stubborn to tell him or her. But it's not too late. Begin writing your letter: "I will never see you again after today. There are some things I want to say. . . ."

What did this exercise show you about your relationship? Did you write your letter in the heat of anger or with extreme sadness? How do you feel now? Different from the way you felt before you started writing? Put your letter aside for two days, then read it again. In the calmness of another day, you may feel like leaving your letter labeled "Pretend letter. Can we talk?" on your partner's pillow.

This exercise acts as a catharsis, or cleansing, releasing the pent-up emotion that has always been at the bottom of your relationship with your partner. It allows you to experience your genuine feelings for your partner so you can express them to him or her.

Your Home Loveplay

This week, you'll progress further on your journey toward intercourse. I want you to try a technique that helps people who have many different kinds of sexual problems, especially those with premature ejaculation, painful sex, and vaginismus (involuntary spasms of the muscles in the lower third of the vagina). In this technique, the woman mounts her partner's soft, nonerect penis.

Here's how the technique is done. After several minutes of sensuous total-body caressing, with plenty of kissing and loving touch, have your partner lie passively on his back, relaxing all of his muscles completely. Generously lubricate his soft penis and your vaginal area with saliva or a store-bought, water-based lubricant to make penetration easier (if you are unsure what to use, ask your pharmacist). If your partner has an erection, cuddle until it subsides. Now swing one of your legs over your partner's body and sit across his hips, facing him. Stuff his flaccid penis into your vagina as far as you can. You may have to try a few times before you succeed—the technique is awkward and the penis is soft and floppy. Be sure to keep your sense of humor—you will probably need it right now!

Once you have stuffed your partner's soft penis into your vagina, adjust your position until you and your partner both feel comfortable. Now contract the muscles in your vagina as though you were stopping the flow of urine and hold the contraction for a count of ten. Repeat this action a few times. Then do what I call the "flick exercise," that is, contract your vaginal muscles briefly and relax. Contract and relax, counting "one, one, one" ten times. Repeat several times. It will feel good for both of you.

At this point, a number of things can happen. The repetition of your contractions may stimulate your partner to have an erection. If this happens, hug, caress, and wait; the erection will subside. Wait for thirty seconds, then contract your vaginal muscles again. The goal is to relax your vaginal muscles so intercourse can feel good and to extend your partner's erection for your mutual pleasure. Try this exercise two or three times this week.

Some men may feel threatened by the woman-on-top position, and some women may feel uncomfortable doing it. But this technique is important because it relaxes the man and gives control to the woman. She puts the penis in; he is not initiating penetration. She cannot blame him for hurting her. The man with premature ejaculation can avoid the anxiety and "spectatoring" I talked about in chapter 1 ("Am I doing it right?" "Will I be able to last long enough?"). The man with erection problems does not have to worry about the lack of an erection during this technique. He can relax, turn off his anxious thoughts, use sexual fantasy, and feel each erotic sensation that arises. It also helps the woman who feels pain during intercourse because of vaginismus. She learns that the involuntary muscle spasms she once felt can now come under her control. Even the woman who has not experienced orgasm can be helped. While her partner's penis is inside her, she (or he) can stimulate her clitoris manually or with a vibrator. She feels good and learns to associate this good feeling with having her partner's penis inside her.

If you have any physical problems, such as arthritis or an artificial hip, that make this technique painful or difficult, do not try it. But if it is just a matter of frustration at not being able to succeed at your first attempts, that is not a good excuse for stopping the exercise. Relax and don't worry about it. Try and try again until you can master this most valuable technique for building up sexual pleasure and self-confidence. Remember when you learned how to ride a bicycle? You fell at least ten times until you learned how to ride. Be as patient and persistent in the bedroom.

I remember one woman who tried this technique but insisted that it didn't work. She claimed she tried and tried but could not stuff her husband's soft penis into her vagina. Finally, I asked her to show me, using two dolls made from pipe cleaners, exactly how she was attempting to mount her husband. From the placement of the dolls, I could see that she had been sitting across her husband's knees instead of across his hips. No wonder she could not do the exercise; her husband's penis would have had to be twenty-four inches long! I told her to try sitting closer to her target. She did and met with much more success.

How One Couple Got Through Week 4

Rick, thirty-six, and Tricia, thirty-four, entered sex therapy because of Rick's loss of interest in sex, which led to erection problems. Rick was a social worker who chose his field because he thought he could help people and "change the system." The job was tough, and

Rick discovered that some of his patients needed lifelong help. Over the years, he became disillusioned with his work, but he couldn't find another job. Tricia was a struggling actress; the couple had met when Tricia organized a charity performance for Rick's social service agency. Rick now envied Tricia for her glamorous job.

Sex was good before the couple got married, but shortly after the wedding, Tricia got a part in a play in another city. They struggled through a commuter marriage for three years. Living apart was tough, but the sex was exciting—as if they were still dating. Then Tricia landed a good part back in Chicago and she and Rick were once again living together full time. "That's when our sex life began to decline," said Tricia. "I'm afraid of losing Rick, but I don't want us to go on this way any longer."

During the miming exercise in week 4, the therapists asked Rick to show them with his body what he thought his biggest problem was. He had a hard time conveying his answer nonverbally, but the therapists eventually saw that he was trying to describe his job. They asked him to show how he felt about his work, and he rubbed his eyes as if he were crying. Then he moved his arms up against an invisible barrier and tried to push through with his entire body, but had no success. It was obvious to the therapists that Rick felt frustrated and powerless at his job. The same feeling of impotence transferred over to his sex life and manifested as sporadic erection difficulty.

We asked Rick if he could find something in his job that would give him satisfaction, some small goal he could attain. He expressed doubt, so we asked him if he had considered another line of work. Rick said that his "dream job" would be operating a restaurant but that he was afraid to make the leap for many reasons: an uncertain economy, the competition, the loss of his professional status. Tricia encouraged him to consider seriously giving it a try.

By the end of the seven-week sex therapy program, Rick's sexual symptoms began to improve. His interest in sex increased as his outlook brightened, although the couple still had some underlying power issues to resolve.

"When you start sex therapy, you just feel that everything you're going through is so abnormal," said Tricia. "But the therapy normalizes everything for you. It's something I have a hard time remembering, that what I've gone through is normal. It made me feel like we weren't the only ones in the world with problems like these, that we weren't alone."

Your Assignments for Week 4

1. Take turns doing the miming exercise (see page 201), including the role-reversal session (see page 204). Then do the Gestalt exercise together (see page 205).
2. Write each other a farewell forever letter (see page 207).
3. Continue with your home loveplay several times this week and incorporate the technique I describe in which the woman mounts her partner's soft penis (see page 210).

9

Week 5: The Turning Point

A Crucial Week

At this point in sex therapy, many couples panic. "It's week 5. It's almost over." They worry. They fight. They wonder if they've done the exercises right. That kind of reaction is normal; it's called "separation anxiety." Yet often just knowing that the end of sex therapy is near makes a couple focus more and work harder during the time they have left. If you feel anxious because your seven weeks of home sex therapy are drawing to a close, use that feeling as a reminder to give the next three weeks your full time and effort. I know that finding time is always a problem, but it's important to make the time to improve your relationship. Reaffirm your commitment to sex therapy. After all, if you've been doing your home loveplay exercises these past four weeks, you've already made a big investment in your relationship. Keep it up and see it through to the last day.

For some couples, week 5 is a turning point. Something just seems to happen, without effort. That's how it is in life when you try to change. Remember when you tried to lose weight? You tried, you worked at it, but nothing seemed to happen for a while. Then, all of a sudden, things improved—you saw a change on the scale. It was like a gift because you weren't expecting it right then. But it wasn't really a gift because you worked hard for it. It can be the same with sex therapy in week 5.

"In the fourth week of sex therapy, we hit a fence," said Lisa. "But in week 5, something clicked. I'm not sure what it was. Maybe not having sex for four weeks opened something up—whatever it was, a little bulb went on. Jeff noticed it too. We both felt more peaceful and relaxed, and my interest in sex blossomed for the first time since our courtship. This is the only time—really since our honeymoon—that I've focused on the two of us as a couple."

Don't be discouraged if week 5 is not a turning point for you. Some couples just don't experience an "ah-ha!" in week 5. That's OK. Sex therapy is different for everyone. But do take a few minutes to look back on the last four weeks of your at-home sex therapy. Did you and your partner put as much into those weeks as you could have? Did you do your home loveplay regularly? Do you remember that I said back in chapter 5 that the success of your sex therapy is directly related to the number of times you do your home loveplay? If you have not been doing your loveplay faithfully, start doing it now—this afternoon or tonight. You may even want to consider starting your loveplay over from week 1, spending one session together on each stage, rather than a full week. It's a great refresher.

But some couples who *have* been cooperative and steadfast in doing their home loveplay regularly feel no particular change in week 5. In fact, some couples experience week 5 as a blue-funk week. They may complain that their first attempts at long-awaited intercourse fail or go sour. Their first-week hopes are tempered by fifth-week reality. They may be anxious about intercourse or angry at the children or about something at work. Many problems enter the bedroom with you. I usually tell our patients that this letdown is not unique to them. Many people before them have experienced similar feelings of frustration. If you and your partner feel discouraged about a lack of progress, you should join hands, climb the "little hill of funk" together, and continue with your home loveplay in spite of your low spirits. The loveplay is the key to successful, permanent change. It is OK to feel discouraged, but I want you to continue your exercises anyway. Just don't get into a bout of sustained negative thinking about your slow progress. Remember the small improvements you have seen—the talking, touching, and learning about your body and that of your partner. To help energize you, I've included some tips in this chapter on ways to combat the negative thinking that can sabotage you.

How to Correct Negative Thinking

Your thoughts can trigger your moods. The thought of going on vacation can fill you with excitement and optimistic anticipation, even if you're stuck at home or the office for the next six months. Negative thoughts—whether or not they are true—can trigger depressed or angry moods. Depressed or anxious people think that their perceived gloom and fears are real. They see their situation as hopeless. For pessimists, negative thinking is automatic. It's a habit that they may have learned from mom or dad without realizing it. But the good news is that you can train yourself to change the way you look at the world. Then you can improve your mood, which can improve your relationship. Negative thoughts can also trigger angry words: "Stop being such a wet blanket." When you learn to control your negative thinking, you will communicate better with your partner.

The first step in learning to correct negative thinking is to recognize it. Remember that it can take many forms and that it directly affects your relationship with your partner. In his book, *Feeling Good: The New Mood Therapy*, David D. Burns tells his readers about some common manifestations of negative thinking. You can benefit from this knowledge too.

- *Self-blaming*, in which you blame yourself for a negative event over which you had no real control: "If I had taken the day off, this would never have happened."
- *Black-or-white thinking*, which causes you to discount your performance if it falls short of perfect: "I lost five pounds, but I wanted to lose ten."
- *Generalization*, when you see a single negative event as a never-ending pattern of defeat: "Pat didn't tell me she'd be home late. She always forgets important things."
- *Flaw-finding*, in which you let one negative detail cloud the overall picture: "Larry bought me an expensive birthday present, but he didn't bother to wrap it."
- *Dismissing the positive*, when you insist that positive experiences don't count for some reason: "We had a nice time last night, but that doesn't make up for the last time."
- *Jumping to conclusions*, when you draw a negative conclusion for no good reason: "He said we'd go out to dinner so I won't have to cook, but I'll bet he forgot. He probably doesn't really want to go."
- *Enlarging or diminishing*, which causes you to exaggerate the importance of negative events or downplay the importance of positive events: "Paula looked like a sourpuss when I got home. That means the whole evening is shot."
- *Emotional rationalizing*, when you assume that your negative feelings are a true reflection of the facts: "I have a feeling Frank is untrustworthy, so it must be true."
- *"Should" statements*, which cause you to motivate yourself by self-blame: "I should have gotten a baby-sitter. Then we wouldn't have had a fight in the restaurant." The end result of "should" is guilt or shame.
- *Name-calling*, an extreme form of overgeneralization that causes you to stereotype yourself or someone else: "I'm a loser" or "He's a lazy bum."
- *Excessive expectations*, like "happily ever after" that set unattaina-

ble or impossible goals: "After we get married, I know I can change him."

Julie, a beauty-shop owner, and Stan, a nursing-home administrator, both age thirty-two, entered sex therapy because of the big difference in their sexual drives. Stan wanted to have sex every day, while Julie was satisfied with having it once a week, sometimes every other week. Stan never wanted to ask Julie to do anything she did not want to do, and he was comfortable masturbating in secret to fulfill his stronger sex drive. One day, Julie saw Stan masturbating in the shower and she reacted very strongly. Stan admitted to her that he masturbated regularly, causing Julie to blame herself for what she saw as a serious flaw in their marriage: a very common difference in their level of desire for each other. "I'm a failure," she told Stan. "And I'm making our marriage a failure too."

Julie had fallen prey to negative thinking about her relationship with Stan. She used magnification to exaggerate the importance of the difference in their sex drives beyond its true significance. Then she labeled herself and her marriage a failure. She didn't know that having a different sex drive from her husband was not abnormal—in fact, it's very common—and that there were ways of dealing with the situation. She automatically assumed her relationship with Stan was doomed. "Ever since I was a kid, I thought I was being more realistic when I saw things negatively," she said, "like I was kidding myself if I was positive or cheerful." With the help of her therapists, Julie learned that, on the contrary, her gloomy, inaccurate predictions were actually contributing to her increasingly depressed mood and to Stan's withdrawal from her.

We educated Julie and Stan about the natural difference in sexual desire that can occur between two people. This difference is neither good nor bad—it's just different. Julie had no idea that Stan wanted sex as often as he now said he did. "I never told Julie because I didn't want to upset her," he said. "It wasn't really her problem anyway. I think she's a wonderful wife and mother."

Couples who experience libido differences need to negotiate a mutually satisfying compromise. For example, Stan and Julie agreed to bring each other to orgasm, with or without intercourse, three times a week. Stan said he would continue masturbating if he felt he needed to release his sexual tension more often than that. Both partners said they felt closer and were happy about their more honest communication with each other.

A simple exercise can help you see if you have negative ideas about yourself. Take a piece of paper and write down your good points and your bad points. Now look at what you've written. Where did you start? With the bad points? That may show you give more weight to the bad in yourself than to the good. Maybe you had a hard time coming up with any good points. Think about it. Are you kind to your parents, your children, your friends? If so, you have much to admire in yourself. There is a lot about you that is positive if you only look deeply enough and in the right places.

Here are some suggestions you can use to counteract your own negative thinking:

1. *Try to become more aware of your negative thoughts*. Listen to yourself when you speak, to detect any of the forms of negative thinking I outlined on page 218. Maybe it would help to tape-record yourself during a conversation. You may be surprised at what you hear! You could also try becoming more aware of the way you constantly talk to yourself in your mind. We all self-talk. Is your inner dialogue negative? Are you telling yourself unproductive things like "I'll never be good enough" or "I'm a rotten lover"?

2. *Replace your negative thoughts with positive thoughts*. Once you've recognized your gloomy or pessimistic thoughts, consciously substitute more positive and productive ones. When you hear yourself thinking, "My sex problems are hopeless," instead try thinking, "I'm learning new ways to improve my sex life."

3. *Use humor to defuse your negativity*. Taking yourself too seriously

can be dangerous. Humor will help you relieve the "woe is me" syndrome: "We'll both probably put our backs out if we try the woman-on-top position, but I'm willing to give it a try at least once."

The Let's Look at Us Questionnaire

We usually don't slow down enough in our busy day to think or feel. We just rush through the day and then collapse in bed. The purpose of the following exercise is to make both of you think about some issues surrounding your relationship and your sex life that you may have never considered before. I want each of you to make a copy of this exercise and complete it today.

LET'S LOOK AT US QUESTIONNAIRE

What would you like to change most about yourself?

How could you achieve this change? (Think of two answers.)

    1.

    2.

What would you like to change most about your partner?

What could your partner do about changing for the better? (Think of two answers.)

    1.

    2.

What could *you* do to help him or her change? (Think of two answers.)

    1.

    2.

What pleases you most about your partner? (Think of two answers.)
1.
2.

What was the best thing you and your partner did together in the last month?

What was the hardest thing you did together in the last month?

What is the best thing about your relationship?

What is the worst thing about your relationship?

What could you do about the worst thing? (Think of two answers.)
1.
2.

What are the best things about your sex life?
1.
2.

What are the most difficult things about your sex life?
1.
2.

How can you help to change the hardest things?
1.
2.

How can your partner help to change the hardest things?
1.
2.

How can sex therapy at home help you change the hardest things?
1.
2.

List four things about sex you enjoy:
1.
2.
3.
4.

List four things about sex you find difficult:

1.

2.

3.

4.

List four things you enjoy doing socially:

1.

2.

3.

4.

List four things you have difficulty doing socially:

1.

2.

3.

4.

List four things you enjoy doing around the house:

1.

2.

3.

4.

List four things you have difficulty doing around the house:

1.

2.

3.

4.

Would you let your partner read this questionnaire? yes ___ no ___

Read over your answers carefully. You've given yourself a lot to think about. Could your answers help you make some positive changes in the next few weeks? For example, let's say you answered that the worst thing about your relationship is a lack of communication. Then you said one of the things you could do about it is set aside fifteen minutes after dinner every night just to talk to each other instead of watching TV. Now try it! The exercise forced you to look for ways to improve your relationship. But you must take it a step further and actually do it in your life.

Letter to a Significant Someone

This week, I would also like you to write a very special letter to someone, dead or alive, who had a significant, but negative, influence in your life. It could be anyone—a parent, your partner, an ex-spouse, a relative, or a teacher—but it should be someone who held you back or harmed you in some way. (Remember the letter Mary Jane wrote to her Uncle Eddie in chapter 1?) Tell the person exactly how you feel, now, about what he or she did to you. Don't hold back. But see if there are any healing or forgiving feelings hidden in yourself behind the hurtful ones.

Do not mail this letter; it is for your own awareness and growth. The act of writing the letter will help you come to terms with whatever disturbing feelings you have about the person you are writing to.

To show you what I mean, I've included a letter that one of our patients, Celeste, wrote to her estranged older sister, Luanne, who had had a brief affair with Celeste's husband:

Dear Luanne:

We have never spoken since you had the affair with Jack. I feel the need to write for my own peace of mind. I have never understood how two sisters who were once so close could end up like this. I've turned it over and over a hundred times in my mind. I felt betrayed when you slept with Jack. That could have broken up my marriage. But I wouldn't give Jack a divorce, and he stayed with me, impotent. I never forgave you for that. Even now, so many years later, tears are burning in my eyes. Sometimes I still think, "I hate her and I hope she gets what she deserves: a life full of pain and misery like she gave me." But I keep trying to let go and forgive you because I love you. I hate you, and I love you. You're my sister. I was angry at Jack for a long time too, but right now, I just want to forget about what happened and start over. Jack is a wonderful person, and he loves me. I'm going to stop dwelling on the past and look forward to a better future with him.

Your sister, Celeste

Celeste and Jack entered sex therapy to work on Jack's erection problems. The couple grew much closer over the course of the seven-week program. Jack's ability to have an erection improved as he overcame his guilt about his infidelity.

Is there a significant someone in your past or present to whom you would like to write a "get-it-off-my-chest" letter? Do it now, but don't mail it. It's for you alone. Write down exactly how you feel so you can rid yourself of the emotional grudge you've been carrying around for so long. Bad feelings are corrosive, and both parties involved lose. When you let go, both win.

The Relationship Expectations Questionnaire

At the beginning of a relationship, people have high hopes for the future. Even if they are having problems, they believe that love will conquer all. Sometimes one partner might say, "I know he lies, but I think I can change him" or "She spends every cent she earns, but it will be different after the wedding." These people have unrealistic expectations of their partner and the future of their relationship.

This short questionnaire will help you to gauge whether the expectations you had at the beginning of your relationship were realistic, or whether, like Don Quixote, you dreamed an impossible dream. It also shows you how your expectations change through the years. When you are both finished, share your responses with each other.

RELATIONSHIP EXPECTATIONS QUESTIONNAIRE

Write down the three most important expectations you have now about your relationship:

Expectations of myself	Expectations of my partner
1.	1.
2.	2.
3.	3.

Write down the three most important expectations you had about your relationship on your wedding day or at the time you began this relationship:

Expectations of myself	Expectations of my partner
1.	1.
2.	2.
3.	3.

Are you ready to show this to your partner? yes _____ no _____

I want to show you how one couple, Jill and Marty, completed this questionnaire. Jill had been a regional sales manager for a large hotel chain, and Marty was an architect. This was Marty's second marriage, but he had no children from the first. The couple had two young children, only fifteen months apart. "I was so furious at the second pregnancy," said Jill. "Marty didn't want me to go back to my job after the first baby, which we both wanted. And he made sure I wouldn't go back by having sex with me one night before I had time to insert my diaphragm. I protested, but he said he'd withdraw before he came. I felt betrayed when I conceived the second time," she continued. "Sex has never been the same for me since. My tubes are tied now, but it's like my desire got tied before that." Jill became so apathetic about lovemaking that she feared Marty would take a lover "and bring home herpes or AIDS."

. . .

Here are Jill's answers to the Relationship Expectations Questionnaire:

The three most important expectations I have now about our relationship are:

Expectations of myself
1. To go back to work when our youngest is in preschool.
2. To resolve my extreme anger at Marty
3. To get our sex life back on track

Expectations of Marty
1. To accept my wanting to work, not for the money, but for my mind
2. To go through sex therapy with me
3. To think of me as his equal, professionally

The three most important expectations I had about our relationship on our wedding day were:

Expectations of myself
1. To be a good life partner for Marty
2. To have kids
3. To keep on working

Expectations of Marty
1. To be truthful with me
2. To be faithful to me
3. To let me keep on working

Now let's take a look at Marty's answers to this questionnaire.

The three most important expectations I have now about our relationship:

Expectations of myself
1. To support Jill and the kids financially
2. To help Jill get through this bad period
3. To help out with the kids more

Expectations of Jill
1. To be fair with me
2. To work on her anger
3. To "be my wife" again, that is, have sex with me

The three most important expectations I had on our wedding day:

Expectations of myself
1. To do everything I can to make this marriage work
2. Not to let my job get in the way of our time together
3. To be a good lover

Expectations of Jill
1. To always be a good lover
2. To be my companion and playmate
3. To be a sweet mother

Jill was angry that parenthood had compromised her career, unlike Marty's. She was resentful that Marty, whom she thought of as a good father and excellent provider, was able to continue his profession. Marty protested his innocence. "I truly did not intend to derail your career," he said. "I just wanted to make love to you again. Having Sean (their second child) was . . . I don't want to call him an accident, but I didn't mean to trick you into having him. He's a wonderful baby, and we both love him."

Jill's early expectation of being a "good life partner" for Marty was well intentioned but vague. She had expected him to be truthful and felt that he had betrayed her trust, but she had not thought to suggest he use a condom. Marty did not force her to get pregnant a second time. She was partly angry at herself for having been so impulsive. Obviously, she hadn't known on her wedding day how important her career was to become (that goal was third on her list) until it had been threatened by the second pregnancy.

Jill could have returned to work, but admitted that she truly enjoyed those early months with their first child. Part of her anger at

Marty hid anxiety about her own reluctance to go back into the deadline-heavy business world. When Jill was honest with herself, she said, "It was easier to blame Marty." Her apology to him was the turning point in their relationship. After their youngest child turned one year old, Jill found a nanny and returned to work full time. Her sex drive slowly returned, but fatigue now replaced her anger at Marty as a dampening force on their sex life together.

Your Home Loveplay

This is the week you've all been waiting for! After large doses of closeness, kissing, and caressing everywhere on the body, I give you and your partner my blessing to proceed to full intercourse and orgasm if you want. You don't have to have intercourse every time you do your home loveplay this week, but try to have it a few times this week. See how it goes. Remember to spend half an hour or so on your mutual loving and sensual touch *before* you attempt to have intercourse. Savor your loveplay. Kiss, touch, relax, kiss again, and tell each other how you feel. Use lots of sexual fantasy—or whatever else you need—to preserve your sexy mood. Enjoy!

I remember one couple who decided to go to a motel for their first attempt at intercourse. The walls of their room were covered with ceiling-to-floor mirrors. "It could have been real sexy," said Gus, "but we're both nearsighted!" Humor helped this couple defuse the tension surrounding their sexual encounter.

Having intercourse for the first time in at least five weeks is a big event. Talk to each other about how it felt. Tell each other what you liked and disliked about the experience so you can improve on it next time. You may think that if you have not had sex in years, you will be more likely to fail at your attempts, but that's not true. It all depends on the two partners and their commitment to sex therapy and to each other. Sometimes people who have deep-seated emotional problems may have more difficulty succeeding at their first try, but that is not necessarily true for everyone. Sex may now be fine but you may be struggling with other emotional difficulties. Contact a professional who can help you work through them. Set a goal of six visits and then evaluate your situation. Continue on if you need more help.

If your first attempts at intercourse fail, try again. Don't be overly concerned if your first attempts at having sex are awkward. Have a sense of humor, be optimistic, and stay persistent. Anger or anxiety will only make your situation worse. Try to relax (see page 160 for relaxation exercises). If you get stuck, wait until tomorrow or next week and then try again to make love.

How One Couple Got Through Week 5

Rosemary and Alan, both forty-six, entered sex therapy because Rosemary had never experienced an orgasm. The couple had been married for twenty years and had three children. Alan was a civil engineer, and Rosemary worked part-time as a dental hygienist.

Rosemary had been brought up in a strict Catholic home. Her parents never talked to her about sex, and she had never explored her own sexuality through masturbation or fantasy. She had been a virgin when she married Alan, a Protestant. Her family had nearly disowned her for marrying a non-Catholic, but they reconciled after Rosemary and Alan had their first child, about ten years before.

"I was totally ignorant about sex when I got married," confessed Rosemary. "Sex was evil, a temptation of the devil. My body was unknown territory. I always tried to be a 'good girl' and that meant denying my own sexuality, but I thought I had to submit whenever Alan wanted sex. I know that sex is an important part of marriage, but I derive little pleasure from it. It's just become one more job I have to do. But I truly love Alan, and I want sex to be a 'want' instead of a feeling of 'I have to.' "

We told Rosemary to be the one who initiated the home loveplay every other night, so she could feel more in control. "At first, our home loveplay was clumsy," said Alan. "I guess I have a lot of old-fashioned ideas about the woman being compliant. So when we had to take turns beginning the loveplay sessions, I felt funny just lying there. But I think it was good for Rosie to take charge for a change."

We were able to help Rosemary simply by giving her objective medical information about her sexual anatomy and by encouraging her to explore her sexual self. "By the fifth week, I was ready to have sex," said Rosemary. "I had masturbated four or five times since the beginning of therapy and had learned a lot about my body's responsiveness—I had my first orgasm at age forty-six! I wanted to try that new knowledge out with Alan." The couple had intercourse several times during week 5, and Rosemary experienced an orgasm twice that week—a turning point not only in the couple's sex therapy but also in Rosemary's life.

Intercourse with your partner may not be as groundbreaking this week as it was for Rosemary and Alan, but it's a major step in your sexual self-improvement program. Encourage and support each other in your attempts at lovemaking. Tell your partner what felt good and what still needs to change. Remember to use honest "I" language instead of accusatory "you" language.

Your Assignments for Week 5

1. Fill out the Let's Look at Us Questionnaire (page 221) and the Relationship Expectations Questionnaire (page 225).
2. See if you've fallen into the habit of negative thinking. If you have, follow the steps I recommend to change those unhelpful patterns (see page 220).
3. Continue your home loveplay exercises and include intercourse (see page 229).

10

Week 6: The Light at the End of the Tunnel

Is Your Goal In Sight?

The weeks of your do-it-yourself sex therapy are drawing to a close. It's as if you can see light approaching at the end of a long tunnel. The anxious among you ask, "Is it really almost over?" The optimists anticipate a bright future. This is the last full week you have to be your own sex therapist. There are no questionnaires to fill out this week and no exercises to do, unless you want to repeat some just for fun or to help solve a specific problem. There's just you and your partner and your home loveplay. Be as inventive and imaginative as you can be.

Resist the impulse to forgo your home loveplay just because this is the last week of sex therapy (the seventh week is for review and reflection), especially if you already progressed to intercourse last week. Home loveplay is still important because it's a transition between the previous weeks—which built up to intercourse—and the following weeks and months when you will be enjoying your newfound intimacy together day by day. Don't cheat yourself! Give your relationship the chance it deserves to flourish and grow.

Your Home Loveplay

How did your attempt at intercourse go last week? Did either of you reach orgasm? Whether you succeeded or not is less important than whether you experienced closeness and sharing during your home loveplay. The loveplay is the special key to learning about your body and that of your partner, discovering your responses and those of your partner. If you didn't have intercourse, try again this week. If you did have intercourse last week, keep up the good work. You are overcoming your difficulties, and you are enriching your and your partner's sex life.

What specifically should you do in your home loveplay this week? Everything. Repeat the stages from week 1 until now. Please remember to include plenty of sexual fantasy to keep your desire burning strongly. And don't forget about erotic surprises. You and your partner can continue to use this technique to bring some sparkle and surprise into your relationship, as I suggest later in this chapter.

"I remember that, during the sixth week of sex therapy, we were feeling pretty good about ourselves," said Rob, a thirty-six-year-old science instructor at a junior college. "The week before, Penny and I had intercourse for the first time in months, and she said she hadn't felt so aroused since we dated."

Penny, age thirty, worked as a customer service rep for a manufacturing company. She experienced a severe drop in sexual desire after the birth of the couple's only child, about four years before they came to sex therapy. "I had the postpartum blues really bad," Penny explained. "After I started feeling better, I had more energy, but my sex drive just seemed to stay in neutral. I stopped being affectionate toward Rob because every time I touched him, he took it as a sign that I was ready for sex. I don't blame the guy. We hadn't made love for ages. But I just couldn't talk about it. I didn't know any other way of getting the message to him that I wasn't interested in having sex—even though I still loved him," Penny said.

"We used to walk around the house avoiding each other. It was awful. When we came here, you persuaded us to talk openly and honestly, and that defused the tension," Penny continued. "Having to massage each other everywhere except the genitals was a great idea. It was relaxing, and I didn't tense up because you said, 'No intercourse for a few weeks.' I felt relieved, but that was silly because we hadn't even tried to have sex for eight months. But because *you* said 'no intercourse' I didn't feel scared that Rob would want it or that I had let him down. Somehow his tenderness for me this week was different from when he used to look like an injured husband every time I pulled away. Last week, I really *wanted* to make love to him, and that felt wonderful."

Plan Another Erotic Surprise

Remember what fun you had planning an erotic surprise for your partner back in week 2? Maybe it kindled something interesting. Maybe it backfired. Either way, you learned about your partner's likes and dislikes and your own. It's time to recapture that experience by planning another sexy fun surprise for this week. I want each of you to plan a surprise for the other. Here's how an older couple we treated approached the task.

Florence and Fred were a seventy-two-year-old couple who came to sex therapy because of Fred's increasing erection difficulties. The ability to have an erection naturally declines as a man ages. But Fred wanted to know if there was anything the couple could do to minimize that decline.

We told the couple that the diminishing rigidity of an erection as a man gets older doesn't indicate any kind of disorder. We also taught Florence to lovingly stimulate Fred's penis more strongly and to do it long enough for him to have a robust erection that he could sustain.

With longer and stronger stimulation from Florence, Fred improved his erections, which boosted his confidence dramatically.

In the meantime, the couple brought a little romance back into their relationship by planning an erotic surprise. This is the way Fred thoughtfully surprised Florence with a touching and nostalgic evening at home.

"We had an old 78 RPM record of our favorite song in the attic," Fred told us. "It was warped and sounded terrible when I played it, so I heated the record up for a short time in the oven and put it between two big books to flatten it out overnight. It worked! Then I cooked a nice supper while Florence was away at her afternoon bridge club meeting. When she got home, she heard that old record playing and saw the candles I lit on the dining room table. She was so surprised. We played our song three times and danced to it the way we used to years ago. Florence said it was real romantic."

How One Couple Got Through Week 6

Ken and Nancy, both in their mid-thirties, had been living together for five years. Each had been married before; Ken had a young daughter who lived with his ex-wife. Nancy was insecure and hostile, and she had a sharp tongue. She verbally upbraided Ken at every opportunity, then complained about his lack of interest in her sexually. Ken very deliberately withheld sex to get back at Nancy. "I won't make love to her until she gives me some respect," said Ken.

This couple had had regular sex until about eighteen months before coming to therapy. Then Nancy's increasingly belligerent behavior began to put Ken off sexually. But Ken and Nancy didn't have a sexual problem. They had a relationship problem that caused misery in the bedroom. Their sex life together would not improve until they healed the rift between them.

During the first few weeks of sex therapy, Ken and Nancy made very slow progress. The Gestalt exercises during weeks 3 and 4 helped bring out certain factors in Nancy's past that still influenced her behavior. Her father had periodically left home to live with various lovers, returning when he was thrown out for drinking. Nancy's mother always took him back, and so did Nancy, despite a string of broken promises. Nancy's first husband and a boyfriend had also exploited her financially. "I was as bitter as my mother," said Nancy, "only she kept it in and I just let it all out."

Now, in week 6, the barriers between Ken and Nancy were beginning to break down. "The questionnaires Dr. Renshaw asked us to fill out really opened my eyes," said Nancy. "I always thought I was a kind, people-oriented person, but the therapists said that some of my answers showed deep anger. I know I've hurt Ken, but I feel so humiliated when he refuses to have sex with me."

During the miming session in week 4, when they could not hide behind sarcasm and biting words, both Nancy and Ken showed true tenderness and caring for each other. Ken displayed such nonverbal affection that Nancy burst into tears when he stroked her face. He continued to embrace her as she wept on his shoulder. Ken realized that his withdrawal from Nancy had deeply wounded her, and Nancy understood how her angry words had caused him to retreat in pain. The therapists reminded Nancy to keep telling herself that Ken was not her father. We also recommended to Ken that, when Nancy began one of her long, angry speeches, he put his arms around her for as long as it took to calm her down. Spending ten minutes to dispel her anger in this quiet way would be far more effective than ten weeks of arguing.

By week 6, Ken and Nancy had come to realize that resolving their sex problems was hard work. "But it may be the most productive hard work we've ever done," said Ken.

How Another Couple Got Through Week 6

Bernie and Michelle were in a troubled marriage. Bernie's mail order business had failed and he declared bankruptcy. Then, he over-ran the credit line on the couple's personal charge cards and wrote several bad checks to pay for luxury items such as good cigars. Michelle was forced to pay off Bernie's debts from her own limited earnings as a clerk typist and she resented it greatly. But, instead of talking about her fears and anger, she lost all interest in having sex with Bernie. In fact, she told us she could no longer stand the sight of him. She started sleeping on the fold-out sofa in the family room.

Bernie was angered by Michelle's lack of interest in him sexually. It had been his idea to come to our clinic. Oblivious to his own behavior, he wanted us to "fix" Michelle. We told him that their relationship was the problem, not Michelle. And Bernie had to take responsibility for his share of their relationship problems.

During the first week of sex therapy, Michelle refused to do the home loveplay. "Bernie revolts me," she told us. "I don't want him to touch me." We knew that this impasse had to be crossed so, in week 2, we told the couple to spend thirty minutes together on the couch one night talking about their problems, without the TV or radio on to distract them. They were to take turns listening to each other finish the following statements, "I feel hurt about . . ."; "I feel scared about . . ."; "I feel upset about. . . ."

During his Gestalt exercise, Bernie realized that running away from problems had been a pattern in his life, learned when he was very young. Bernie put his father in the chair and asked him why he hadn't forced Bernie to be more responsible as a child. "Why did you let me get away with so much? You never set limits for me. Kids always need limits, even an only child like me." Bernie didn't see that blaming his father was another way of avoiding responsibility for his own actions now.

By week 6, Bernie's defenses began to break down. He told us his swaggering financial extravagance had just been a cover-up for his intense feelings of insecurity and failure. "Men aren't supposed to show weakness," he said. "So, when the business failed, I tried to act as if nothing happened. Inside I was scared out of my wits, but I couldn't let Michelle see me like that. So I got defensive and just spent more. I guess I went too far."

Michelle's response to this revelation was disbelief. "Did you really think you were being strong when I was trying to pay the bills?" she asked. Still, she was thankful that Bernie was at last communicating honestly. The couple began talking, without rage, about ways to cope with their problems and Michelle's anger gradually lessened as her understanding grew.

Although Michelle and Bernie did do some home loveplay, they did not have sex by the end of the seven-week program. They decided to meet with their cotherapists for three follow-up sessions and, by the last meeting, they had progressed to intercourse. Bernie's expression of remorse, along with getting a part-time job, helped Michelle to respond to him with less resentment. Only then could she respond to him sexually. "He really is a good person underneath it all," she said. "But he has some growing up to do."

Sex therapy is an ongoing process; your work doesn't end this week. In the following chapter, I'll tell you how to sustain the gains you've made so far and how to avoid falling back into your old, ingrained habits.

Your Assignments for Week 6

1. Do your home loveplay (see page 233) several times this final week, including intercourse.
2. Plan another erotic surprise for your partner (see page 234).

11

Week 7: Life After Therapy

Facing the Future

How are you doing now? Do you and your partner feel as if you're stand-
ing hand in hand at the beginning of the road to a bright future? Or are
you both wobbling on a tightrope that's suspended over a deep chasm?
Relax and don't give up. Our program marked the beginning of your
new life together. You may still have some individual or couple problems to work out along the way. But you have already taken the hardest
steps.

In many ways, you have had a more difficult task than people who
come to our sex therapy clinic at Loyola. Our patients have two therapists to encourage them and coax them on, but you have had to discipline yourselves. I know that it may have been hard for you. Our
patients also have the benefit of being able to come back for follow-up
therapy after they complete the program, while you can only give yourselves a rereading of this book. Changing something as intricate as a

sexual relationship is difficult. It requires finding your own sexual style, just as you have to find an eating style to maintain your ideal weight. Change must be reinforced by practice until it feels natural to you both.

Now let's see just how far you have progressed. First, try to think about exactly what the sex therapy program has or has not done for you. Then, to find out how much your sex life has changed, fill out the following short questionnaire.

THE "HOW HAVE YOU CHANGED?" QUESTIONNAIRE

What were your initial expectations of the home sex therapy program?

Were your expectations fulfilled?

Do you think your expectations were realistic?

Do you have any unmet expectations?

What were your first reactions to participating in the program?

How much did you learn about the following things?

How your body is made	not much	a little	a lot
How your partner's body is made	not much	a little	a lot
How your body works	not much	a little	a lot
How your partner's body works	not much	a little	a lot
Your feelings	not much	a little	a lot
Your partner's feelings	not much	a little	a lot
Your attitudes	not much	a little	a lot
Your partner's attitudes	not much	a little	a lot
Sexual problems in general	not much	a little	a lot

How did you change over the past weeks?

How would you describe your ability to handle your problems now?
worse   same   a little better   a lot better

What do you think your or your partner's sexual problem was when you started the program?

How would you describe the problem now?
worse   same   a little better   a lot better

How do you think the problem will be in six months?
worse   same   a little better   a lot better

How do the following things compare now to the way they were seven weeks ago?

	Then			Now		
Nudity in bed	never	sometimes	often	never	sometimes	often
Lights on during sexplay	never	sometimes	often	never	sometimes	often
Kissing during sexplay	never	sometimes	often	never	sometimes	often
Touching own genitals	never	sometimes	often	never	sometimes	often
Touching partner's genitals	never	sometimes	often	never	sometimes	often
Foreplay (over three minutes)	never	sometimes	often	never	sometimes	often
Trying new positions	never	sometimes	often	never	sometimes	often
Talking about sex with partner	never	sometimes	often	never	sometimes	often
Guilt about sex	never	sometimes	often	never	sometimes	often
Anxiety about sex	never	sometimes	often	never	sometimes	often
Shame about sex activity	never	sometimes	often	never	sometimes	often
Enjoyment of loveplay	never	sometimes	often	never	sometimes	often
Enjoyment of intercourse	never	sometimes	often	never	sometimes	often
Frequency of masturbation	never	sometimes	often	never	sometimes	often
Frequency of intercourse	never	sometimes	often	never	sometimes	often
Frequency of oral sex	never	sometimes	often	never	sometimes	often

Frequency of anal sex   never sometimes often   never sometimes often

How often did you do your home loveplay per week? week 1 ____
week 2 ____ week 3 ____ week 4 ____ week 5 ____ week 6 ____

Which of the following factors do you think most helped you overcome
your sexual problems? (Circle all that apply.)

Your changed attitude

Your partner's changed attitude

The sexological examination

Talking about sex with your partner

Your home loveplay

Reading about other couples' sex problems

Knowing other couples had overcome their sex problems

Other _____

Overall, how would you rate the sex therapy program?
poor   fair   good   excellent

Backsliding

After a honeymoon period, some couples find themselves having
the same problems they had before they tried to change. It's sort of like
being on a train that gets derailed. I like that comparison because couples who begin repeating their problems really do get off the track.
Backsliding can happen to anyone who has been through sex therapy,
just as it happens to people who try to stop smoking or lose weight. But,
just as with weight control or quitting smoking, slipping doesn't mean
you've failed.

People who come to therapy with a lack of interest in sex seem
most prone to backsliding. I think it's because they fall back into their
habits of avoidance more easily than do people with performance types

of sexual problems, such as premature ejaculation. Let me illustrate what I mean by telling you about our former patients Scott and Caroline.

Scott was a thirty-seven-year-old real estate agent who had had a severe lack of interest in sex for several years. His wife, Caroline, an attractive thirty-two-year-old receptionist, could not understand how any man could lose interest in sex. She was convinced Scott must have a physical problem and asked us to give him testosterone shots, but his physical exam showed normal levels of the hormone. "Does that mean he's not attracted to me anymore?" she asked tearfully. We assured Caroline that Scott's problem was not a reflection on her. Instead, it was his body's response to the conflict that was going on inside him, between the two of them, and at work.

From the responses Scott gave on his questionnaires, the therapists suspected that he suffered from severe anxiety about what he perceived to be his own sexual inadequacy. Rather than confront his anxiety, he chose to avoid sex with Caroline as much as he could. He would go to bed after he knew Caroline was asleep so he wouldn't have to risk having her approach him for sex. In the morning, Scott would slip out of bed before Caroline so he wouldn't wake her up. He used his bad back routinely as an excuse not to have intercourse. "I work late selling real estate," Scott rationalized, "so we don't have a lot of time for sex. Besides, I don't have to prove I love Caroline. She knows I care about her. I give her everything she wants."

"Wake me up!" said Caroline when she heard that Scott did not want to wake her. "I'd love to just have some cuddling. Forget the intercourse; it's been so long since we cuddled." This reaction from Caroline forced Scott to confront his years of anxiety and avoidance; it was quite painful for him to hear about Caroline's longing and loneliness. But, through regular home loveplay, he slowly regained his self-confidence about giving Caroline affection—without sexual activity. Caroline stopped demanding sex. Scott stopped complaining of back pain. By the end of the program, they were having intercourse twice per week. Our follow-up six months later revealed that Scott and Caroline had both become comfortable with having sex about once per week on Sunday night (Monday was Scott's day off).

Two years later, I received a call from an again-tearful Caroline, who said Scott had reverted to his old patterns of avoidance behavior—working late, going to bed late, and waking early. His backaches had returned, worse than before. "What can we do?" she asked.

I told her to try scheduling certain aspects of their loveplay on Sunday nights. For example, they could plan to take a shower or relax in a tub together and massage each other to keep their loveplay fresh and lighthearted. I advised they say openly to each other, "No intercourse tonight—this is just for relaxation." They could also repeat the entire sex therapy program in two-day segments instead of in one-week segments. In other words, they could repeat the exercises and home loveplay contained in week 1 for two days, then repeat the exercises I recommend in week 2 for two days, and so on.

Six months later, Caroline and Scott requested a visit with me. They had resumed having sex about once every two weeks. I reminded them that they must vigilantly take the steps I had outlined at the first sign of backsliding, not only now but throughout their life together. This was especially important for Scott. As a child, he had learned to withdraw passively as a way of avoiding problems with his parents. While such behavior may have been a convenient way of adapting in his youth, it caused problems in his marriage because it prevented him from having a close relationship with Caroline. I told Scott he was lucky Caroline pushed for intimacy. Otherwise, they would only be two lonely roomers sharing a boardinghouse.

As I've said, sex therapy can be like weight loss. Just as the lost pounds can come back if you don't permanently change your eating habits, your sexual problems might come back if you don't change your style of loveplay for good. Here are a few suggestions for avoiding backsliding by permanently changing your sexual habits:

Be creative in the way you approach each other for sex. Tease each other. Reminisce about a special moment that pleased you both. Experiment with positions, locations (sex in the dining room? in the kitchen? outside?), and times (meet at home for a sexy lunch). Reread the section of this book that describes erotic surprises (see page 157) and set your imagination free. Being in a committed relationship does not mean that your bedroom is "dead serious." Playfulness and humor are normal and healthy.

Schedule your loveplay, like a date. Why not make an appointment with each other for sex? You may think that this kind of structure will take the spontaneity out of your lovemaking, but remember, you must always schedule the things that are important in your life. The anticipation of your encounter can even enhance your excitement. Surprise and spontaneity can surround your sexual appointments: wear something unusual, try a new position, turn on all the lights, or make love by candlelight.

Repeat any stages of your home loveplay. Go back and reread parts of this book to each other. Start at week 1. Kiss and touch all over the body, except the breasts and genitals, but instead of doing this for a week, do it once, with zest, as if it were your final day on earth. All you have is this moment. Savor it. The next time, try another stage for a few days, maybe one that includes breast and genital touching. Finally, include intercourse in your loveplay. Feel free to repeat any of the exercises in past chapters, such as the Fantastic Voyage, Gestalt, or miming exercises. Use your creativity to come up with another erotic surprise for each other. Sexy surprises make you think lovingly of each other on the days before the surprise as well as during and after it. Communicate, communicate, communicate, so each of you knows how the other feels all along the way—throughout the years.

Watch out for negative patterns of behavior. These include blaming, withdrawal, put-downs, or "it's no use" thinking. When you slip back into your old thought processes, you may also fall back into your old unhappy bedroom patterns. Replace those critical, resentful thoughts with ones that recognize your strengths. For example, instead of thinking, "We're right back where we were. We'll never change!" try thinking, "It's hard to change, but I know we can do it. Our relationship is the most important thing we have. We've invested years in each other. We should at least take a few months to try to change." Your burden is halved when you share it with your partner.

Make a date to talk about your progress. I often suggest to couples that they make a special date a month after completing sex therapy to gauge whether their sex life has improved, stayed the same, or gotten worse. "I'm too busy" is the most common excuse I hear, but you've got to make the time; talking things over can make your relationship not only survive but thrive. Try to remember the things you learned or did during the seven weeks that touched you emotionally. Was there a special moment of tenderness with your partner? Did one of his or her sexy surprises touch you in a certain way? These are the things that will stay with you and help you get back on track again.

Where to Go for Additional Help

If, after reading this book, you feel that you still have not resolved your sex problems satisfactorily, I urge you to seek further help. There are many excellent books on relationship problems; browse through your local bookstore to find one whose style appeals to you.

Here are a few books that I recommend to our patients. You might find them helpful too.

Sex and Human Loving by W. Masters, V. Johnson, and R. Kolodny (Little, Brown & Company, 1986, paperback); *The New Our Bodies, Ourselves* by The Boston Women's Health Book Collective (Simon & Schuster, 1992); *The New Male Sexuality* by B. Zilbergeld (Bantam Books, 1992); *For Yourself* by L. G. Barbach (Doubleday, 1992); *The Dance of Anger* by H. G. Lerner (Harper & Row, 1983); *The Sexual Healing Journey: A Guide for Survivors of Sexual Abuse* by W. Maltz (HarperCollins, 1991); and *When a Woman's Body Says No to Sex: Understanding and Overcoming Vaginismus* by L. Valins (Penguin Books, 1992).

Call your local community hospital. Ask to speak with a social worker who can refer you to a local therapist. Or ask to speak with a doctor who specializes in sexual problems. But first, a word of caution. Remember to use common sense when seeking out a therapist. Find someone who respects your values. Be especially wary of someone who tries to coerce you into sexual acts that make you feel uneasy. Always check out the credentials of anyone you are considering as a therapist before you see him or her. If you need further help, the following two organizations may be able to help you find local treatment for and more information about your sex problems:

American Association of Sex Educators, Counselors,
and Therapists
(AASECT)
435 N Michigan Ave
Suite 1717
Chicago, IL 60611-4067
AASECT is a not-for-profit professional association that certifies sex educators, sex counselors, and sex therapists. The organization will send you a list of certified sex therapists in your area for two dollars and a self-addressed stamped envelope.

Sex Information and Education Council of the United States
(SIECUS)
130 W 42nd St
Suite 2500
New York, NY 10036-7901
SIECUS was founded to provide comprehensive information on all aspects of sexuality. It offers a wealth of information about sexuality not otherwise available to the general public. Write for the organization's free publications catalog.

Part 3

Sex and Special Needs

12

Sex, Disability, and Long-Term Illness

People with long-term illness or disability often struggle with special problems when it comes to their sexuality. There are 35 million disabled people in the United States. Millions more have heart disease and cancer. If this is your situation, you know that you have exactly the same sexual needs as anyone else, but your conditions often make it difficult for you to express yourself sexually. In this chapter I will explore the sexual issues of people with special needs. I'll also try to answer some of the questions that you may be afraid to ask your doctor or that your doctor may be uncomfortable answering. The list of conditions I have included in this chapter is not exhaustive; I have tried to cover the conditions that affect the largest number of people, based on my experience.

Heart Disease

Sex is vigorous physical activity. When you are aroused, your blood pressure temporarily rises, your heart rate increases, and you begin breathing heavily. That's why people with heart disease are sometimes afraid to have sex. They and their partners fear that the physical strain and excitement of intercourse might be too much for them, causing chest pain or even a heart attack. But most heart patients can have intercourse and orgasm safely. If you can walk up a flight of twenty steps, you can probably have intercourse without physical problems. Ask your doctor. If you take the heart drug nitroglycerin to help you engage in physical activity without pain, take a dose before you make love. Unfortunately, many doctors, in their discomfort over talking about sex, never tell the person with heart disease that it's OK to have intercourse, so both partners remain sexually frustrated and unhappy.

I remember one woman telling me she used to lie in bed, longing to touch her husband. But she was afraid that if she did, it would arouse him and either make him angry (because he was too afraid to have sex) or be dangerous for him. "I was frightened," she said. "I thought it would be too much for his heart."

Her husband suppressed his desire by following a suggestion of his old football coach: when aroused, take a cold shower. None of this was necessary. The man was perfectly capable of having sex, but he had never asked his doctor about it and the doctor had never told him or his wife that it was permitted. When we phoned the man's doctor, we explained the situation and the doctor gave the couple the go-ahead. With great relief, the couple resumed sexual activity, tentatively at first. "Now I know my touch can't hurt him," said the wife. "It never could," he responded.

Sometimes, avoiding sex can cause more stress than intercourse itself. One of our patients, Gary, a forty-eight-year-old commodities broker, had undergone bypass surgery four years previously. Two years after his surgery, he met his second wife, Beverly, and they got married.

Sex was a serious problem for the couple almost from the beginning. Beverly avoided it because she feared it might injure her husband's heart. Gary started masturbating. Then he began having frightening episodes of rapid heartbeats at bedtime. A long and expensive series of tests failed to reveal any physical cause, so Gary's cardiologist (heart specialist) assumed that anxiety was causing the problem and put Gary on a tranquilizer.

The new drug made things worse. Gary now began having erection problems, a common side effect of some tranquilizers. The impotence heightened his anxiety, which increased the episodes of rapid heartbeats. When the couple entered sex therapy, we took Gary off the tranquilizer (with his cardiologist's consent) and his erection problems vanished. A few weeks later, after much counseling from his therapists, Gary's rapid heartbeat problem also disappeared. Clearly, wanting (yet avoiding) sex, coupled with the fear of losing his new wife, had caused Gary's anxiety. We contacted Gary's cardiologist, who gave the couple the green light to have sex, based on Gary's current physical condition. Heartened by this permission, the couple began having regular intercourse with no further difficulty.

Of course, severe heart disease can limit the sexual activity of some affected people. If you have heart disease and you cannot walk up four steps without becoming breathless, your doctor will probably advise you to refrain from having intercourse. But don't stop there. Talk to your doctor about your sex life. Ask him or her exactly what your limits are and how you can be affectionate and sexual with your partner within those limits. For example, ask your doctor if you can bring your partner to orgasm through hand or mouth stimulation. That way, you can get pleasure out of giving your partner pleasure. Even if heart disease prevents you from having intercourse, it does not prevent you from having a loving, caring relationship with your partner—and showing it by helping your partner reach orgasm.

Cancer

No matter what part of the body it affects, cancer is a life crisis for the person who has it. Almost every person with cancer responds to the disease with fear: fear of pain, fear of it spreading, fear of being disfigured, fear of surgery, fear of rejection by the partner, and fear of death itself. You may experience only minimal discomfort and few symptoms before the cancer diagnosis. But the treatment—radiation therapy, surgery, chemotherapy—can cause pain, weakness, and major changes in your lifestyle. While you may temporarily table sexual feelings during the "crisis phase" of treatment and emotional adjustment, these feelings never disappear completely. You can still have sexual desire, and you should express it as fully as you can.

People who have cancer—and their partners—have many questions about the way the disease will affect their sexual relationship: "When can we resume intercourse?" "Will I still be able to have children?" People also have many misconceptions about cancer and sexuality. For example, in cases of cancer of the vagina, cervix, or uterus, you or your partner may believe that intercourse will be impossible or harmful. Your partner may feel that he or she has somehow caused your cancer through sexual activity. You may even fear that your partner might "catch" cancer from you if you have sex.

None of these ideas is true. But these misconceptions can sometimes cause sexual problems. For example, a man may begin having erection problems after his partner's breast (or cervical) cancer diagnosis. A woman may lose interest in sex when her partner develops cancer of the bladder or prostate. Cancer is not contagious, although couples should use a condom until the treatment site of cervical, bladder, or prostate cancer is completely healed to avoid infection. Such fears are normal, and misconceptions are understandable. Once again, if you have cancer, I urge you to talk to your doctor about how the disease will affect your sexuality to clear up any possible misunderstanding.

There are two types of cancer that affect sexuality in very specific ways: breast cancer and prostate cancer.

Breast Cancer

Some cultures regard the female breast as simply an organ designed to feed the young. For these people, the breast symbolizes nurturing and mothering. But our Western culture has always eroticized the breast. To us, the female breast is mainly a symbol of beauty and sexual attractiveness. That's why, when the appearance of a woman's breasts is threatened by disease and disfigurement, the woman struggles with serious body image problems that can affect her sexual relationship with her partner.

In the early stages of arousal, a woman's nipples usually become erect. But women vary in the amount of erotic pleasure they derive from having their breasts stimulated during loveplay. Some women can have an orgasm just by stimulating their own nipples or by having their partner stimulate them. Others feel more pleasurable sensations when other parts of their body are touched. Most women in our society feel an inevitable loss when breast cancer disfigures or takes away one or both of their breasts.

The depression and anxiety about death that accompany a diagnosis of breast cancer can be severe enough to produce a loss of interest in sex, at least temporarily. Your doctor can treat your depression with counseling and medication. But pain caused by the cancer can also dampen your desire. And the treatment needed to fight the cancer can cause problems of its own. Radiation therapy and chemotherapy can cause hormonal side effects that produce early menopause—even for women in their twenties and thirties. When taking these treatments, not only does the woman stop menstruating, she also experiences all the other symptoms of menopause, such as thinning of the vaginal walls and vaginal dryness, which can cause pain during intercourse if added lubrication is not used. Treatment can also cause hair loss, another blow to a woman's self-image.

These symptoms can cause you to avoid sex at a time when both partners especially need closeness. Your partner may feel uncertain about when to renew sexual activity and may even have difficulty having an erection. The penis is a sensitive barometer of the relationship. If you are experiencing pain caused by changes in your vagina, try the exercise I prescribe for women with vaginismus on pages 85–86. Open-

255

mouthed breathing, relaxation, and insertion of your well-lubricated finger into your vagina will help you overcome your fear of pain during intercourse.

Tammy was a thirty-nine-year-old woman who had had her cancerous left breast removed. The chemotherapy she underwent to treat the cancer made her weak and nauseous. She temporarily lost all of her hair. Her doctor told her that the chemotherapy would also cause her to enter menopause prematurely. Initially, Tammy didn't mind that bit of news because she and her husband, Mike, already had two children and did not want more. But when Tammy began experiencing the symptoms of menopause on top of all the other pain and discomfort she was having, she became depressed. She also felt disfigured because of her surgical scar and was afraid to let Mike see her naked. Two years after Tammy's surgery, the couple entered our sex therapy program because Tammy was afraid that Mike would leave her if their sex life did not improve.

Tammy and Mike completed the same exercises and home loveplay sessions as every other couple in sex therapy. In addition, the therapists openly discussed the loss of Tammy's breast and gave the couple reading materials to educate them about her condition. This frank discussion helped prevent further physical distancing between Tammy and Mike.

While filling out the My Body Questionnaire in the first week of sex therapy, Tammy realized that all the words she circled to describe Mike's body were positive (healthy, active, strong) but that all the ones she chose to describe her own body were negative (unhealthy, disabled, useless). When she got to the question that asked what one thing she would change about her body if she could, she had answered, "to be whole again." The therapists gave Tammy information on reconstructive breast surgery and tried to help her understand that, even though her body had undergone a devastating change, it was still lovable.

We encouraged Tammy to lie naked next to Mike with a light on in their bedroom during their home loveplay so Mike could see her surgical scar. On the first night she undressed, she cried inconsolably.

But on the next few nights, she bravely complied with our instructions. "On the fourth or fifth night, Mike touched and kissed my scar," said Tammy. "That made me cry again, but this time it was because he was so sweet and loving." Tammy was lucky to have such an accepting partner. With time and the help of a breast cancer survivors' self-help group, Tammy slowly began to accept herself as Mike did. The couple came in for two follow-up visits, and we saw that they were progressing well.

If you and your partner face the same kind of emotional strain as Tammy and Mike, you must first grieve over the loss together. Accept yourselves as you are, and try to recapture the playfulness that characterized the earlier stages of your relationship. Take turns massaging each other in bed or take a shower together as part of your foreplay. Such lighthearted moments will help lift your spirits so you can face your problems with renewed energy together.

Prostate Cancer

More than one hundred thousand men are diagnosed with prostate cancer in the United States each year. Many have no symptoms; the cancer is discovered during a routine rectal examination or after a blood test. Men have many questions about prostate cancer's effects on their lives: "Will I lose bladder control?" "Will I have pain?" "What about my sex life, my erections, my orgasms, my desire, my sperm?" "Will I still be able to father children?" The doctor usually responds by saying something like "The progress of prostate cancer has many patterns, from rapid spread to ten years or more of survival. Let's be optimistic and work together to control yours."

The sexual side effects of prostate cancer vary from man to man. If you have had prostate cancer, the likelihood of developing sexual side effects depends on the type of treatment you receive, your previous sexual functioning and frequency, your age, the medications you are taking, whether or not you smoke, and how much alcohol you drink. The three most common types of prostate cancer treatment are surgery, hormone therapy, and radiation therapy. All of these treatments can affect your ability to have an erection, sometimes permanently. Hormone therapy can also lower your sexual desire because the hormone used to treat prostate cancer is the female hormone estrogen, which blocks the effects of the male hormone testosterone, responsible for tumor growth and needed for sexual desire in a man.

If you had an active sex life and if your erections, ejaculations, and level of desire were satisfactory before your treatment, then your sexual outlook will be more positive after treatment. Even if you do have sexual problems, some may be only temporary during your treatment. Erection problems, for example, may improve with time (within three to twelve months) and healing. If you have had prostate surgery, especially if the internal valve of your bladder no longer shuts tightly, your ejaculations may become retrograde. This means that, instead of ejecting semen out, the muscle contractions that take place during orgasm will propel the semen back up into your bladder. Retrograde ejaculation will make you infertile, but you will still be able to feel your internal ejaculations, which will feel like an internal sensation of release, and learn to enjoy them. Radiation therapy can also affect your ability to have children. If you want a child, you might consider storing some of your sperm before you begin treatment. The surgical removal of both testosterone-producing testicles will permanently affect your sex drive and potency.

What no treatment can change is your love for your partner and hers for you. Keep your morale and your mood high by continuing to share closeness, touching, kissing, talking, laughter, and playfulness. *Prostate cancer is not contagious, but self-pity may be.* Tender words, the awareness of your partner's sexual needs, and hand or mouth stimulation are good alternatives if you can no longer have intercourse. Use them regularly to nurture closeness. Remind yourself that *an active and fulfilling sex life does not have to include intercourse.*

Some men with prostate cancer are good candidates for one of the three treatments used to help men with erection problems: implants into the penis, injections into the penis, or the vacuum erection device (see page 61). Talk to your doctor to find out if these treatments can help you.

Alcoholism

Many people think that alcohol is an aphrodisiac because it can break the chains of inhibition that often surround sex. But drinking too much alcohol can actually hamper sexual function, as Shakespeare put it so well when he wrote, "It [alcohol] provokes the desire, but it takes away the performance."

Alcohol is not a stimulant drug, as some people think. It briefly causes a state of confident well-being as it dissolves your inhibitions, but then it quickly becomes a central nervous system depressant, slowing your responses, dulling your sense of touch, and making you sleepy. When you drink alcohol, it takes longer for you to become sexually aroused. Drinking alcohol can temporarily affect a man's ability to get an erection or to ejaculate and can reduce a woman's sexual drive and her ability to achieve orgasm.

But the problems caused by social drinking are nothing compared to the effects of chronic alcoholism. In men, alcoholism can cause long-term erection problems because of changes in blood circulation to the penis and its nerve supply. The liver damage produced by alcoholism can even cause a hormonal imbalance in a man that produces increased levels of the female hormone estrogen and reduced levels of the male hormone testosterone, leading to enlarged breasts, shrinking of the testicles, and a lower-than-normal sperm count. Female alcoholics sometimes experience infrequent orgasm, an inability to reach orgasm, and reduced sexual drive.

If you or your partner has a drinking problem, you need to get help or support. Talk to your doctor to find out what help is available in your community, or call the local chapter of a self-help group such as Alcoholics Anonymous or Al-Anon.

Harvey was a fifty-two-year-old man who came to our sex therapy program with his wife, Eva, because he had been having erection problems for about two years. He said he and Eva previously had had intercourse almost every day. Harvey had been a heavy drinker for thirty-two years and was diagnosed with alcoholism and cirrhosis (damage from scar tissue) of the liver.

Harvey was the only child of a domineering widow who was also an alcoholic. He had completed high school, served a stint in the navy, and had a stable job as a railroad union officer. Harvey had married Eva, now age forty-eight, seventeen years earlier; she also had a drinking problem. They had no children together (Harvey had a low sperm count), but Harvey had adopted Eva's three children from a previous marriage. The couple insisted their relationship was mutually satisfying and that Harvey's erection difficulty was their only problem.

Harvey and Eva enthusiastically began their home loveplay exercises and surprisingly reversed Harvey's erection problems in the second week of therapy. They said their "quick cure" occurred for three reasons: because we had told them not to have intercourse, because they put their mattress on the floor to keep the bed from squeaking, and because Harvey consumed only two, instead of his usual twelve, beers each night during the seven weeks of sex therapy. Of all of these, which really did the trick? We were not sure, but we suspected that cutting back on his intake of alcohol helped Harvey the most. Whatever the cause, Harvey remains free of his erection problems two years after the completion of therapy.

If you are having erection problems or difficulty with arousal and orgasm that you suspect may be related to your drinking habits, try not drinking for three or four weeks to see if your sexual problems resolve. Again, I urge you to ask for help from your doctor or from a self-help group such as Alcoholics Anonymous if you think your drinking has gotten out of control.

Diabetes

In a person with diabetes, the pancreas fails to produce sufficient insulin, a hormone that helps the body absorb and store the essential sugar glucose. Glucose remains unabsorbed in the blood, producing such characteristic symptoms as excessive thirst and increased urination.

Diabetes impedes blood flow in the body's small blood vessels, including those in the genital area, so the vessels cannot supply enough blood needed for an erection. Although not all diabetic men will develop erection problems, the most common diabetes-related sexual difficulty in men is the inability to have an erection. Diabetes can also cause some loss of sensation, so that the man needs longer stimulation to get an erection. These physical changes produced by diabetes can be more or less severe and are sometimes not reversible. Also, many other factors—depression, anxiety, medication, a drinking problem—can compound the health problems of diabetics, so doctors often have difficulty determining whether a man's sexual problems are caused exclusively by the diabetes or by a combination of factors. To restore the ability to have an erection, diabetic men who are impotent can take advantage of one of the three medical treatments I discussed in the section on erection problems starting on page 61: surgical implants in the penis, injections into the penis, or the vacuum erection device.

Women who have mild or early-stage diabetes usually have no sexual problems directly related to their diabetes. Those with more severe diabetes may sometimes experience dryness in their vagina, so they need to use lots of artificial lubrication or saliva during intercourse. Some medical studies suggest that diabetic women can have difficulty reaching orgasm because of the loss of sensation the disease can produce, but other research contradicts this claim.

Hysterectomy

Hysterectomy, the surgical removal of a woman's uterus and sometimes also her ovaries and fallopian tubes, is not really a disability, but many women and their partners fear that it can affect their sex lives. Doctors perform a hysterectomy to treat women who have extensive and painful fibroids (noncancerous tumors in the uterus), heavy menstrual bleeding and severe menstrual pain, cancer of the uterus or cervix, or severe endometriosis (in which fragments of the lining of the uterus grow outside the uterus). Women and their partners have many misconceptions, concerns, and fears about hysterectomy: they may believe it causes the loss of womanhood and attractiveness, inability to have sex, weight gain, and more. Sometimes the woman's partner views the hysterectomy as a blow to his manhood because the woman can no longer bear children.

A hysterectomy that leaves the ovaries intact does not lead to any loss of sexual desire or function because your ovaries continue to produce female hormones. But if your ovaries have been removed, you will experience all the symptoms of menopause (see page 50), including a possible loss of desire—even if you are under age fifty—because of the loss of hormones. Hormone replacement therapy helps maintain your sexual function—after hysterectomy or menopause—by restoring lubrication and reversing thinning of the vaginal walls. Regardless of whether or not you are undergoing hormone replacement therapy, your ability to have an orgasm will not be affected, even if your ovaries have been removed, because arousal occurs in your clitoris and in your mind.

Having intercourse before your surgical wound is healed is painful and carries the risk of infection. If you have had a hysterectomy, your doctor will probably tell you to refrain from having intercourse for about six weeks or until the area is completely healed. But that doesn't mean that you need to be distant and unaffectionate! You can have plenty of good sex without intercourse. The comforting and caressing you receive from your partner promotes healing and bonding. Once you resume sexual relations, try the L-shaped position for intercourse. Lie with your trunks at right angles to each other and legs interlocked (see illustration below). This position frees you from bearing your own weight or your partner's on the scar during intercourse.

Having a hysterectomy does not make you fat, contrary to many people's beliefs. You become fat only when you take in more calories than you use during physical activity. Hormone replacement therapy may cause a temporary weight gain from fluid retention if the dosage is incorrect. If this occurs, ask your doctor to adjust the dosage to resolve the problem.

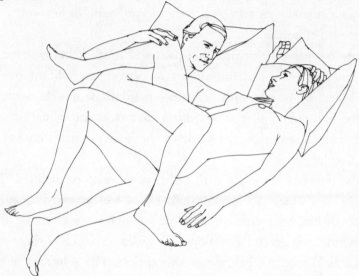

The L-shaped Position

Arthritis

People with severe arthritis (inflammation of the joints) often experience pain, stiffness, deformity, and limitation of movement. These symptoms can affect your emotional adjustment and body image. But the pain and deformity that can accompany arthritis need not bring your sex life to a halt. Effective medication and an accepting sexual partner can help you enjoy a satisfying sexual relationship in spite of your physical difficulties.

Arthritis can strike the very young as well as the very old. The age at which arthritis strikes strongly affects your social life and sexual development. Teenagers need the approval of their peers as part of their development process. Physical appearance and the ability to take part in activities such as sports and dancing are also extremely important to adolescents. Teens who have juvenile arthritis cannot share in these physical activities. Many withdraw socially or limit their socializing to other disabled peers. Denying the disability can cause an adolescent to become sexually promiscuous, either to prove his or her worth or to find needed closeness.

Adults with arthritis find that pain and restricted movement can both dampen desire and impede sexual performance. Many medications taken by people with arthritis—painkillers, muscle relaxants, sleeping aids, tranquilizers, and drugs that treat inflammation—can lessen physical sensation, reduce desire, or cause physical changes that affect your appearance.

The partners of people with arthritis can also be affected. They may consider illness a personal weakness or feel ashamed socially by your condition. Your partner may avoid sexual relations because of fear of inflicting pain on you. Emotional complications such as those experienced by the couple below can also appear. The solutions to their problems may help you.

Edwin was a sixty-year-old former butcher whose arthritis had forced him to retire three years before he entered sex therapy. His wife, Faye, age fifty, was an attractive woman who wanted to continue having sexual relations with Edwin, but who thought that his claims of pain and limited movement were just a ploy to avoid intercourse. Edwin complained that Faye's tossing and turning during the night hurt him, so the couple now slept in separate rooms.

During therapy, Faye said, "Ed runs hot and cold. Sometimes when I approach him for sex, he's ready and eager. At other times, he complains that he's in too much pain. I feel as if he's rejecting me and using the arthritis as an excuse. And sometimes when we do have sex, he cries out in pain," she went on. "That spoils it for me. I don't know whether I'm really hurting him or if he's just not in the mood. Either way, it's easier just to forget about sex altogether."

Faye did not understand that people with arthritis often go through periods of intense pain and immobility, followed by periods of remission, in which they feel much better. Edwin assured her that he was not exaggerating his pain just to avoid having sex with her. "I want to have sex with you more than anything," he told Faye. "That's why I came to sex therapy." Edwin's sexual desire was still strong.

We gave the couple some advice on sexual positions that could lessen the pressure on Edwin's painful joints. If you have arthritis, you could benefit from this knowledge too. In the L-shaped position, you lie on the bed, facing each other, with your trunks at right angles and your legs intertwining (see illustration on page 263). This position also makes it easier for you to caress breasts and genitals. Another good position for people with arthritis is the woman-on-top position, unless the woman has arthritis in her knees or hips. The spoon position, in which the woman lies parallel to the man with his chest facing her back, also works. He then enters her vagina from the rear, with her guidance.

Edwin and Faye were as elated as a honeymoon couple when they successfully had intercourse in these positions. Faye's suspicions that Ed was avoiding her were replaced by contrite and caring concern for her husband. They spent many hours making up for lost time and lost closeness.

Physical Disability (Including Stroke)

Many of the things I have said about arthritis and sexuality also apply to physical disability and sexuality: deformity can affect your body image, and limited movement can make successful sexual activity difficult (but not impossible). Even so, disabled people usually retain their sexual desire. Many enjoy a satisfying sex life with an understanding and cooperative partner.

Bruce was a forty-nine-year-old former ironworker who had fallen off a scaffolding four years earlier. He was now in a wheelchair and had lost control of his bladder, so he had to wear a tube, called a catheter, inserted into his penis and connected to a drainage pouch strapped to his thigh. Bruce could no longer work at his trade, so he and his wife, Clare, age fifty-one, had started a small lumber supply business. They came to sex therapy because Bruce had refused to have any sexual contact with Clare since the accident.

Bruce was depressed and wept often. He was no longer able to have an erection. He would not sleep in the couple's bedroom, preferring to stay in the family room, and refused to let Clare share the sofa bed. "I'm too humiliated to let her see me like this after twenty-two years of marriage," he said at our first meeting. After much reassurance from the therapists, Bruce agreed to visit Clare in their bedroom once each day to do their home loveplay. "But I make such a mess [because of his catheter] that I'll go right back to the den afterward," he warned.

The physician therapist showed Bruce how to remove his catheter temporarily and instructed him to empty his bladder more completely by pressing on his pubic area with the palm of his hand. This procedure would allow Bruce to remain dry and free of the tubing for about thirty minutes.

On the second visit, Clare was smiling and radiant. "This week has been like our honeymoon," she exclaimed. "It was wonderful to be together again, loving and touching." Bruce interrupted her to say, "But I didn't have any erections." She replied, "I didn't marry an erection. I married you. Now you're back. I don't care about any erections."

During the seven weeks of sex therapy, Bruce discovered that, even though he could no longer have an erection, he could still have a physically close and affectionate relationship with his wife. Bruce and Clare enjoyed massaging each other before bed, and Bruce discovered that he could give Clare pleasure by stimulating her clitoris until she reached orgasm. He began sleeping in their bedroom once again. Clare was ecstatic.

Another disabling condition, stroke, occurs when a blood vessel inside the brain ruptures or becomes blocked, causing bleeding and obstruction of the brain's circulation. Many cases of stroke are caused by severe and uncontrolled high blood pressure.

Upon leaving the hospital, the person who has had a stroke experiences much anxiety. The person's brain and body have been damaged, and the sense of self has been severely shaken by changes in the ability to move, talk, and see. The person might be afraid that another stroke could occur, might be dejected about the future, and could be demoralized at the condition of his or her body.

A common result of stroke is paralysis on the left or right half of your body. If the right half of your body is affected, your ability to speak can also be impaired. These effects may be minor or severe, but there is usually some permanent loss of function on one side. You may also have a significant loss of sensation on the affected side. If the stroke was very severe, men may experience erection problems, delayed ejaculation, or retrograde ejaculation (see page 258). Women may have decreased vaginal lubrication. These problems are unusual, but they do happen.

Muscle weakness and limited movement can make it extremely awkward and difficult for a person who has had a stroke to perform sexually, but there are some common-sense ways of overcoming these problems. Use pillows to prop up your weakened side, a handle on the headboard of the bed, or a trapeze hung over the bed to help you maneuver more easily during sex. Nonverbal cues or signals can help someone whose speech or vision has been affected to better communicate his or her needs or loving thoughts to the partner.

Many partners of disabled people are frightened by the person's disability, but I want to emphasize again that, *although the outside person has changed, the inside person is the same as before*. Your task is to accept your partner as he or she is now. As difficult as it may seem to do, try introducing some humor into your bedroom. Tease and laugh with your partner because it tells him or her, "I have confidence that you're strong enough to laugh about it. Let's not be so serious. I don't want to treat you like porcelain." Beware of self-pity. It will drag you both down.

Ostomy

People who have long-term bowel disease, such as colitis (inflammation of the colon, or large intestine) or cancer of the rectum may sometimes require a type of surgery that removes a section of intestine near the anus. Such people can no longer have a bowel movement the usual way, so the surgeon must create an opening (called a stoma) in the wall of the abdomen through which the intestines can eliminate waste. The waste then passes out of the body into a plastic collecting bag. Sometimes the stoma is temporary, and sometimes it is permanent. This surgical procedure is called ostomy. If the surgery is done on the large intestine (the colon), the procedure is called a colostomy. Surgery done on the final end of the small intestine (the ileum) is called an ileostomy.

People who have had this type of surgery must deal with a dramatic change in the way their body works. They usually feel shock, denial, and shame. It may take months or years for them to adjust and accept themselves the way they now are. Guilt and worry about the sounds and odors produced by the stoma are normal.

The stoma is never located near the vagina, clitoris, or penis, so it usually does not affect your sexual functioning physically. But it can have serious emotional effects on your sexuality. You may withdraw from sex out of fear of offending your partner, fear of damage to the stoma, or fear of rejection. Your partner may indeed reject your sexual advances. He or she may not want to look at or touch the stoma, may be upset about body secretions or odors, or wrongly fear catching the underlying cancer or colitis. People cannot overcome these obstacles faster than their personalities will allow. Neither partner should coerce the other. Instead, you should take the time you need to sort out your feelings and find new ways to express and fulfill yourselves sexually.

I often tell people with ostomies that they should empty their stoma, put on a fresh collecting bag, and then place a towel or wrap a scarf over the bag like a cummerbund before sexual activity. This helps them overcome the worry over appearance and prevents the plastic bag from shifting. If a spill does occur, they need only use some soap, water, and a sense of humor. Experimenting with positions also helps. A person with an ostomy may find that an upright, kneeling position takes the pressure off the plastic bag. The L-shaped position depicted on page 263 can also work well.

If you find that intercourse is impractical or if you're uncomfortable about it, remember that you can still approach lovemaking for the joy of togetherness, without the goal of intercourse. Kiss, touch, cuddle, and caress, and then touch and stroke each other's genitals with your hands or a vibrator to elicit and satisfy your sexual feelings. *The inability to have intercourse does not mean the loss of ability to have an orgasm or the loss of the ability to love.*

Sexually Transmitted Diseases (Including Genital Herpes)

Sexually transmitted diseases (STDs) are rampant, and many can have lifelong or tragic consequences. For example, chlamydia, the most common STD in the United States, often causes no immediate symptoms, but can later produce a serious infection in women that sometimes causes infertility. Genital warts have been linked to cancer of the cervix in women. If you think that there is a possibility that you have become infected with an STD, see your doctor and get tested. Treatment, usually with antibiotics, is simple and effective for many STDs.

Most STDs affect your sex life either temporarily or permanently.

But the STD that I have seen most often in our clinic is genital herpes. No cure for genital herpes has yet been found, and this disease can permanently affect your sex life.

Caused by the herpes simplex virus, genital herpes produces a painful rash on the genitals. Small blisters appear, which burst and form painful ulcers that heal in three to seven days. In some people, the outbreak never recurs, but most people with herpes have occasional recurrences for the rest of their lives, although, over time, the outbreaks may become less frequent. Doctors treat genital herpes with a drug called acyclovir, which helps the ulcers heal faster and makes them less painful. But there is currently no treatment that prevents recurrence of the disease.

People with herpes may find it embarrassing to tell their partner about their condition, but a frank discussion is the only way to avoid spreading the disease. If you have genital herpes, you should avoid having intercourse during the stage when blisters and ulcers are present (when herpes is highly contagious) *even if you use a condom*. The blister phase only lasts for a few days at a time, and abstinence is the only way you can be absolutely sure you are not infecting your partner. Many people feel a tingling just before the blister phase, and this is the time to stop having sexual activity. Spend the time during outbreaks exploring your sexuality without intercourse but with plenty of love and affection.

. . .

If you have a disorder that I have not covered in this chapter and the disorder is affecting your sex life, talk to your doctor. Don't be afraid to ask questions about your sexuality, because he or she can give you the information and guidance you need. If not, ask your doctor to refer you to another doctor in your area who has had special training in human sexuality (see page 247).

Your sexuality is an important part of your life. Don't let disability prevent you from discovering new ways to express yourself sexually or from giving and receiving sexual pleasure.

Epilogue

It's not easy to admit that your sexual relationship needs serious help. I have seen people approach sex therapy in several unhealthy ways. Some pretend to engage in the program to convince themselves that "not even sex therapy can help us, so we can give up on sex." A few use sex therapy as one more means of controlling their partner, to make the partner change. Others drop out of the program because they think sex therapy is silly or boring. But those who are willing to take the time and make the effort to go through the painful self-examination needed to assess honestly their relationship's strengths and weaknesses begin to relate at a level of mature, mutual sharing that enriches both partners.

I want to congratulate you on having the courage and commitment to get the help you need. You have completed your course of home sex therapy, but your sexual exploration does not end with the last page of this book. In fact, this is only the beginning. It's the beginning of a new level of understanding about each other and the start of a greater closeness between the two of you.

You have learned many new things, but not just with your mind. Your body learned, and your feelings learned too, through your love-play and the other exercises in this book. This kind of learning by experience brings not only knowledge, but also understanding. And, because you learned the things in this book together, the experience has probably brought the two of you closer together. Shared experience always creates a special bond.

So you see that you have worked on your relationship as well as on your sex life. Now use what you have learned to work on it some more. Sex therapy is a dynamic, ongoing process. That means that you will have to use this knowledge and understanding all throughout your relationship to keep your sex life as interesting and satisfying as you want it to be.

I wish you a lifetime of love, smiles, and fulfilling sex. Good luck!

Index